Healing Together

A volume in the series
The Culture and Politics of Health Care Work
Edited by SUZANNE GORDON and SIOBAN NELSON

Healing Together

The Labor-Management Partnership at Kaiser Permanente

Thomas A. Kochan
Adrienne E. Eaton
Robert B. McKersie
Paul S. Adler

ILR Press
an imprint of
Cornell University Press
Ithaca & London

First published 2009 by Cornell University Press
First printing, Cornell Paperbacks, 2009

Printed in the United States of America

Library of Congress Cataloging-in-Publication Data

Healing together : the labor-management partnership at Kaiser
Permanente / Thomas A. Kochan . . . [et al.].
    p. cm. — (The culture and politics of health care work)
Includes bibliographical references and index.
ISBN 978-0-8014-4798-3 (cloth : alk. paper) —
ISBN 978-0-8014-7546-7
(pbk. : alk. paper)
    1. Kaiser Permanente—Personnel management.   2. Labor-
management committees—United States.   3. Health services
administration—Employee participation—United States.
4. Health facilities—United States—Personnel management.
5. Collective bargaining—Health facilities—United States.
6. Medical personnel—Labor unions—United States.
7. Industrial relations—United States.   I. Kochan, Thomas A.
II. Series: Culture and politics of health care work.

    RA971.35.H43 2009
    362.11068'3—dc22   2008048071

Cloth printing   10   9   8   7   6   5   4   3   2   1
Paperback printing   10   9   8   7   6   5   4   3   2   1

To the memory of Susan C. Eaton

Contents

Acknowledgments

When leaders of the Kaiser Labor Management Partnership first approached us about studying their experiences, we had no idea the project would turn into an eight-year effort, much less this book. We are grateful to the initial leaders of the partnership and to their successors for giving us free reign to explore and document their experiences without conditions. Special thanks are due to the early partnership leaders John Stepp, Leslie Margolin, Peter diCicco, and their successors Tony Gately, Anthony Wagner, Mary Ann Thode, Martin Gilbert, and John August. Support for the research was provided by the Kaiser Permanente Labor Management Partnership Trust Fund.

We could not have provided the detailed account that follows without the cooperation and participation of the hundreds of labor and management representatives whom we interviewed, worked with to collect data, and observed in action in negotiations, meetings, conferences, and with whom we occasionally shared a drink late into the night. The open access we had to people at all levels of the management, physician, and labor organizations from headquarters in Oakland to all the regions across the country gave us a full, 360 degree view of this initiative. The talent, commitment, hard work, and perseverance of these leaders and representatives are the heart and soul of this partnership. American labor relations would be well off indeed if their individual talents and the relationships they built with each other could be replicated across the country.

Special appreciation goes to the staff from Restructuring Associates, Inc., the team that has facilitated partnership activities at Kaiser from the start. Relations between researchers chronicling processes like these and those guiding and facilitating them can often be tense or guarded, with each party feeling the other is getting in the way or second guessing the others' work. This was not the case here; we worked together, cooperated where we could and shared information where it was appropriate and useful to do so, and built lasting friendships with RAI facilitators. They guided the partnership through the normal crises we document in the pages that follow. Without their skillful work, the partnership could well have ended in any number of these pivotal events.

We were also aided by a number of research colleagues along the way. Paul Gerhart and Phyllis Segal carried out case studies of specific regional developments and projects for our 2004 report on this project. George Strauss, Marty Moran, and Teresa Sharpe joined us to observe and analyze the 2005 negotiations and Saul Rubinstein joined us in the study of the union coalition. These efforts provided the basis for the symposium devoted to the partnership published in the January 2008 issue of *Industrial Relations*. We are grateful for their help and their insights into these aspects of the partnership. We thank the editors and publishers of *Industrial Relations* for permission to use several charts and tables from those papers. Adam Seth Litwin did yeoman work in studying the key role that HealthConnect, Kaiser's medical records technology initiative, plays in the partnership. Chapter 9 of this book was drafted by Adam. His PhD dissertation on this topic represents perhaps the most careful analysis of the effects of these technologies on health care outcomes completed to date.

Throughout the project Jacalyn Martelli provided administrative support and coordinated the efforts of our far-flung and evolving research team with her usual skill and persistence. We thank her for her continued good work on our behalf.

Phil Primack did us and our readers a great service in editing our first draft into a narrative that we hope tells a compelling and coherent story. Suzanne Gordon and Sioban Nelson, the editors of this series, likewise helped us find our voice in summarizing what we have learned about partnerships and health care through our work at Kaiser Permanente.

We dedicate this book to the memory of our dear friend and colleague Susan C. Eaton. As we note in chapter 1, Susan was a member of our original research team but we lost her to leukemia about two years into the project. Dedicating this book to Susan is only one of the many tributes already paid to her memory. She truly was a renaissance woman, a passionate advocate for justice at work and an inquisitive researcher who left no stone unturned. Her interview notes and write-ups provided much of the material in this book on the early years of the partnership. But more than anything, Susan lived a life dedicated to advancing the cause of worker voice and progressive relationships between labor and management. We can think of no better way to honor her and her memory than to see this partnership continue to thrive and advance in the years ahead.

Healing Together

CHAPTER 1

To Fight or Talk?

The union leaders came prepared for a fight on that cold December day in 1995. They represented a coalition of twenty-seven unions and 55,000 workers employed by health care giant Kaiser Permanente (KP), the nation's leading not-for-profit health maintenance organization. Both sides faced enormous pressures—and an enormous choice.

At the time, Kaiser was losing more than $250 million and was being advised by a management consultant to break itself up and to take steps to better match the cost structures of competing HMOs. But if he followed such advice, Kaiser's CEO Dr. David Lawrence would be abandoning Kaiser's historic commitment not only to being an integrated health care provider and insurer, but also to its hard-earned reputation as an employee and union friendly employer. As it was, Kaiser's response to mounting competitive pressures facing all health care providers was already transforming its long history of positive labor-management relations into one of intensifying conflict, with Kaiser demanding wage and benefit reductions and the unions responding with strikes.

Peter diCicco, who for the next decade would be the executive director of the Coalition of Kaiser Permanente Unions, faced similarly high stakes. On the one hand, the twenty-seven Kaiser union locals represented in the coalition were increasingly impatient and unhappy. On the other hand, it might not serve either Kaiser employees or the broader labor movement for the coalition to go to war with Kaiser.

In an attempt to find neutral ground to frankly discuss each party's concerns and possible options, John Sweeney, then president of the Service Employees International Union (SEIU) and on his way to becoming president of the American Federation of Labor–Congress of Industrial Organizations (AFL-CIO), called on the nation's top mediator, John Calhoun Wells, to arrange and facilitate a top-level, off-the-record meeting. The outcome was that crucial December meeting, which was held deep inside Dallas's sprawling airport.

Led by Sweeney, the labor delegation was set to warn Lawrence and other top Kaiser executives of the consequences of continued hostility and escalating conflict. "We went to that meeting ready to blast Kaiser Permanente for its behavior," said diCicco. "At the top of our list was patient care. That's where the frustration was the greatest among our members." Lawrence clearly recognized the stakes. "It was almost a make-or-break meeting," he would later recall.

But the labor leaders were in for a surprise. Lawrence opened the meeting with a statement that disarmed them. "He said all the things we were prepared to say," said diCicco. "It was clear that there was almost total alignment of objectives."

Thus began what would become the largest, most complex, ambitious, and broad-based labor-management partnership in U.S. history. "What I remember thinking about at that meeting was that we've got nothing to lose by being forthcoming about what I believed needed to happen in terms of our relationships . . . [and] the kind of collaboration required to deliver modern medical care in all of its complexity," said Lawrence. "[T]here are no answers to these things; they grow out of the collective effort of teams of people who are working on specific areas of medical care delivery."

This book tells the story of the first ten years of the Kaiser partnership and its implications for two of the greatest challenges facing the nation today: how to at least improve, if not fix, a broken health care system; and how to revive a labor-management relationship that has collapsed. The Kaiser partnership informs both issues. As the chapters that follow make clear, the partnership is a living thing, constantly facing threats as well as opportunities. In those early days of 1995, the parties chose to convert threat into opportunity. And as seen in the challenging contract negotiations of August 2008, this pattern of managing to become stronger in the face of even dire economic and other circumstances continues. Details of the 2008 agreement are impressive in their own right. They include a wage agreement that keeps workers whole in a period of rising inflation and an innovative Health Retirement Account that allows workers to apply unused, accumulated sick leave at retirement to purchase health insurance benefits. But what is most striking is how the new agreement positions the partnership to move to the next level. It establishes a jointly developed new performance improvement program that strengthens the line of sight between worker efforts on the front line and teams that improve quality and other operational health care outcomes to performance based wage increases. It also creates a high-level labor-management committee to work on marketing, product development, and other strategic issues needed to attract the new customers and to secure Kaiser Permanente's future.

In such ways, the partnership has expanded the frontiers of U.S. labor-management relations in health care. It is an important model for how to engage the workforce and its representatives in joint efforts to improve health care delivery through major organizational reforms and efficiency improvements—and how to do so without imposing the suffering and economic losses that have afflicted workers in other industries that are also struggling to restructure themselves. Within this context, the partnership story is especially resonant because it has grown within a sector—health care—that can be especially adverse to such collaborative approaches.

At the same time, the lessons of the Kaiser partnership have implications for improvement of health care delivery. It is, after all, impossible to talk about true reform of the health care system without including those who actually deliver and manage health care services. And with health care providers facing major shortages of nurses and other front-line workers, finding ways to improve and better manage the health care workplace is more important than ever. The partnership has produced positive and lasting benefits for patient, employee, and health care provider alike.

This is no theoretical story. By 2007, the Kaiser partnership covered more than 90,000 employees. Three path-breaking collective bargaining agreements had used state-of-the-art negotiations and problem-solving tools to address topics normally beyond the purview of union-management relations, such as quality and performance improvement. Policies continue to be set at Kaiser by labor-management forums on a wide variety of issues, from improving work and family balance to responding to incorporating electronic medical records into the care delivery process.

What makes such accomplishments especially noteworthy is their achievement within an industry—health care—where power is so highly decentralized and dispersed among doctors who defend their autonomy, and across medical care units that have long traditions of tailoring practices to fit their seemingly unique needs. A labor-management partnership would seem to be especially hard to implement and sustain in such a context. Distrust borne out of past conflicts and/or ideological differences does not melt away with the announcement from leaders at the top of management or labor organizations that a partnership has been formed. Doctors, managers, nurses, and other employees must first feel the same pressure to change for them to even consider commitment to partnership principles and processes.

The pre-partnership relationship between Kaiser and its employee unions reflected such challenges and mutual distrust. Now, more than a decade later, Kaiser Permanente and the union coalition have succeeded in sustaining their partnership, demonstrating that it is not only possible to negotiate path-breaking labor agreements in innovative ways, but to work together to implement new medical technologies and team-based work systems that health care experts see as central to reducing costs and improving the quality of health care in the United States.

To be clear: We do not present the Kaiser partnership as a panacea for the nation's labor-management problems, let alone for its health care crisis. Nor do we suggest it is the best or only way to structure employment relations in health care or other industries. Indeed, as we will discuss, major disagreements exist within the labor movement about the proper role of health care unions and health care employers in meeting the challenges facing the industry. One major union, the California Nurses Association, has refused to join the partnership and is highly critical of it, Kaiser, and the coalition of unions. We are critical of some of the bureaucratic features of the partnership that have slowed progress in improving health care delivery. Partnership efforts such as Kaiser's can indeed be slow, hard, and fragile. Their success can be difficult to measure.

All that said, the advantages and limitations of the partnership offer some core lessons that can be applied across sectors and in the design and administration of national labor policy, especially within the health care industry, 80 percent of which remains unorganized. No one is served by a return to the adversarial traditions of the past, or by the turmoil seen in other sectors that have undergone significant restructuring through adversarial processes, such as the airline industry. The Kaiser partnership points to a better way.

This book brings together our collective observations about and experiences with the Kaiser partnership. These go back to early 2001, when head of the union coalition at Kaiser Peter diCicco, lead negotiator and key executive at Kaiser Leslie Margolin, and their lead consultant John Stepp visited MIT to ask whether our group would be interested in conducting an independent study of the then four-year-old Kaiser Permanente labor-management partnership. They approached us because of our prior work on industrial relations, especially on innovations in labor-management relations. Although we had heard about the partnership, none of our research team members had any prior involvement in it. Given its importance, we prepared a proposal to which the partnership leaders agreed.

Among other things, we required that consistent with standard MIT research requirements, our team would have full access to the parties and the data available and we would be free to reach our own conclusions and publish our results subject only to review for factual accuracy (not interpretations) and for proprietary information. The project would be supported by the Kaiser Permanente Labor-Management Partnership Trust Fund that was set up to administer the partnership. In early 2001, the original research team of Thomas Kochan, Robert McKersie, and Susan Eaton began working on the project.

In the 1980s, Kochan, McKersie, and another colleague—Harry Katz—conducted a series of case studies of innovations in labor-management relations for the U. S. Department of Labor,[1] data from which featured prominently in our 1986 publication, *The Transformation of American Industrial Relations*. In that book we argued that the traditional New Deal system of collective bargaining was undergoing significant changes that were both necessary to its future viability and yet at risk for lack of a supportive public policy.[2] In the 1990s, our group continued to study and be involved in partnerships in the steel, clothing, telecommunications, and other industries. One project was a long-term study of the Saturn Corporation, the effort by General Motors and the United Auto Workers that was the most ambitious labor-management experiment of its era.[3]

Our role in these projects was similar to the one we proposed for the Kaiser project. We would retain our independence as outside researchers, while providing periodic feedback and recommendations to the parties on how to address challenges they were experiencing as their efforts unfolded. To us, this mixed role of research and engagement was consistent with our team's goal of acting on the conclusions that had emerged from our 1980s research: Labor-management relations needed to change in ways that fostered both expanded worker voice and improved organizational performance. Unless innovations could be sustained, our analysis suggested unions would continue to decline and labor-management relations would become more rigid and less effective in meeting the needs of workers, employers, and society in general. This project was thus consistent with our interest in continuing to pursue this line of research and with our goal of fostering innovations and improvement in labor-management relations.

To us, the central intellectual question in this project was whether the partnership the parties were building would yield the improved results for workers, unions, Kaiser as an employer, and the members (patients) Kaiser Permanente served.

The project is now in its eighth year. Over time, our research team has both changed and expanded. Less than three years into the project, we lost our close friend and colleague, Susan Eaton, to leukemia. Aside from the enormous personal loss, this left a big void in our team. Fortunately, we had already begun to work with Adrienne Eaton (no relation to Susan) before Susan's death. Adrienne also had a long history of studying the role of unions in labor-management partnerships[4] and, as a consultant, had been helping the Kaiser union coalition assess the partnership. Adrienne agreed to join our project while continuing her work with the coalition. In 2004, Paul Adler, an organizational sociologist who had worked both on partnerships and on work processes in health care, joined the team to bolster our West Coast presence as we began working on a report on partnership developments between 2002 and 2005.[5]

Our methods of research can best be described as a mix of standard social science research—case studies, surveys, interviews, participant observation, and analysis of documents, reports, presentations—and action research through our feedback to those involved in the partnership processes. We have produced four interim reports on the partnership. Though written largely for the parties themselves, each of these reports was published independently, circulated widely to people in our profession, and posted on the MIT Institute for Work and Employment Research website (http://mitsloan.mit.edu/iwer). We have also published a number of peer-reviewed journal articles.[6]

In the following chapters, we detail the people and pivotal events that illustrate both the power of partnership and its precarious, often fragile, nature in the face of often resistant management, labor, and public policy traditions. We delve into the leadership styles, governance structures, and organizational changes needed to initiate, sustain, and derive benefits from a labor-management partnership. By highlighting how these issues were addressed by those involved in the Kaiser partnership, we hope to show that there are ways for labor and management to work together, not in total harmony or under naive notions that conflicts would magically disappear, but by surfacing and addressing issues, challenges, and conflicts as they arise to improve patient care and the lives of those who deliver it.

Chapter 2 reviews the history of health care labor relations, followed by a discussion of how that history has informed and complicated the establishment of labor-management partnerships. Chapter 3 presents a profile of Kaiser Permanente. Chapter 4 summarizes the partnership's early years, focusing on some early achievements and challenges that had to be addressed if it was to make it beyond the initial stages. Chapter 5 discusses the struggles associated with diffusing a partnership across an organization as complex and decentralized as Kaiser Permanente.

Chapter 6 provides a description and analysis of one of the signature breakthroughs and achievements of the partnership—the negotiation of two of the largest, most complex, and most innovative collective bargaining agreements in U.S. labor relations history. Chapter 7 reviews the challenge of building and maintaining a coalition of the various Kaiser unions, made all the more difficult by the 2005 split of the major unions at the national level. Chapter 8 analyzes the partnership at a more personal level, looking at the role of upper- and middle-level leadership of Kaiser and the unions. Chapters 9 and 10 take up two major initiatives on the front lines of health care delivery—efforts to introduce and expand the use of teams of health care workers to solve problems and improve care and efforts to introduce and expand the use of electronic medical records technologies. In chapter 11, we assess Kaiser's overall performance as a health care delivery organization and how Kaiser's workforce and unions have fared over the first decade of the partnership's existence.

The final chapter summarizes the lessons—both for the health care industry and for the nation's labor relations system—that we hope policy makers and others will take away from the partnership. The partnership can serve as a road map. The route may not be direct or without detour and obstacles, but it can lead to success for those who choose to work in partnership to improve both health care delivery and the lives of those who deliver it.

CHAPTER 2

Partnerships:
Great Challenges, Greater Opportunities

The issues that engaged Peter diCicco and David Lawrence in 1995 in Dallas were symptomatic—then and now—of a crossroad facing U.S. labor-management relations. To put it bluntly, the nation's labor law is broken.[1] Workers who want to join a union face enormous hurdles. Relations between labor and management have become increasingly adversarial, less innovative, and less responsive to what workers want not only from their jobs, but from their unions and employers as well.[2]

When the Kaiser partnership effort began, relations between Kaiser and its unions were at a low point. Workers felt devalued and angry. Management faced absenteeism, low morale, and other problems, none of which were good for operations, let alone quality of care for patients.

In examining the partnership's results—successes and otherwise—we address three fundamental questions. First, how do partnerships actually work and what ups, downs, and uncertainties do the parties face as they begin working together? Second, based on the successes and frustrations of this and other partnerships we have studied over the years, should labor-management partnerships be available and supported as one option for workers, employers, and unions? Third, if labor-management partnerships do have sufficient merit, how can they be initiated and sustained?

The Kaiser partnership offers important insights into these questions. It serves as a model of how to go about engaging the workforce and its representatives in joint efforts to improve labor-management relations which, in the case of a major health care provider, also means improving the quality of health care delivery on a more cost-effective basis. That matters not only to labor relations specialists, but to those concerned about the crisis in this nation's system of health care delivery.

The Coming Choice: Which Way for U.S. Labor Relations?

Union membership has been declining for decades. Now representing only about 7.5 percent of the private sector labor force, unions have reached a nadir not experienced since the depths of the Great Depression. Also harkening back to the 1930s, some commentators today believe labor's decline will continue into oblivion, that unions are a relic of a past economy and are neither needed nor wanted in today's modern workplaces.

We believe otherwise. An increasing number of workers, now reaching a majority of the non-union workforce, express a desire for representation.[3] The evidence that U.S. labor law is broken is so overwhelming that it is beginning to gain wider attention from conservative and liberal journalists, academics, and even business leaders.[4] In 2007, the U.S. Senate and House of Representatives both voted favorably on a labor law reform proposal, though not by sufficient margins to survive the Senate delaying tactics or a likely presidential veto. A new Congress and a new president may finally break the long impasse over labor law reform.

But even absent such long overdue action at the federal level, unions and other worker advocacy groups—including newer coalitions of religious, community, and ethnic/immigrant organizations—are expanding the array of innovative strategies used to pressure employers to recognize and respect worker rights, to afford them a voice, and to meet accepted standards of behavior and conditions of work.[5] Often, these groups have had to work around the constraints of current labor law. They pressure employers to be neutral in organizing drives or negotiate rules that provide a fair process. In other cases, unions and other worker advocates lobby for local or state ordinances or laws to counterbalance the problems with federal labor law.

Given the breakdown in federal labor law, they have little choice. Take the example of the 650-person Service and Maintenance Unit at the Enloe Health Care Center in Chico, CA. In an April 2004 election, supervised by the National Labor Relations Board (NLRB), the workers voted to be represented by the Service Employees International Union. But management contested the election results and won hearings, first from the NLRB regional office, then from a federal administrative law judge, and finally from the NLRB in Washington which, in August 2005—nearly eighteen months after the vote—certified that the union had won the election and directed the parties to negotiate a first contract.

A month later, management announced through its attorneys that they would refuse to bargain with the union. In January 2006, the NLRB issued a final order to bargain, as well as a complaint against Enloe Health Care for failing and refusing to bargain with the union. A U.S. Court of Appeals found no merits to the employer's objections to the election process or results and granted the NLRB's request for a summary judgment to enforce the Board's order to bargain.

The outcome? Enloe laid off 173 bargaining unit employees. The union called a strike, which drew support from local religious and community groups and political leaders. The health care center replaced its CEO; the new one recognized the union and reinstated the laid-off workers with back wages. The new CEO also fired the attorneys who had billed the hospital more than $3 million up to that point. In September 2007, bargaining for a first contract finally began. Such cases are routine across the nation, triggering calls for labor reform and for better ways to think about—and implement—labor-management relations.

For all the talk of the death of labor, history is not on the side of those who see workers' voices silenced indefinitely. This nation's historical pattern has been one of long periods of gradual union decline, followed by rapid bursts in new organizing and new approaches to labor relations, often triggered by a combination of national crises, shifts in union organizing strategies, and changes in the political and legal climate.

To us, the question is not *whether* there will be a shift in the patterns of labor organizing and worker representation but *when* and, even more important, *what forms* of representation will emerge and shape the future of labor-management relations. Are we destined to witness the emergence of a replay of the adversarial labor relations of the past or can we learn from both positive and negative experiences to shape a labor relations system that better fits the modern workforce, economy, and larger societal needs and expectations? That is what was at stake as diCicco and Lawrence and their colleagues met in Dallas. And it is what is at stake in comparable debates taking place over labor policy and organizational relationships across the country today.

Health Care Labor Relations

To many union activists, Enloe Health Care typifies not only the sorry state of federal labor law, but the health care industry's resistance to workers and unions. In fact, considerable variation in employment practices and relationships exists in the health care industry, in both unionized and non-unionized organizations. We briefly describe examples of such relationships in this chapter.

Bringing partnership principles to bear in health care poses some unique challenges—and opportunities. The creativity and shared commitment that a partnership can foster is especially needed in health care, where nurses, physicians, and other employees interact, presumably to make patient care their top priority. In practice, however, building such a partnership faces several challenges, including one that is unique to health care. Beyond the usual labor-management differences that must be overcome, another powerful party must also be engaged: doctors. Teamwork, especially teamwork with unions, does not come naturally to doctors. Their training prepares them to make quick, individual, and often unchallenged decisions on how to best care for their patients. Only since the late 1990s have there been calls to change physician education to encourage and train them to work more effectively in teams with nurses and other professionals. The Institute of Medicine, for example, envisions "a new health system for the 21st century" in which:

> The delivery of services is coordinated across practices, settings, and patient conditions over time. Information technology is used as the basic building block for making systems work, tracking performance, and increasing learning. Practices use measures and information about outcomes and information technology to continually refine advanced engineering principles and to improve their care processes. The health workforce is used efficiently and flexibly to implement change.[6]

Although recommendations such as this are leading some medical schools and residency programs to educate doctors about how to adapt to a more coordinated view of medical care, we know of no such efforts to date to educate doctors about how to work with unions, much less with unions that now expect doctors to treat them as partners in health care delivery. Moreover, it is not just the attitudes or behaviors of individual doctors that need to be factored into how to build a partnership. As we describe in more detail in the next chapter, physicians at Kaiser Permanente (KP) have their own organization, with elected leaders who share decision-making power with managers and executives from the front lines in individual clinic and hospitals, to the top levels of the organization.

Health care has been a growth industry for jobs and for the labor movement. From 1995 to 2005, employment in hospitals grew by more than 13 percent, from 4.97 million to 5.74 million workers. Over that same period, the number of hospital workers covered by collective bargaining agreements rose from 821,321 to 883,659, an increase of 7 percent, though there was a small decline in percentage of the workforce covered (from 16.5 percent to 15.4 percent). Growth in the employment and unionization of registered nurses (RNs) was even more substantial. The ranks of employed RNs grew by 23 percent, from 1.95 million in 1995 to 2.4 million in 2005 and the number of nurses with collective bargaining coverage grew by more than 32 percent, from about 300,000 to almost 400,000; union density among RNs also grew slightly.[7] Of course, the statistics on density mask incredible geographic diversity. In some large cities in the Northeast, the Midwest, and on the West Coast, union density rates are considerably higher for the hospital industry, whereas the South remains largely unorganized.

Though 80 percent of the health care industry remains unorganized, Service Employees International Union (SEIU) now boasts one million health care members working in hospitals, nursing homes, and home care. Aside from SEIU, a member of the national breakaway labor federation Change to Win, other unions with substantial—20,000 members or more—health care representation include these AFL-CIO affiliates: American Federation of Teachers, United American Nurses, American Federation of State, County and Municipal Employees, Communications Workers of America, and the formerly independent but recently affiliated California Nurses Association. Another Change to Win affiliate, the United Food and Commercial Workers, also represents health care workers.

There is wide variety in the quality of jobs in the hospital sector. A strong hierarchy characterizes medical work where, traditionally, doctors have the greatest power and prestige. Much has been written about the situation nurses face: although pay rates have been rising for RNs, working conditions have deteriorated. Indeed, statistics support the view that the nursing shortage is as much a function of heavy flow *out of* the profession in response to working conditions as the inadequate flow *into* the profession. As of 2008, more than one in five licensed nurses was not working in his or her chosen profession. Through both collective bargaining and legislation, nurses' unions have been addressing major issues, such as mandatory overtime, staffing ratios, and related scheduling issues, in order to enable nurses to provide high-quality patient care, have a decent personal and family life, and take care of their own mental and physical health.

Not all hospital workers are well-paid professionals. The hospital sector also employs a substantial body of low skilled, low wage workers. The largest job categories within this group are nursing assistants, housekeepers, and food service workers. The ranks of nursing assistants, who are replacing RNs in many direct patient care functions, have grown substantially in the past decade. Appelbaum et al. report that "in 2000, the median wage for food service workers was $8.25 an hour, for housekeepers $8.15 and for nursing assistants $9.00." Further, "[a]nnual turnover rates among these occupational groups at some hospitals approached 100 percent [and r]ates greater than 50 percent were common."[8]

For our purposes, more important than the number of jobs and union members in health care is the quality of labor-management relations. Here we also find wide variation, from examples of true labor-management partnership, to more traditional arm's-length relationships, to all-out wars over organizing. Although we focus on the Kaiser partnership, other labor-management partnerships exist, including the Labor-Management Project initiated in 1997 by SEIU Local 1199 and its multiemployer association, the New York League of Voluntary Hospitals and Nursing Homes. Funded by the League contract, the Project formally covers more than 125,000 local union members who work in dozens of non-profit hospitals and nursing homes belonging to the League. The Labor-Management Project sits within a broad strategic alliance, a cooperative relationship aimed at improving patient care, assisting workers in retaining their employment if hospitals close, protecting and increasing public funding for the health care system, and achieving union organizing goals. At the facility level, labor-management partnership activities take a variety of forms, depending on the interests and readiness of management and labor leaders. In some cases, this has meant improving labor relations, including the use of interest-based problem-solving skills. In other instances, it has gone much further, with projects focused on expanding opportunities for worker participation to improve quality and safety of patient care, the quality of jobs, and patient satisfaction scores. In some facilities, other unions—including the Committee of Interns and Residents and the New York State Nurses Association—have joined hospital-based partnership activities.

Strategically, SEIU Local 1199 has used its considerable political muscle in Albany and in Washington to leverage repeated infusions of federal and state dollars into New York City's non-profit hospital system for investment in both capital improvement projects and human capital. Such efforts have supported extensive, jointly administered training activities as well as higher wages and benefits. In addition, in 2002, the League and 1199 negotiated a limited neutrality agreement covering new union organizing. Some individual members of the League have also signed organizing agreements that are more advantageous for the union, a phenomenon explicitly allowed under the League agreement.[9]

Other large health care providers have also negotiated their own versions of partnership agreements. One of the more interesting involves the Allina system in Minnesota. In the 1990s Allina was part of a multiemployer and multiunion partnership involving fifteen hospitals, SEIU Local 115, and the Minnesota Nurses Association. Although this complex partnership was ultimately impossible to hold together—due in no small part to conflict within the employer group and between the two unions—Allina management and SEIU have continued to pursue a non-traditional approach.[10] The latest iteration of the partnership that began in 2006 is, in certain respects, an outgrowth of the Kaiser partnership. Allina CEO Richard Pettingill was, as president of the California region of Kaiser's health and hospitals organization, heavily involved in the early years of the Kaiser partnership. The SEIU local involved in the Allina effort studied the Kaiser partnership, and the parties hired John Stepp, the lead consultant to the Kaiser partnership, to provide assistance in developing the Allina partnership. The Allina partnership initially focused on service and other performance improvements, better workforce development, income security, and management neutrality to minimize labor-management conflict around union organizing.[11]

A starkly contrasting situation involves another SEIU affiliate. In March 2006, SEIU Local 1199/New England and Yale New Haven hospital and community leaders signed an agreement to govern the organizing of low-paid service workers at the hospital as well as to provide training to local residents. The agreement—which called for neutrality by the employer and a code of conduct for both parties—was the product of a bitter fight waged by the union for several years, in alliance with New Haven residents and local politicians and clergy. The alliance scrutinized the hospital's financial practices, worked to block the building of a new cancer center, and argued that poor pay and poor patient care were linked. In the process, Yale University, formally a separate entity from the hospital, found itself pulled into the battle. While the March 2006 agreement was greeted with much fanfare, by the end of 2006, it was in tatters. An arbitrator found that the hospital had violated both federal labor law and the organizing agreement by allowing managers to conduct mandatory work meetings about the organizing drive. As a result the union decided to postpone an upcoming election and the union's allies expressed their anger at, and sense of betrayal by, the hospital. "[I]t raises serious issues in my mind about the hospital's management and about the hospital's intention all along," said New Haven mayor John Stefano. "This serves nobody. The most I feel is sad. It just hurts the community, it hurts everybody."[12] In August 2008, the hospital paid SEIU two million dollars to settle—at least legally—the case.

Cedars Sinai, one of the largest hospitals in Los Angeles and a recognized leader in health care research and teaching, serves as another illustration of the battles that often occur when employees attempt to unionize. Cedars Sinai has traditionally been a high-wage employer, stating its intent to pay in the upper 20 percent of the area's wage distribution. At the same time, it has consistently fought unionization efforts, starting in 1976 when interns and residents sought to organize. The hospital successfully argued before the NLRB that interns and residents were not "employees" covered under the National Labor Relations Act (NLRA) because they were students being trained by the hospital. In 2002, the hospital again successfully challenged the results of an election in which the majority of nurses voted to join the California Nurses Association (CNA). The hospital and the CNA have continued their stand-off ever since. The CNA has argued that the hospital intimidates union supporters and relies on union avoidance consultants to the detriment of patient care, while the hospital has argued that it is the union that "engages in very aggressive tactics." Cedars Sinai's CEO added, "we believe that our ability to deal directly with our staff, nurses and others is the best way for us to achieve the institution's mission and achieve high quality health care."[13]

For years, trade unionists have maintained that the Yale and Cedars Sinai scenarios are typical in hospitals: health care workers who seek to organize unions usually meet intense resistance. Although SEIU has successfully negotiated neutrality agreements in a limited number of hospital chains, most notably the California operations of Tenet and Catholic Health West, most hospitals have remained resistant to union organizing.

Once organized, most hospital labor relationships feature more traditional arm's-length relationships, similar to those in other industries. Since the mid-1990s, unions and management have engaged in contract fights over health and pension benefits. Health care employers have traditionally spent less on benefits than other employers. For example, in 2000, "health care employers spent only 1.5 percent of their payrolls on pensions," compared to 6.8 percent by other "non-manufacturing" employers.[14] As is true in other industries, benefits disputes in the health care sector have sometimes resulted in work stoppages. Demands for decent health care benefits for both active and retired workers are especially emotionally laden in this industry—representing a variant of the Biblical proverb, "Physician heal thyself." At the same time, hospitals face tremendous challenges with declining reimbursement rates from both Medicare and private insurance companies as well as greater patient acuity resulting from the increasing use of outpatient treatment for many procedures.

A similarly wide variation in practices and patterns of relationships also exists in the 80 percent of the health care sector that is unorganized. Although cases of low pay and strong suppression of union organizing exists, particularly in the lower wage nursing home segment of the industry, the picture is more varied among non-union hospitals, which have seen some instances of exemplary employment relationships. One example was Boston's Beth Israel Hospital. Prior to its 1996 merger with neighboring Deaconess Hospital, Beth Israel was listed among the top 100 best places to work. It had a well-known gain-sharing program, in which employees received bonuses as productivity improved, and was characterized by progressive human resource practices, with resulting low turnover. But after the merger the management changed, financial pressures intensified, and human resource policies shifted. Nursing morale plummeted as the staff experienced increasing patient loads and decreasing managerial support.[15] Could it be that the absence of a union and collective bargaining at Beth Israel meant there was no check on such a downward spiral? More recently, under new management, Beth Israel has been working to rebuild its reputation as a good place to work, but its management still vigorously opposes unionization.

These examples show that there is no preordained trajectory suggesting that relations between health care workers and their employers—union or non-union—will inevitably improve or deteriorate. That depends on the choices industry and labor leaders, employees, and policy officials make as they go about the task of expanding coverage and managing costs. Partnering is one such choice—but as we discuss next, it is not without controversy.

Partnering: Difficult for Both Labor and Management

Since at least the mid-1980s, there has been an active debate, largely an ideological one, within the labor movement over the value of labor-management partnerships. Critics within the movement fear that partnerships would undermine member support for unions and union representation of worker interests both within companies and society at large. They fear that unions engaged in these relationships would push toward an "enterprise" focus rather than focusing solely on workers' interests. In our view, however, the last twenty years of union experience has not borne out these fears, though the debate continues.[16]

For unions that do choose to form partnerships, the challenge is to develop the capacity needed to build effective and sustainable partnerships that expand union influence and power in order to address issues that are important to their members, but that are normally off-limits in traditional bargaining, *and* to add value to the enterprise, while not losing their ability to represent members in traditional ways when necessary. In presenting the story of the Kaiser partnership we focus on these challenges by examining how the unions in the Kaiser coalition sought to expand their influence, add value, represent member interests, and address the voice of internal and external skeptics and critics of partnerships.

Building and sustaining partnerships between labor and management in the United States has not come naturally or easily. Formed voluntarily and without any public policy supports, labor-management partnerships generally occur in settings where unions are already strong and employers do not have the option of either avoiding or getting rid of the union and where one or both parties are dissatisfied with the current state of their relationship. Often, it takes a crisis to provoke a departure into a new relationship. And strong leadership on both sides is necessary to launch and sustain a partnership.

Partnerships normally entail efforts to improve cooperation and trust at the workplace, both between workers and supervisors and between union and management representatives. Although some partnerships focus on working together to introduce changes that improve productivity, product or service quality, and worker satisfaction, others go further and seek to improve the *process of negotiations* by introducing more problem-solving techniques in bargaining new labor agreements and resolving problems during the term of an agreement, which otherwise would have become formal grievances.

A smaller number of partnerships, which call for higher levels of consultation and input by union leaders into managerial decisions beyond the normal scope of labor relations, involve departures from the dominant model of labor relations that has evolved under the NLRA. But regardless of their form or scope, partnerships must be built and sustained by mutual trust and respect, shared power, and achievement of tangible results on goals important to each party, which they cannot achieve without each other's help.

To understand why such partnerships are rare requires a quick glance at U.S. labor history and labor law. Compared to European countries, the United States was slow to develop a modern labor relations system. Prior to the 1930s, labor relations were characterized by extremes—violent labor conflicts by frustrated groups of miners, craftsmen, and others with labor market power seeking to gain recognition and modest improvements in their working conditions or just to defend existing standards, only to be met with repression and dissolution of the union when the economy weakened and power shifted back to employers. The surge of labor conflict during the Great Depression and the fear that the U.S. economic way of life could be lost finally led to the passage of the first comprehensive national labor law, the National Labor Relations Act of 1935. The NLRA promised workers that they could exercise their rights to join a union and engage in collective bargaining. The goal was to eliminate the violent battles over union organizing and structure an orderly negotiating process for reaching agreements over wages, hours, and working conditions. In 1974, this law was extended to health care workers employed by private sector and non-profit organizations.

Unfortunately, the NLRA did not eliminate conflicts over union organizing. Indeed, countless studies and a mountain of evidence show that today workers cannot exercise their right without having to endure long, high-risk, highly tense battles with their employers to join unions and achieve collective bargaining contracts. Only one in five organizing efforts are successful in reaching a first contract; if the employer resists and commits an unfair labor practice, the chance of getting a contract drops to below one in ten.[17]

There are multiple reasons for this dismal record. Unionization of the workforce is viewed in most management circles as a black mark on an executive's career and a sure ticket out the door. Most managers thus do whatever it takes to avoid unionization. Labor leaders, for their part, assume management hostility will greet any organizing effort; therefore, they prepare their potential members for the fights that lie ahead. Where unions do exist, managers often try to minimize their influence, protecting management's "prerogatives" by keeping unions out of day-to-day decision making and administrative affairs. At the same time, many union leaders are leery of being perceived as getting too close to management, an attitude that serves to reinforce arm's-length relationships.

Outside the walls of labor, management, and the legal specialists who advise them, most workers, citizens, and thoughtful leaders wish for a better approach, one that respects workers' rights to exercise their legal rights to association and their desire to have a voice at work and a management approach that generates cooperation, not conflict. Historically and currently, the majority of U.S. workers expect more out of labor-management relations than is often delivered. Polls over many years consistently indicate the majority of Americans disapprove of strikes and a majority of workers want management and union leaders to create workplaces that are productive, relationships that are respectful, not fraught with conflict and tension, and organizations that meet the needs of their customers and the community in general.[18]

Lessons from Other Partnerships

To meet these higher expectations and hopes, labor and management leaders have turned to a range of partnership strategies. Indeed, partnerships have waxed and waned throughout most of U.S. labor-management history. In the 1920s, a number of leading railroads and their unions worked together to put their history of violent conflicts behind them as they sought to expand passenger service across the country. During World War II, productivity and safety committees were created in plants across the country to foster production and ensure that those contributing to the war effort labored under safe working conditions.

Another wave of partnership activity occurred in the 1980s and 1990s in response to intensified competitive pressures in steel, automobile, and other manufacturing industries. Partnerships were credited with reviving companies. For example, by working in partnership with the International Association of Machinists and Aerospace Workers and United Steelworkers of America, Harley-Davidson was able to recover from near bankruptcy and to once again become an icon of the motorcycle industry. In 1982, a joint venture between General Motors and Toyota was formed to reopen a failed GM plant in Fremont, CA. Out of the ashes of that GM plant, which had the worst labor relations and performance record, emerged the New United Motors Manufacturing, Inc. (NUMMI). By working together and implementing the Toyota Production System, within two years the same union and most of the same workers were producing cars at world-class levels of productivity and quality.[19]

The Harley-Davidson and NUMMI partnerships remain in place more than two decades after their creation. But many partnerships do not survive, at least in the forms in which they were first conceived.

Consider the Saturn Corporation, perhaps the most ambitious and visible example of a labor-management partnership created in the 1980s.[20] Saturn was created as a new division of General Motors in 1985 and began producing cars in 1990. It was conceived as a partnership from the outset, with a joint team working together for several years to design both a new organization and a new small car for the U.S. market, which GM could not do profitably at the time. Saturn was to be a "new kind of organization," designed with partnership principles from top to bottom. Union partners worked side by side with executives in manufacturing, marketing, human resources, product development, and other functions. Union representatives served on both a strategic advisory committee and a manufacturing council. Work teams were jointly led by labor and management partners.

Saturn's early years were highly successful. The concept of a "new kind of organization and a new kind of car" created a buzz among U.S. car buyers and the parties produced and sold vehicles that achieved top quality ratings from consumers. But leadership turnover, ambivalence about sharing as much power as was called for in the Saturn agreement, and delays in authorizing new products eventually led to considerable resistance from those at the top of both the United Auto Workers (UAW) and GM. In 2003, GM and UAW brought the Saturn division back under the national collective bargaining contract. Nonetheless, labor and management leaders at Saturn continued to work together in a modified and simplified partnership that carried over many of the principles of the initial model. And Saturn once again regained momentum, producing new models that were well received by customers and experts alike. In 2006 one of its models was named the "car of the year" at the Detroit Auto Show. By 2008 Saturn, like all of GM, was again in decline.

Another instructive partnership experience comes from the steel industry. In 1993, as the United Steelworkers of America (USW) began preparing to negotiate separate contracts with major steel companies, USW president Lynn Williams was convinced that a new approach was needed. LTV, one of the largest steel companies, had already been through bankruptcy and other companies were in trouble. During the 1980s, the parties had implemented labor-management participation teams at the plant level that had, in some instances, been quite successful in dealing with production problems. Given the state of the industry, a strategy that moved above the shop floor was needed. The concept that emerged was labeled "New Directions," envisioning a strategic partnership with each of the major integrated companies. Inland Steel, now part of Acelor-Mittal Corp., was the first company to agree to the concept and stipulated that the union would be apprised of all important capital decisions, that a union-nominated director would sit on the corporate board, and that a standing committee of the board would track the partnership. The company agreed to maintain a neutral posture in the face of union organizing (distribution was not unionized), employment security would be assured, and the parties would work cooperatively to increase productivity. The agreement called for joint committees from the top of the organization to the shop floor.

Though successful in its early years, this partnership floundered when the union belatedly became aware of the company's bid to acquire some assets in Venezuela. The union also maintained that Inland Steel had violated the neutrality provision during organizing campaigns on the distribution side of the business. An additional reason for the union withdrawing from the partnership to a posture of what it referred to as "professional adversarialism" was the fact that when the parties attempted to negotiate a wage increase in 1996 they reached an impasse, which had to be resolved by an arbitrator.[21]

An even sadder story comes from efforts to build and sustain a partnership between AT&T and two of its unions—the Communications Workers of America (CWA) and the International Brotherhood of Electrical Workers (IBEW). Beginning with a contractual Quality of Work Life (QWL) program established in 1983, AT&T and its unions went through a number of iterations of union and worker involvement in decision making. The QWL program was undermined by various organizational stresses, including the breakup of the Bell telephone system and rapid and substantial technological changes within the telecommunications industry. In 1992, the parties revived and expanded the quality of work life efforts in the form of Workplace of the Future (WPOF). The WPOF partnership involved union-management committees at the top level of the corporation as well as within business units where significant business decisions were being made. In addition, union members participated in teams and committees at various levels of the organization. WPOF included a system for integrating collective bargaining and partnership by providing a high-level labor-management committee that could approve local experiments that were in conflict with collective bargaining agreements.[22]

Although the WPOF story is replete with many local success stories involving improved organizational outcomes for the company, workers, and customers, it too proved ultimately unsustainable. The decision by AT&T to eventually split itself into three separate companies is symptomatic of the severe competitive pressures it was under; and the fact that the unions received notice of the decision only shortly before the news media was emblematic of the limits of partnership at the strategic level. Partnership continued to struggle along at the pared-down AT&T and at its spun-off manufacturing operation, Lucent Technologies, taking different forms depending on the business context. But the union-AT&T partnership ultimately collapsed with the CWA's withdrawal in the face of continued allegations over management's conduct in resisting union organizing campaigns in the parts of AT&T's business that were growing and represented the future of the business (and of union membership). Even without that proximate cause, the partnership would likely have been unsustainable, given the incessant size and shape shifting—trivesting, merging with new partners, spinning off business lines while adding others—that AT&T has undergone in recent years.

These examples suggest that partnerships are vulnerable to the departure of their original champions, who challenge traditional management precepts for maintaining "control" over the workforce and labor relations. They challenge traditional labor union precepts that stress the need to avoid getting too close to management or being co-opted into supporting unpopular management actions. They require considerable leadership skills and training of both management and labor representatives to change their traditional behaviors toward each other. They require adopting new ways to negotiate, resolve conflicts, and solve problems. They require the resources and fortitude to invest in infrastructure and joint processes that take time to show results. And they require patience, acceptance of occasional setbacks, and periodic reinforcement of the recognition that working together is better than the alternative of either suppressing workers' desire for a voice and rights or arm's-length, adversarial engagement.

Federal labor law remains a major constraint on the adoption and sustainability of partnerships. The whole premise of the NLRA as enforced by the NLRB is that labor relations will be adversarial. The Act draws a clear line of demarcation between management responsibilities and rights to allocate resources and direct the workforce and labor's rights to negotiate over the impacts of management decisions on wages, hours, and working conditions. Figure 2.1 illustrates both the constraints of existing labor law and the

Here's how it sizes up ...

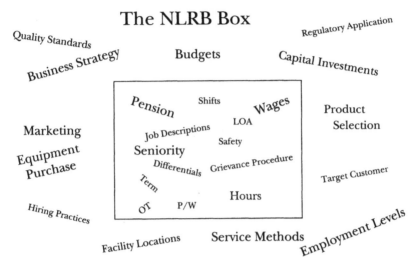

Figure 2.1. The "NLRB Box," courtesy of Peter diCicco

potential of a partnership in health care for breaking out of what Peter di-Cicco describes as the "NLRB Box." Inside the box are the issues that current NLRB rules require unions and employers to negotiate. Outside of the box is a plethora of issues central to the quality and cost of health care. These are the kinds of issues being taken up jointly by labor and management in the Kaiser partnership.

Such efforts are restrained by twentieth-century thinking about how work is organized, organizations are structured, and goods and services are produced and delivered. To the modern workforce and those designing modern organizations, such thinking may seem to belong in a museum. Workers today expect to have a voice at work and they expect management to listen to their ideas. Organizational design specialists emphasize the importance of building networks that draw on the knowledge of the full workforce and coordinate their efforts. Rather than dividing people into management and labor camps, contemporary models of work organization stress teamwork among people who bring different, specialized knowledge to bear on the tasks at hand. This is the potential creativity and shared commitment that labor-management partnerships in general and the KP Labor-Management Partnership in particular, seek to mobilize.

Unfortunately, even recent decisions by the NLRB—the agency charged with enforcing and interpreting labor law—undercut such attempts. In 2006, for example, the NLRB ruled in a series of cases to exclude charge nurses (nurses assigned the responsibility of organizing and overseeing the work of fellow nurses on a given shift) from union membership and collective bargaining coverage. This ruling has had the effect of driving an artificial wedge between nurses who work side-by-side and often in teams. Such a view by the NLRB defies all recent evidence that teamwork contributes to quality care and the consensus of countless reports that argue teamwork among nurses and among nurses, doctors, and other health care workers should be encouraged.[23]

In summary, this brief trip through the history and current context of U.S. labor relations illustrates why partnerships are rather rare, live such a precarious life, and are hard to sustain. Yet, despite such history, from time to time both business and labor leaders turn to partnerships when faced with the recognition that their current relationships are not meeting their needs. This is exactly the situation that led labor and management leaders to decide to try partnership at Kaiser Permanente.

CHAPTER 3

To Fight or Partner: Forming the Partnership

Against such an uneven history of labor-management partnership success and with federal labor law increasingly working against organized labor, establishing a labor-management partnership between a coalition of twenty-seven unions and an organization as complex as 8.6 million-member Kaiser Permanente (KP) was no easy task. This was especially so because the choice to partner rather than to fight was made in an environment of growing anger and frustration among Kaiser's workers, increasing competitive pressures on health care insurers and providers, and rising concerns about the quality of care of health maintenance organizations in general and Kaiser in particular.

That the partnership was created at all—let alone that it continues to thrive, even with problems and criticisms—speaks to a longer tradition of positive relations between Kaiser and the labor movement, a tradition born in the late 1930s on the Columbia River in Washington state.

In 1938, Henry J. Kaiser, who left his native New York at the age of 24 in 1906 to move west, led a consortium of construction companies building the Grand Coulee Dam. Kaiser and his partners had also won contracts to build the Hoover Dam, a project that typified the labor conflict growing across the nation. As recounted in Rickey Hendricks's 1993 history of Kaiser Permanente, it was during the Grand Coulee project that Kaiser became a believer in and supporter of unions. During World War II, Kaiser was recognized not only for delivering ships from his California shipyard in about one-third of the time allotted by the government, but for establishing child-care centers to meet the needs of the growing number of women employed in the shipyard.

As he had done for an earlier public works project—the Colorado River Aqueduct—Kaiser asked his partner Sidney Garfield, MD, to provide health care to the 6,500 workers engaged in the Grand Coulee Dam project.

Workers paid for the plan with a 50 cent per week payroll deduction (about $7 in current dollars) for health care not related to work injuries. Workers' families, however, had to access health care through traditional, fee-for-service arrangements that were unaffordable for most of them. The unions representing the workers pushed successfully for a medical plan to cover the workers' dependents, at a cost of 50 cents per week for wives and 25 cents per week for dependents.[1] Although popular discussions rarely highlight this fact, Kaiser Permanente, one of the first HMOs, was created largely by union pressure.

The Grand Coulee Dam project represented a transition in Kaiser's approach to dealing with unions. Kaiser's earlier public works projects had seen union organizing in the radical western, rural tradition. Kaiser and his partners had aggressively resisted the union demands, at the same time improving some of the horrendous conditions that inspired militancy in the first place. At Grand Coulee, the Kaiser company took a different approach:

> Henry Kaiser, an ambivalent witness to union organizing at Hoover Dam in the early part of the decade, now committed himself to establishing good labor relations. Garfield later remembered that at Grand Coulee Kaiser "surprised" him with his views on the role of unions in the new industrial order. "It was his feeling," Garfield said, "that unions were absolutely necessary in the industrial world of today. He felt that the unions were a great contribution to that; he felt they were necessary and he was 100 percent for them."[2]

Henry Kaiser did not invent prepaid medical plans but he was the first to build to large scale an integrated model that included prepaid group health insurance and medical care provided by groups of physicians in the organization's own medical facilities and hospitals. He also left his personal imprint on the organization he founded. Like most successful entrepreneurs, Kaiser had strong views and a significant flare for promoting causes he championed.

He attacked with vigor those who opposed him—at times, including the physicians who partnered with him in providing health care. As such, the sometimes tenuous and often fractious relationship between the Kaiser organization and its physicians can be traced all the way back to the founder of this institution.

In the years following the completion of Grand Coulee Dam, Kaiser and Garfield took the model of a prepaid group health care plan to the rapidly expanding (and unionized) Kaiser ship-building enterprise. The first Kaiser shipyards were in Richmond, California, and the Portland, Oregon, area. In 1942, Garfield opened clinics and hospitals to serve the thousands of workers employed at these facilities. From this base, the health plan and medical facilities (run by what was called the Permanente Foundation) moved rapidly into Southern California. Shortly after the war, the plan was opened to the general public and gradually expanded, largely by adding union health plans and union members to its customer base. The International Longshoremen's and Warehouseman's Union (ILWU) became a particularly strong supporter of the Kaiser plan, helping establish it in port communities where they had substantial membership. By the mid-1950s, ILWU, as well as the Retail Clerks and Culinary Union members and their dependents, represented one-third of KP's Southern California "members" (as KP calls its individual customers). The United Steelworkers throughout California, beginning with the local representing workers at Kaiser's steel plant in Fontana, chose the KP health plan when it was offered.

Henry Kaiser remained closely involved in the operations of the organization and in 1951 pushed to have his name added to the various Permanente organizations. The Permanente Medical Group successfully fought off this proposal, but Kaiser's name was attached to the health plan and hospital foundation. In the mid-1950s, Permanente doctors sought to gain greater independence and control from the Kaiser Foundation and eventually negotiated the modern-day Kaiser Permanente organizational arrangement. Thus was born the structure that remains in place today known as Kaiser Permanente: a partnership between the Kaiser Foundation Health Plan and Hospitals (KFHPH) and the various regional Permanente Medical Groups (PMGs). The PMGs today have more than 13,000 physicians and a large number of other health care providers, whereas the first partner is made up of the health maintenance organization (HMO) insurance plan and the twenty-nine medical centers and many other health care facilities owned by Kaiser.

The Structure of Kaiser Permanente

Kaiser Permanente operates across several states, and is internally managed as eight regions—Northern and Southern California, Colorado, Georgia, Hawaii, Mid-Atlantic (Washington, DC, Maryland, and Virginia), Northwest (Northwest Oregon and Southwest Washington), and Ohio. The national headquarters (known as the "Program office") is located in Oakland, CA.

Each of the regions comprises several separate but interdependent legal entities. All the regions have their own Kaiser Foundation Health Plans, which sell prepaid health plans to employers, employees, and individual members. These health plans are legally not-for-profit public-benefit corporations, and they fund the Kaiser hospitals and pay for the services of the medical groups. All the regions also have their own Permanente Medical Groups, which are physician-owned for-profit partnerships or professional corporations through which 13,729 doctors serve only the Kaiser health plans. All the regions operate outpatient facilities—a total of 416 medical offices, and four of them also operate their own hospitals—a total of 32 in Northern and Southern California, Oregon, and Hawaii. The hospitals are managed by regional, not-for-profit Kaiser Foundation Hospitals.

The Permanente Medical Groups are coordinated through the Permanente Federation, which is a separate entity focusing on systemwide care policies. The PMGs also created the Permanente Company to pursue investment opportunities, most notably through Kaiser Permanente Ventures—a venture capital firm that invests in emerging medical technologies.

Regional membership (as of 31 May 2007) included:

- Northern California: 3,286,230
- Southern California: 3,248,933
- Colorado: 475,913
- Georgia: 283,001
- Hawaii: 223,284
- Mid-Atlantic states: 507,630
- Ohio: 149,745
- Northwest: 483,552

Source: Kaiser Permanente Office of Labor-Management Partnership

---

The various Permanente Medical Groups operate as for-profit corporations or limited partnerships, contracting services solely to Kaiser Foundation Health Plans and Hospitals, while the latter retains its not-for-profit status.

However, this massive and complex structure did not come easily. As detailed by Hendricks, Kaiser took on one public battle after another for forty years after the Grand Coulee Dam project. He defended Permanente doctors against the vehement attacks of the American Medical Association as he fought an ongoing battle to gain greater control over the doctors. He worked with unions to expand health care coverage while simultaneously battling John L. Lewis over union efforts to gain a greater voice in the governance of their health plans. He battled to keep KP doctors from being drafted in the Korean War, but he responded to the McCarthy era by requiring his own version of a loyalty oath from employees. After moving in 1958 to Hawaii, where he lived until his death in 1967, he created—in the face of opposition from the Hawaii Medical Association—Kaiser Permanente's Hawaii region.

Kaiser faced resistance from organized medicine early on. "[The American Medical Association] condemned contract practice, even as the trend grew in the region," wrote Hendricks. "AMA and labor leaders both charged that company-paid doctors were unsympathetic to patients and represented employer 'intrusion . . . into intimate family relationships.' . . . The AMA vehemently defended the traditional system of solo fee-for-service practice because it preserved values of individualism, voluntarism, and doctor-patient trust. Direct payment for care signified this trust, giving both participants a stake in the healing process."[3]

This battle would continue for the next thirty years, with national- and state-level medical societies seeking to deny membership to KP physicians as communists or communist sympathizers during the McCarthy era or later as advocates of "socialized medicine."

Despite their organizational alliance and dependence on Kaiser for their employment and financial well-being (Permanente physicians were generally paid well above the income levels of solo practitioners), the doctor-Permanente relationship was fraught with continuous tension and conflict. Early on, the Permanente physicians developed their own norms and philosophy separate from Kaiser management, in part to build the power they needed to deal with Kaiser (the company employing their patients) and in part to ward off the criticism of their medical colleagues for deviating from the traditional solo practitioner model. The differences reached a peak in the early 1950s, when the Northern California Permanente Group demanded independence. A series of heated negotiations produced the current organizational arrangement: Permanente doctors would have their own organizations and governance structures and freedom to make their own financial arrangements (including for-profit group practices and clinics), and would contract with the Kaiser Health Plan and Foundation for the delivery of health care to members of the Kaiser health plans.

The legacy of Henry Kaiser is thus the largest, non-profit prepaid integrated health care program in the country, one created in partnership and with the support of union employees and union customers. Kaiser's efforts led to the acceptance of HMO plans around the country. This legacy has played a key role in helping attract idealistic and dedicated physicians, nurses, and other employees to Kaiser Permanente over the years. And as we will see, it also exerted a significant impact on labor leaders in 1996 as they contemplated whether to go to war or to form a labor-management partnership with Kaiser Permanente.

"The HMO That Labor Built"

Given its origins, it is not surprising that workers and Kaiser Permanente embraced collective bargaining shortly after the non-profit organization was created, which was long before non-profit hospitals were required to recognize unions under federal labor laws. SEIU Local 49 in Portland signed its first contract in 1946. By 2007, KP employed approximately 130,000 workers, of whom more than 100,000 were represented by unions. Of these, 86,000 were represented by unions in the Labor-Management Partnership (LMP).

The complexities involved in building and sustaining a coalition among a widely diverse set of unions representing Kaiser workers is discussed in more detail in chapter 7. Table 3.1 presents a complete list of the local unions involved in the coalition. SEIU represents the single largest group, accounting for 60 percent of union members in the coalition, representing mostly lower skilled workers (e.g., maintenance, food service, nursing assistants, and unit clerks) in both California regions, the Northwest, and Colorado. Consistent with the strategic restructuring undertaken by SEIU under the Andy Stern administration, on 1 January 2005, the two large locals representing KP California members were merged into a "mega local"—United Healthcare Workers-West (UHW)—creating the nation's second largest health care local, with about 126,000 members at that time, 40,000 of whom worked for KP. UHW also represents health care workers throughout California, including hospital workers at the Sutter, Tenet, and Catholic Health West systems.

The United Steelworkers represents workers at Kaiser's Fontana facilities, reflecting the historical relationship of that service area to the early Kaiser company's manufacturing plant and the union that represented its workers. The United Nurses Association of California (UNAC) was born when unorganized

Table 3.1. Coalition Unions at Kaiser Permanente

Union	1997 membership	2006 membership	KP region	Main occupations represented at KP
United Nurses Association of California (UNAC- AFSCME)	4,500	9,519	S. California	RNs
Oregon Federation of Nurses and Health Professionals (AFT)	1,238	2,577	Northwest	RNs/professionals
International Brotherhood of Teamsters	N/A	317	S. California Ohio	Technicians Nursing assistants
International Federation of Professional and Technical Engineers	826	1,133	N. California	Optometrists, lab scientists, technicians
KP Nurse Anesthetist Association	250	300	S. California	Nurse anesthetists
Office and Professional Employees International Union	5,300	10,525		
LOCAL 2			Mid-Atlantic	
LOCAL 17			Ohio	All groups
LOCAL 29			N. California	Clerical and other
LOCAL 30			S. California	
LOCAL 277			Texas	
SEIU	29,130	50,033		Maintenance, food service, nursing assistants and unit clerks, and others, except 535
LOCAL 49			Northwest	
LOCAL 105			Colorado	
LOCAL 250 (merged into UHW)			N. California	
LOCAL 399 (merged into UHW)			S. California	
LOCAL 535			California	Professionals including RNs
United American Nurses	N/A	140	Ohio Northwest	RNs RNs
UFCW	3,332	6,831		
LOCALS 135, 324, 770, 1036, 1167, 1428, 1442			S. California	
LOCAL 7			Colorado	RNs, professionals
LOCAL 27			Mid-Atlantic	RNs, professionals
LOCAL 400			Mid-Atlantic	RNs, professionals

(*continued*)

Table 3.1 (*continued*)

Union	1997 membership	2006 membership	KP region	Main occupations represented at KP
LOCAL 555			Northwest	Technicians
LOCAL 1996			Georgia	All groups
USWA 7600	2,800	4,663	S. California	Most groups other than nurses

Source: Coalition of Kaiser Permanente Unions.

Fontana RNs formed their own union after witnessing the power of unionization among other workers. The Fontana nurses allied with other Southern California hospitals' RNs to form UNAC as an independent union in 1972. UNAC affiliated with the American Federation of State, County and Municipal Employees (AFSCME) in 1989. Similarly, the RNs at KP's Sunnyside hospital in Portland, OR, organized in 1979 into the Oregon Federation of Nurses and Health Professionals (OFNHP), an affiliate of the health care division of the American Federation of Teachers (AFT). The Kaiser Permanente Nurse Anesthetist Association, representing nurse anesthetists in the Southern California region remains a small, independent union.

The Office and Professional Employees International Union (OPEIU) represents the second largest block of Kaiser workers after SEIU. Small OPEIU locals represent KP workers in Southern and Northern California and Ohio. Twelve locals of the United Food and Commercial Workers (UFCW) represent a few thousand workers across five Kaiser regions. The UFCW operates substantial health and welfare funds; the union's relationship with Kaiser and its representation of Kaiser workers stem from the choice of Kaiser as a provider under the union's health plans.

Almost all of these local unions represent non-Kaiser workers in addition to their Kaiser members. Some represent only other health care workers (e.g., SEIU-UHW, UNAC, OFNHP). Others represent various kinds of workers. Interestingly, the largest OPEIU local represents clerical staff working for the United Healthcare Workers-West—SEIU. UFCW locals are typically large amalgamated locals with members from a wide array of sectors and employers. For instance, one of the two Washington, DC area (Mid-Atlantic region for KP) locals representing KP workers has 40,000 members working for over sixty different employers, only a handful of which are other health care employees. That particular local represents about 1,000 KP workers. This diversity in the makeup of the local unions creates challenges for union leaders in serving members who work in very different labor-management environments—ranging from highly cooperative to very adversarial.

All of the unions described thus far were founding members of the coalition that participates in the partnership. Since the coalition's formation, affiliates of two other national unions have joined: United American Nurses (UAN), the AFL-CIO affiliate, which is also the collective bargaining affiliate of the American Nurses Association with members in Kaiser's Ohio and Northwest regions, and the International Brotherhood of Teamsters, which represents a small group of technicians in Southern California and nursing assistants in Ohio.

As we discuss later, other unions that represent Kaiser workers are, for various reasons, not part of the coalition or the partnership. The most significant of these is the California Nurses Association, which represents nearly 12,000 nurses in Kaiser's Northern California region. Also not part of the partnership are most of 2,000 Kaiser workers in Hawaii, who are represented by UNITE-HERE. Another 2,000 non-partnership employees are represented by the independent Pharmacists Guild. Most of the remaining unions not involved in the partnership represent small units of skilled trade workers (painters, operating engineers, laborers, carpenters). Despite strong opposition from SEIU, the Communications Workers of America organized a KP call center in 2004. At that time, SEIU had begun its campaign to better align union structures with industries, and thus opposed this entry of yet another union into the Kaiser jurisdiction. To demonstrate its seriousness in this regard, SEIU opposed CWA joining the coalition, effectively blocking its entry.

1980s and 1990s: Growing Competitive Pressures

Besides its roots, another factor explains why labor-management relations have been generally positive for most of KP's fifty-year history. Until the 1980s, KP was one of the nation's lowest-cost health care providers. It was also able to pass on the costs of improvements in its labor contracts to its customers. Unions continued to find Kaiser Permanente attractive as a service provider for their members and negotiated KP options into many contracts. And as an innovative HMO, KP focused on preventive services at reasonable cost, which served working families especially well.

In the late 1980s and early 1990s, however, KP began experiencing severe competitive challenges, particularly from for-profit health care insurers aggressively seeking to increase their market share. As then SEIU president John Sweeney summarized the situation in the mid-1990s:

> [O]ver a period of nearly 50 years, organized labor is an outright sponsor of Kaiser Permanente as a low-cost, high quality health plan for working families. We bring members in by the hundreds of thousands through our Taft-Hartley plans because Kaiser promises to buy union, build union, and hire union—a great social compact. Then suddenly, HMOs enter a new world of competition, similar to what corporations encountered in the early 1970s. Kaiser decides to take the same low road to the bottom by slashing labor costs—restructuring, outsourcing, closing hospitals, and changing patient care standards—without consulting either plan members or the workers that deliver their care.[4]

KP also decided to pursue an expansion strategy around the country, including moving into some predominantly non-union areas, such as Atlanta and North Carolina. This expansion created problems. For one thing, KP was moving into areas where it had no track record and thus could not take advantage of its reputation for quality care. Moreover, quality problems sometimes emerged as these new units ramped up and quality problems also appeared as operations in better established regions came under increasing cost pressures. When KP posted substantial losses, totaling $900 million from 1995 to 1997, Kaiser pulled back from Texas, Kansas City, New York, New England, and North Carolina. These setbacks were a shock to an organization that had grown steadily since World War II.

KP responded by hiring the well-known consulting firm McKinsey and Co. The consultants recommended that Kaiser abandon its integrated model of care and begin selling off hospitals. Rather than following McKinsey's advice, Kaiser lowered prices to attract new members. Although this pricing strategy did foster membership growth, it resulted in additional revenue losses because the pricing strategy was not matched with a strategy to build the internal capacity necessary to efficiently serve new patients. From its beginnings, Kaiser has been able to be cost-effective when members' medical services are kept in-house; but it pays a heavy price when members are referred outside of Kaiser facilities and networks. Reflecting both a changing context and business strategy, KP began to pursue a new, tougher labor relations strategy that produced a series of layoffs, collective bargaining concessions, and perceived "de-skilling." The result was an increasingly demoralized workforce during the early 1990s. As many front-line workers put it, "This is not the Kaiser we came to work for."

Worker frustration welled up in focus groups conducted for the union coalition in 1998. "It used to be we all worked together to help the patients," said one KP worker. "I used to feel good about myself at the end of a workday. Now they're cutting professional staff and then they come and tell me I'm taking too long to do my job." Other employees cited a lack of job security. "Every time there's a merger, people lose jobs," said another worker.

Many workers said patient care was suffering. "I find I cannot provide patients with the kind of quality I would like to provide because I'm overworked," said one worker. Another worker added, "They keep cutting the staff back, and that puts an extra burden on the remaining staff. The workload stays the same, but now there are less people to do it. So they're going out on disability, or worker's comp, with stress-related problems, because you're overworked, because of the lack of employees. It's a vicious cycle."

Kaiser's unions responded aggressively. Some locals staged protracted and bitter strikes. SEIU Local 250, for instance, conducted a seven-week strike in 1986, primarily to resist a two-tiered wage structure that they ended up having to accept anyway. SEIU Local 535 in Southern California conducted multiple strikes from the late 1970s through 1990. The Oregon nurses union went on strike for fifty-eight days in 1988. UNAC, which had struck Kaiser in 1977 and 1980, facing demands for substantial cutbacks in 1995 negotiations, took a strike vote but ultimately accepted major concessions. The California Nurses Association conducted strikes between 1996 and 1998—the period of the development of the partnership. Besides the effects on employee morale and Kaiser operations, such labor discontent carried another cost for Kaiser—bad publicity. The organization that was long hailed for both quality care and positive employee relations was now generating opposite headlines.

The Unions Come Together

Despite their frequency, none of these strikes were coordinated among the various Kaiser locals, which bargained locally. In this context of historic local union decentralization and growing difficulties with KP, SEIU locals representing KP workers in Northern and Southern California, Oregon, and

Colorado began to meet to strategize and share information. The unions recognized that their disunity created a strategic disadvantage with Kaiser. "We are always catching up with Kaiser," said Sal Rosselli, then-president of SEIU's Northern California health care local. "It took a couple of years until [different locals] had the first Kaiser meeting. . . . We started getting to know each other. We met for a couple of years, periodically. It was useful. We had more information and we brainstormed solutions. But there was no control— every local was autonomous."

According to coalition assistant director Margaret Peisert, top SEIU officials were also looking at the relationship between Kaiser and its unions. "Sandy Polaski [director of bargaining for SEIU nationally] was very interested in [Kaiser,] the largest union health care employer. We're spending all our time fighting with them, everything's going to hell, this is contrary to how we really want to build relationships and build the industry," Peisert said. "We started with the SEIU locals. If we could get them talking to each other and thinking about Kaiser, we might have a shot at getting all the union involved. But we had to get our own house in order first."

Leaders of other unions were reaching the same conclusions. Suffering the consequences of union-by-union bargaining, some local union leaders began to think that inter-union cooperation could improve things. These leaders had seen their positive relationship with Kaiser deteriorate. They had taken layoffs and concessions. With tough negotiations looming in 1995, SEIU—still led by John Sweeney—approached the Industrial Union Department of the AFL-CIO, both because of the department's experience with coordinated bargaining and because a "neutral" body was needed to coordinate the fractious unions. "We really needed someone at the Federation to pull this together," said Peisert. "The IUD was the only department then that really did any kind of coordinated bargaining. That's where we thought we'd start."

In January 1995, Peter diCicco, then IUD secretary-treasurer, asked the presidents of all AFL-CIO unions representing workers at Kaiser to attend an organizing meeting. The first International President's Committee meeting was held in February 1995, followed two months later by what was then called the IUD-Kaiser Permanente Coordinated Bargaining Committee, which was attended by more than 100 delegates. A steering committee composed of local union presidents first met in Denver in June of the same year. At these and other meetings, the unions exchanged information about particular local struggles and began developing a joint strategy and structure.

Plan A or Plan B?

Almost from the beginning, what would become the union coalition pursued two tracks: an adversarial approach focused on a corporate campaign and an approach to Kaiser around a partnership. As Kathy Schmidt, the leader of the OFNHP at the time, and later a coalition staff person, put it, "One was a corporate fight preparation, threatening to attack their quality, and then there was a back door conversation at the same time, 'there must be a better way to do this.'" The local leaders talked about the dual approaches as Plan A and Plan B. "Plan A was to negotiate, to partner," said another local leader from the Northwest. Plan B was to negotiate but to be strategic (in applying public pressure) and aligned for the first time. Plan B would have been a lot of fun."

DiCicco—partly because of his own role in job enrichment when he was business agent of the IUE (International Union of Electrical Workers) local at General Electric's plant in Lynn, Massachusetts—was interested in a partnership approach. In mid-1995, IUD developed a proposal for a "strategic analysis and campaign." It emphasized the dual track approach:

> We feel there is potential—and a great need—for a modified competitive vision that will be successful for Kaiser in the marketplace, will enhance quality of care, and will foster a much more positive relationship between Kaiser and its workforce. By extension, a strategic partnership provides an alternative vision for the industry as a whole to contrast with the non-union, low wage future portrayed in Kaiser's own assessments. Our first and most immediate goal, however, is to forcefully demonstrate to Kaiser that its current competitive strategy, and the labor relations strategy derived from it, will not be successful.

At this early stage, the unions understood that Kaiser had real business problems. But they rejected management's business strategy. Although the unions agreed to fund a corporate campaign against Kaiser, many leaders remained concerned about the impact of such a campaign on KP. "[W]e might do permanent damage to them and to our 55,000 union members if we mount an all-out corporate campaign or use the information we amassed for short-term advantage or leverage," said diCicco.

Kaiser Permanente Management Mulls over Its Labor Relations Strategy

As the unions organized strikes and became increasingly vocal about quality of care issues, consumer advocates were also attacking Kaiser's quality record. The formation of the union coalition and the adversarial strategies the coalition was considering caused consternation among labor relations professionals within Kaiser. According to Tom Williamson, then the vice president for human relations in Kaiser's Northwest region, Kaiser worried about threats of corporate campaigns, further strikes, and bad press. "A number of us close to all this . . . on the management side saw us heading toward a major disaster here. The unions were coming together, working collaboratively, and we had riled them up, and the employees were riled up, more importantly, and were ready to confront us," he said. "While contract expirations were staggered, we saw the possibility they would just let contracts expire and stack up and confront us with a joint strike. Given our values and [the] nature of the organization, locking out people was not an option. . . . I and others were ringing the fire alarm. [A] collision is coming unless we do something."

Al Bolden, the head of Kaiser's labor relations unit at the time, began discussing these issues with Kaiser CEO David Lawrence and other leaders. One option—to preempt a coordinated joint strike by locking out local unions that would not reach agreement—was quickly dismissed as not practical. "The public would go nuts if we locked out hospital workers and closed hospitals," said Williamson. Medical group leaders were also greatly interested in avoiding strikes, which they saw as disruptive to medical care.

Management realized that the unions were also concerned about an adversarial approach and were considering a partnership instead. This mutual realization led to high-level conversations about such an approach.

The partnership was thus not the product of an ideological conversion to labor-management cooperation on the part of either the union coalition or Kaiser Permanente management, but developed out of a pragmatic judgment that the parties would have more to lose separately and jointly by going further down the path of escalating conflict. Nor were diCicco and other union leaders considering partnership in a vacuum. In its 1994 "New American Workplace" report, the AFL-CIO detailed a set of labor principles for engaging in work reform and labor-management partnerships.[5] But consistent with its dual track approach, the union coalition obtained funding for the adversarial strategy, launching its campaign with a joint press conference with the North Carolina AFL-CIO to publicize a negative government agency report on the quality of Kaiser's health care in that state.

By thus intensifying the pressures even while raising the possibility of an alternative—a more collaborative approach—the union leaders set the context for the December 1995 meeting at the Dallas airport, which produced the initial decision to explore the partnership option. John Sweeney and David Lawrence described how their respective organizations approached this choice and came to the decision to try the partnership option.

John Sweeney

What happens? A huge labor-management crisis is created. Suddenly there are 30,000 AFL-CIO members with open contracts in the HMO that labor built. We offer a strategic partnership to CEO David Lawrence to try and end the crisis before it gets out of hand.

After weeks of turmoil, we were not only successful in getting the contracts settled, but our offer to form a partnership was accepted. So sometimes out of crisis and determined effort comes a willingness to try a better alternative.

David Lawrence

I was willing to try anything at that point because it was clear that the path we were on . . . was a dead end. We were going to be facing labor strife in every corner of our organization. We had 54 labor contracts, 36 unions, and if they go south on us, we have a crisis on our hands—at the same time we were in a fair amount of conflict between the Medical Groups and the Health Plan—what I saw was an organization that was starting to balkanize in very serious ways. A lot of this was being driven by external things and a lot of it was being driven by changes we were trying to make in the organization at a strategic level.

It should be noted that even during this stage of the partnership discussion, contracts were still concessionary from the point of view of the unions and the members. Kathy Sackman's union of nurses in Southern California, UNAC, had been gearing up for a strike in 1995 in response to a final offer of 12 percent wage cut but had lost the support of its members. "We went back in, and hammered out a deal," recalled Sackman. "We took some cuts and some reductions in benefits. It was the first time a contract was barely ratified." Dave Bullock, then leader of the large SEIU local representing workers in Kaiser's Southern California region, similarly called his union's 1996 contract "a huge takeaway settlement." No wonder that union members were doubtful about the partnership. "I am very suspicious of the Partnership," said one focus group member. "There has been a lot of doublespeak by Kaiser in the past few years and I think this is just more of the same. We have a union that's supposed to be representing the workers, and now they turn around and say they have a partnership with Kaiser. That raises a lot of questions for me. Who came up with this partnership? Whose idea was it?"

There were other reasons why union members were wary of a labor-management partnership. The recent history of management seeking concessions certainly created an atmosphere of distrust and suspicion. But more fundamental to the unease was the belief held by many union activists that the interests of labor are best served by maintaining an arm's-length posture with employers.

First Steps

After agreeing to pursue a more collaborative approach, the parties sought a consulting firm with significant experience in facilitating labor-management partnerships. After interviewing a number of candidates, they chose Restructuring Associates, Inc. (RAI), a Washington-based firm founded by Tom Schneider. Facilitator and consultant John Stepp, who led RAI's efforts at Kaiser, brought a wide range of experience to the process as a former Federal Mediation and Conciliation Service mediator and a former U.S. Labor Department under secretary of labor, and head of the Department's Bureau of Labor-Management Relations and Cooperative Programs. Stepp was a national expert on how to design and sustain labor-management partnerships. He and Schneider gradually brought in a number of other facilitation experts to the project.

Going from agreement in principle to exploring a partnership to producing an actual partnership agreement required an intensive negotiation and problem-solving process, which took most of 1996 and stretched into 1997 and was led by senior KP executives and union leaders, with significant assistance from Stepp and Schneider. The parties at the table brought both different and overlapping interests to these negotiations. One leading Kaiser physician remembered the goals of the doctors when they first began to hear about the partnership:

> What the Medical Groups [saw] overall, they might get from the partnership, was 1) the possibility of avoiding strikes, which are incredibly bad, especially because the hospitals and clinics have to stay open for business during strikes.

Second, in terms of staffing the units, MDs and RN staff worked closely together. They were always concerned about seniority as the major requirement
for filling jobs, as opposed to skill or experience. . . . In addition union seniority rules screwed up all kinds of good working and team relationships. So
if the partnership meant that there would be more flexibility then the physicians would be able to do their work more effectively.

Like the doctors, management was primarily interested in avoiding more
strikes and a potentially devastating corporate campaign. Although management was interested in developing a more cooperative relationship with the
unions, some managers were very wary of bringing union leaders into management decision making. "Partnership was a word we were familiar with in
our company because of our relationship with the medical groups and hospital," said Williamson. "The unions were very clear [that] it meant consensus
decision making at all levels up and down the organization [as in the Saturn
model]. Management didn't have that in mind. . . . [T]he management people
became pretty skeptical of this joint decision, consensus decision making."

Kaiser management was also facing a rift with the medical groups. Some
observers believed that a major management motivation for entering into the
partnership was to stabilize relations with the unions so it could focus on the
problems with the doctors. Management, at least CEO Lawrence, also had
some general ideas about improving the quality of care through team work
and greater collaboration at the worksite.

As talks between health plan management and unions continued toward
reaching a partnership agreement, the toughest issues—besides agreeing on
the scope of shared decision making—involved employment security and
union security. From the beginning, one of the goals of the coalition was to
organize unorganized workers at KP and among other health care providers.
Some union leaders thought that the positive relations developed with management through partnership would lower management resistance to organizing other workers at Kaiser. When the IUD first formed a Coordinated
Bargaining Committee in 1995, Kaiser's non-physician workforce was about
85 percent unionized. There were still substantial pockets of unorganized
workers, possibly as many as 10,000, including many in new regions in which
KP had only begun to operate. The partnership agreement included a section on "Union Security" that called for Kaiser neutrality in organizing campaigns, an "expeditious" process for recognizing unionization when a majority
of workers indicated their desire for representation, a neutral third-party to

resolve disputes, and a commitment by Kaiser to "encourage subcontractors, vendors, mergers, and alliance partners to adopt the same policy regarding the union representation of their employees." This agreement was later expanded in a much longer and more detailed document.

Other union leaders felt that the partnership could be used to demonstrate to other workers and employers that an alternative to traditional adversarial relationships was possible, while some felt (mistakenly as it turns out) that the partnership would require less union staff support and the time freed up could be reallocated to organizing other workers at Kaiser and in the health care sector more generally.

Employment security proved to be the toughest issue. The language finally agreed to by the parties stated that a key partnership agreement goal was to "provide Kaiser Permanente employees with the maximum possible employment and income security within Kaiser Permanente and/or the health care field." Although this would later require additional clarification, it was an essential element of the initial agreement, especially given the memory of layoffs during the period of financial stress in the ten years prior to the establishment of the partnership agreement. "People felt it was fundamental," said Peisert. "You couldn't ask people to step up to the plate, change the way they were doing things, get involved in joint decision making, redesigning work and figuring out new ways of delivering services, or finding efficiencies, if they were going to be putting themselves or a co-worker out of a job."

Once labor and management leaders agreed to the key provisions of the partnership, it needed to be submitted to a vote of the membership of the twenty-seven unions. An intensive process of education of front-line workers and union members preceded the vote. Most union members had not heard of a labor-management partnership, nor did they know how it would affect their interests. The unions held a national teleconference to brief local and regional union leaders and produced videos that featured John Sweeney—by now AFL-CIO president—describing his vision for what a partnership of this size and scope could mean for the future of labor relations and for the labor movement in the United States.

In June 1997, the partnership was approved by 90 percent of the local union members voting (in a process that pooled the votes of all of the local unions involved). Turnout was high, with over 70 percent of Kaiser employees casting votes.

Opting Out

However, not all unions—including one of the most important ones—would participate in the partnership. In April 1997—two months before the vote—the California Nurses Association conducted a one-day strike against Kaiser's Northern California operations, protesting that they had been working without a contract since January of that year and signaling a very different strategic direction than the coalition unions.

Although CNA had participated in the original discussions with the coalition about coordinated bargaining and even partnership, CNA's leaders chose to withdraw before the partnership was negotiated into its final form. CNA actively opposed the partnership agreement during the membership vote.

CNA had specific quarrels with KP and with the partnership. In an eleven-page document excerpted below, CNA detailed its criticisms, going line by line through the agreement. In brief, the CNA feared that partnership committees would supplant local union bargaining authority and rank-and-file participation. CNA felt the partnership would mean the surrender of union weapons, such as a corporate campaign, in exchange for limited and ineffective participation in managerial decisions.

CNA's Objections to Labor-Management Partnership Agreement

1. The Partnership Agreement authorizes a Senior Partnership Committee (SPC) of Kaiser executives and International Union appointees to reach agreements on mandatory subjects of bargaining that will preclude local bargaining by exclusive representatives.
2. Only the "executive level" SPC will have authority to make decisions and negotiate agreements on terms and working conditions including Kaiser restructuring initiatives. The conditions and rules for the SPC's exercise of supreme collective bargaining authority do not permit rank and file involvement in decisions.
3. Vague promises of "greater job security" are belied by the express exclusion of existing Kaiser initiatives and effective forfeiture of Partnership Union rights to challenge the massive job loss that will result from these initiatives.
4. The Partnership Agreement adopts a "new way of doing business" which changes the basic mission and purpose of the AFL-CIO Unions at Kaiser from exclusive representation of the interests of workers and their families to "labor-management collaboration" to achieve "superior health care outcomes, market leading competitive performance, and a superior workplace for Kaiser Permanente employees"

[quoted from the agreement]. The fundamental change in labor's mission is reflected in new affirmative obligations and duties of loyalty imposed on Partnership Unions to actively promote Kaiser health plans and expand Kaiser's share of the HMO market.

5. The AFL-CIO promotes the Partnership as providing a new voice for workers in "decisions affecting patient care standards" but the Partnership Agreement: a) fails to impose any substantive bargaining obligations on Kaiser regarding decisions affecting quality of care; b) exempts existing initiatives which are largely responsible for the current, rapid decline in Kaiser quality and predictable future trend of decline; c) displaces local bargaining authority over the mandatory subject of the quality of care Kaiser employees receive at the "company store"; and d) eliminates effective means of influencing decisions affecting quality of care by gagging critical public comment about quality and Union opposition to Kaiser restructuring initiatives as dangerous for patients and requiring Partnership Unions to undertake their "best efforts" to promote Kaiser quality regardless of current serious defects in health care services and the inevitable further deterioration of quality that will result from existing and planned Kaiser initiatives to reduce and restrict access to care.

Source: "Is the AFL-CIO/Kaiser Partnership in the Best Interest of Health Care Workers and Consumers?" California Nurses Association, 1997.

In particular, CNA seemed troubled by the unions' agreement to promote Kaiser as a quality health care provider "regardless of the facts, the decreasing quality of care at Kaiser, and the ongoing harm to workers and consumers resulting from current Kaiser business initiatives sanctioned by the Agreement." CNA itself was pursuing an alliance with a consumer group— Consumers for Quality Care—to resist Kaiser's plans for cutbacks in its Richmond, Oakland, and Martinez facilities in California.

At the time, CNA was reshaping itself into a more aggressive, more militant, and more collective bargaining-oriented organization, which would eventually lead to its split from the American Nursing Association. CNA executive director Rose Ann DeMoro has been an outspoken critic of partnerships in general and the Kaiser partnership in particular. As stated in a December 15, 2004, email from Frank Borgers on DeMoro's behalf, "CNA does not believe in partnering with employers. We also believe employees do not want this. . . . Most other unions also do not support partnering with employers. Our job is to fight against corporate power, not partner with it."

Although much less vocal about it, other unions, such as the Guild for Professional Pharmacists, an independent union representing KP pharmacists in West Coast facilities, also chose not to join the partnership. Hawaii's KP region had a pre-existing partnership program of its own, which included labor and management, and so it did not join formally.[6] Overall, of approximately 65,000 unionized employees at that time, 57,000 would initially come under the partnership.

The Partnership Agreement and Structure

Table 3.2 summarizes the key provisions of the 1997 Partnership Agreement ratified by the parties in June 1997, illustrating its breadth. In 2002, senior union and management leaders agreed to an additional LMP goal: to consult on public policy issues and jointly advocate when possible and appropriate.

Figure 3.1 depicts the original LMP structure, the complicated nature of which mirrors the complexity of Kaiser Permanente and its decentralized, regional traditions and the parallel structures of the Kaiser and Permanente sides of the organization. The top two dotted boxes represent the two separate coordinating and oversight bodies for KP and the unions: the Kaiser Permanente Partnership Group (KPPG) and the Coalition of Kaiser Permanente Unions (CKPU), respectively. After considerable internal debate, the KPPG was created in 1995 to better coordinate the work of the Hospital and Health Plan and the Permanente sides of KP. Francis J. Crosson, MD, served as co-chair of KPPG, appointed by the medical groups. Dale Crandall, then president of Kaiser Foundation Health Plan and Hospitals, served as the other co-chair until his retirement in 2002. Leslie Margolin, then senior vice president for workforce development, also served as a member of the KPPG. This group met once or twice a month. Although no union representatives were formally part of the KPPG, diCicco began attending these meetings as an observer several years after the partnership was formed.

The coalition led by executive director Peter diCicco, also had various governance structures. At the top sat the International President's Committee (IPC) later replaced by the Executive Board. More regular governance took place under the auspices of the steering committee, consisting of presidents of the participating locals, some of whom were typically represented by lead staff for the Kaiser portion of their membership. The by-laws of the coalition called for a third, larger representative body—the Delegates Council—to meet at least once a year. Although both the IPC and the steering

Table 3.2. Kaiser Permanente National Labor Management Partnership Agreement (excerpts)

Purpose

- Improve the quality of health care for Kaiser Permanente members and the communities we serve.
- Assist Kaiser Permanente in achieving and maintaining market leading competitive performance.
- Make Kaiser Permanente a better place to work.
- Expand Kaiser Permanente's members in current and new markets, including designation as a provider of choice for all labor organizations in the areas we serve.
- Provide Kaiser Permanente employees with the maximum possible employment and income security within Kaiser Permanente and/or the health care field.
- Involve employees and their unions in decisions.

Process and structure

- Senior Partnership Committee: Executive level of KP Executives and Union Leaders to establish targets, goals, timelines and to discuss strategic issues, and to oversee implementation and review of the process.
- The parties recognize and agree to hold proprietary information in strict confidence and agree information obtained in the course of the Partnership will not be used to the detriment of the other partner.
- The parties will jointly select a third party consultant to assist the Partnership.
- Each business unit participating will establish a Partnership Steering Committee with equal numbers of members from the unions and the company.
- Kaiser Permanente will bear the costs of administering the Partnership. Union officials who are not Kaiser Permanente employees will be responsible for their own costs.

Decision making and scope

- Decision making will vary from situation to situation but should be governed by two criteria: (1) The degree to which the parties' constituent or institutional interests are likely to be affected by the decisions; (2) the level of expertise or added value the parties can bring to bear on the decision to be made.
- If either party's vital interests are likely to be affected by the decision, consensus should be used. If constituent or institutional interests are even marginally affected, consultation should precede a final decision.
- If one party has little, if any, interest in the outcome, and no particular expertise on an issue to be decided, informing is adequate.
- In the absence of consensus, mandatory bargaining subjects will be resolved in accordance with contractual and legal rights. On non-mandatory and non-contractual subjects, management reserves the sole responsibility and right for the final decision.
- The scope of the Partnership should be broad and should include: strategic initiatives; quality; member and employee satisfaction; business planning; and business unit employment issues.

Employment and union security

- The parties acknowledge a mutual obligation and intention to maximize employment security for Kaiser Permanente employees. We recognize that there could be circumstances when such a commitment cannot be achieved. In such cases, the Partnership will make use of attrition, growth of the business, aggressive job matching, short-term training efforts and other mechanisms agreed upon by the Partnership participants. There will be no loss of employment to any employee because of participation in a Partnership program or worksite.
- The parties believe that Kaiser Permanente employees should exercise free choice and decide for themselves whether or not they wish to be represented by a labor organization. Where a signatory union becomes involved in organizing Kaiser Permanente employees, the employer will maintain a strictly neutral position.

Marketing cooperation

- All parties will make their best efforts, as opportunities arise, to market Kaiser Permanente to new groups and individuals and to increase Kaiser Permanente's penetration in existing groups.

Source: Kaiser Permanente National Labor Management Agreement, 1997.

Joint LMP Contractual Committes at K-P

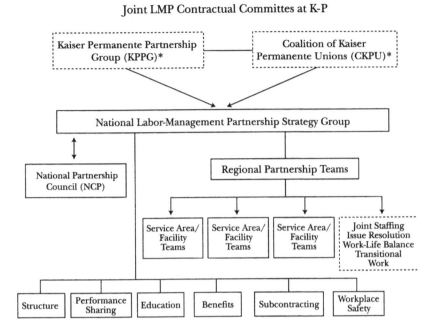

Figure 3.1. The LMP governance structure
Source: Kaiser Permanente Office of the Labor-Management Partnership.

committee were intended to operate by consensus when possible, rules for voting were established. The international unions had one vote each on the IPC, except for SEIU, which, given the size of its KP membership, had three. Each local union received one vote per 500 members on the steering committee, with a minimum of one and a maximum of twelve. The Delegates Council was similarly based on proportional representation.

The top governing body of the LMP in the initial years was known first as the Senior Partnership Committee and later as the Senior Partnership Council. It consisted of twelve union leaders, senior operating managers, and physicians and met eight times a year. At its inception, this body was co-chaired by diCicco and Gary Fernandez, Kaiser's senior vice president in charge of the national labor-management partnership. The National Partnership Council met four times a year and brought together approximately fifty union and management officials to share reports and to enhance coordination across the many parts of KP.

The partnership agreement also created a staff organization—the Office of Labor-Management Partnership (OLMP)—to supply initial support for LMP activities. OLMP employees were technically managerial employees but reported to the two LMP co-chairs. The OLMP staff included fourteen internal consultants, half from labor and half from management, funded by Kaiser and working directly with the Labor-Management Partnership. The OLMP was funded by KP as provided for in the partnership agreement: "Kaiser Permanente will bear the costs of administering the Partnership, including consultants, lost time, and incidental expenses of all Kaiser Permanente employees. Union officials who are not Kaiser Permanente employees will be responsible for their own expenses." In the early years of its existence, the coalition was funded by the member unions and the AFL-CIO. In 1998, for example, the seven international unions contributed close to $500,000 of the budget. At this early stage, the coalition had only a very small staff.

Summary: "Pathways to Partnership"

To direct and support the implementation of the original six goals, the parties developed a five-phase "Pathways to Partnership" plan, which described the phases leading to the full implementation of the vision. (Table 3.3 summarizes the activities for each of the five phases.)

The Kaiser Labor-Management Partnership was thus launched, but not without risks and criticisms. As mentioned, the CNA and some others in the

Table 3.3. Five Phases of Pathways to Partnership

Traditional	Foundation building	Transitional I and II	Vision
• Adversarial • Rule based • Problem settled not solved • Decision making seldom shared	• Education and training • Issue resolution • Establish teams • Involve employees and physicians in decisions	• Input into decision making • Trained in conflict resolution • Collective bargaining • Business education	• All employees and physicians with full understanding of the business • Union leadership integrated into decision making • Interest-based bargaining • Accountable teams • Consensus decision making

Source: Kaiser Permanente Office of Labor Management Partnership.

labor movement opposed partnerships, as did some management groups. From the beginning, diCicco and his union coalition colleagues recognized these risks and responded by insisting that this effort would be more than just "labor-management cooperation." It would be a more effective way to represent their members. The hard work had just begun.

CHAPTER 4

Early Challenges, Early Wins—But More to Do

The structure—and hopes—for the Kaiser Labor-Management Partnership (LMP) were now in place. Now the challenge was to convert promise into measurable progress. That challenge was complicated by the financial pressures on Kaiser, which lost more than $250 million in 1997 and again in 1998. As Kaiser began a process of retrenchment, resources became scarce for implementation of the partnership. Further complicating the picture was the structure of Kaiser, which had a strong, ongoing tradition of decentralized management and regional autonomy. Layered on top of that was the institutional independence of the Permanente Medical Groups relative to the Hospital/Health Plan organization, and the tradition of autonomy of the physicians within the separate medical groups. Effectively, this meant that although top Kaiser management could commit itself to the labor-management partnership, it had limited capacity to force the regions and medical centers to implement it.

LMP leaders also confronted a key choice in the development of any labor-management partnership in a large, multi-unit organization: Is it best to take a broad but shallow approach, gradually progressing deeper into the organization's subunits? Or is it better to have a narrow but deep approach focused on particular units, gradually broadening to a larger number of units? The Kaiser partnership would ultimately pursue a mix of both approaches, building basic partnership infrastructure at the regional level and in service areas, at the same time engaging in several intensive experiments within specific units.

The broad-but-shallow approach would require considerable planning, internal negotiations over who pays for training, consulting services, and other associated costs of taking time away from "normal" work activities to learn how to integrate the partnership principles into day-to-day work. The narrow-but-deep approach involved picking specific projects or "naturally occurring" events or crises and applying partnership principles and processes to address the underlying problems. The advantage of the latter strategy was that fewer organizational resources were needed and chances were higher for visible early successes, which—according to theories of organizational change—would help build the support and confidence needed to sustain the momentum of the partnership.[1] "Early wins" would also bolster the confidence needed to handle difficult times, which were destined to develop down the road. The disadvantage of the narrow-but-deep approach was that it could create political problems for both labor and management by leaving too many people entirely untouched by the partnership.

Thus the dual approach was utilized early in the partnership. As both parties worked to build the partnership infrastructure at the regional and service area levels, they agreed to focus on two potentially fractious issues that could undermine trust: employment security and union organizing. At the same time, the partnership was able to achieve success in two big and visible projects: opening the Baldwin Park Medical Center in Southern California on time and under budget, and negotiating a performance turn-around at Kaiser's Optical Laboratory in Northern California, which faced the threat of closure.

The First Crisis: Employment Security

All partnerships experience from time to time what we call "pivotal events,"[2] that is, crises that come up in unpredictable ways which, if not resolved successfully, threaten to derail or even destroy a partnership, and which, if resolved successfully, build trust and momentum for further progress. The first of what would be a series of pivotal events for the Kaiser partnership was a crisis over the meaning of the employment security language in the initial 1997 partnership agreement. Specifically, the dispute centered on this paragraph on employment security:

> The Parties acknowledge a mutual obligation and intention to maximize employment security for Kaiser Permanente employees. As such, it is the intent

of the parties of the Partnership to avoid the displacement of any Kaiser Permanente employee. We recognize that there could be circumstances when
such a commitment cannot be achieved. In such cases, the Partnership will
make use of attrition, growth of the business, aggressive job matching, short-
term training efforts and other mechanisms agreed upon by the Partnership
participants. There will be no loss of employment to any employee because of
participation in a Partnership program at the worksite.

Not everyone within management endorsed the concept of employment
security. One top management negotiator described concerns held by many
within management in these terms:

> First, I persuaded them that they had confused employment security with job
> security. They thought employment security meant no flexibility for redesign
> and no flexibility for performance. We garnered a lot more support when I
> persuaded them that wasn't the case. Then the second worry was, what if
> something horrible happened? We can't have our hands tied. If there's an
> earthquake or a flood or a hospital closing, we can't guarantee everyone jobs.
> And our labor partners weren't talking about that, something horrible. So you
> see in the language, there is some exception for huge horrible events, and it is
> still defined by management. So that solved that problem. Third, they said, we
> can't afford it. But I asked the management people to figure out . . . how many
> vacancies we have. Typically, we always have an 8 percent to 10 percent va-
> cancy rate. So it's not a question of having too many people. We can be cre-
> ative in retraining and redeploying people. . . . That was critical. The leaders
> and managers just needed time to understand.

In 1999, several issues arose regarding the redeployment of bargaining
unit members. As a result, the National Partnership Council and other union
and management leaders met to discuss how to make the general statement
contained in the 1997 agreement more explicit. The result was a separate,
five-page agreement on employment security dated 20 October 1999, which
laid the groundwork for an issue critical to the developing partnership. The
clarification described in detail the commitment to "re-deploy, not lay-off,
employees who are displaced." The agreement called on the parties to be-
have differently than in the adversarial past: now unions would permit management to increase flexibility, if necessary by reducing staff through attrition,
and management would engage in proactive problem solving and planning
for long-term workforce needs. As discussed in chapter 9, this language

would later serve the parties well as they went about the task of implementing new medical records technologies. It also helped the parties head off an attempt by management in Southern California to respond to a 2003 budget crisis by laying off staff. Such instances gave the workforce and union leaders assurance that they would not be "working their way out of a job" if they engaged in joint processes with management to identify and implement performance improvements.

Union Organizing: Neutrality and Card Check

Labor-management partnerships have often collapsed due to conflicts over union organizing. This partly reflects the complicated and often highly litigious and contested way union organizing and recognition occur under U.S. labor law. From the initial petition to the National Labor Relations Board for an election to the determination of who is eligible to vote to the certification of the election results and negotiation of an initial contract, opportunities to delay or stonewall the process are built into each step of the process.

In partnerships, unions naturally expect a different response to organizing than in the more typical case, where management uses its resources to oppose new organizing. "How can you expect us to cooperate with you in one location when you fight us in another?" is the common union position. Managers, for their part, are rarely unified with respect to partnership, which can require top executives to control managers in an unorganized facility, to tell them in essence, "Be neutral, don't oppose union organizing. And don't worry—your career will not suffer if your employees join the union," a view that runs contrary to the instincts of many managers in the United States.

True to its history and heritage, Kaiser had traditionally not responded aggressively to organizing campaigns in its core regions. But Kaiser's geographical reach was changing. Expansion into the East Coast meant significant numbers of unorganized workers whom Kaiser unions were eager to sign up. More significantly, Kaiser had commenced operations in Georgia and North Carolina—places traditionally hostile to unions. As they sought new accounts, Kaiser marketing managers knew that largely non-union employers would not look kindly on a company that accepted unions and which consequently might pass on higher labor costs. This created a friction between local Kaiser managers and Kaiser unions that were actively organizing in these areas.

The initial partnership agreement did include language stating that KP was supposed to remain neutral in union organizing. But despite this official neutrality, regional management was not embracing unionization. This is shown in a 23 September 1997 memo from Kaiser's Northeast region human resource management to managers and supervisors, which suggested answers to employee questions about union issues. Among the "appropriate" responses listed were:

- "Management is not encouraging unions to organize non-union employees in the Northeast Division. The impetus for organizing will still have to come from the employees themselves."
- "You do not have to talk with a union organizer."
- "You do not have to sign an authorization card. Under the law, you have the right not to join a union and no one can threaten or coerce you into joining."
- "The union cannot promise job security. The only way to ensure job security is if Kaiser continues to grow and remains competitive with other companies."
- "If a union is voted in you will most likely have to become a member, pay dues and be subject to the union's bargaining activity."

By 1999 these tensions led the leaders at the national level to negotiate a more detailed, program-wide agreement regarding union organizing. The labor and management representatives who negotiated the new agreement knew that it would not be easy to put this agreement into effect, especially in a right-to-work state such as Georgia.

The 1999 organizing agreement provided detailed rules for the conduct of organizing campaigns, while still allowing some leeway for the local parties to negotiate specific procedures. It included language regarding unit determination, union access to employer property, campaign commitments and communications, employee information and the card check process by which recognition would typically take place. The unit determination process would begin with local union representatives and managers attempting to reach consensus on the scope of the unit. If that failed, the agreement called for a panel of two labor members and two management members without a direct interest in the outcome (they might, for instance, be drawn from outside the region) to decide it. If that panel failed, a neutral umpire would decide. The agreement laid out factors to be considered in fashioning an acceptable unit. The history and pattern of units in that particular region and the standards used by the NLRB for determining hospital units, including community of interest, were "primary factors." Operational or structural issues were to be secondary factors. Finally, the parties were encouraged to avoid the proliferation of units.

The new agreement also provided union access to KP employees "at mutually agreed upon places and times," at the same time making it clear that organizers could not disrupt work. KP agreed to provide lists of employees and their contact information, if there was enough showing of interest (defined as 30 percent of the potential bargaining unit). The parties committed not to portray each other negatively or to "engage in misrepresentation" or personal attacks. They further committed to keeping campaigns "free from fear and intimidation" and not to discriminate against individual workers. They even agreed to send joint communications to workers about campaigns. To our knowledge, this is the most detailed private agreement governing the organizing and unit determination process found anywhere in the country.

Although the agreement was thorough in dealing with the problems unions had identified in typical organizing campaigns, what was perhaps more important was Kaiser's willingness to stand behind the agreement when local managers took a more traditional, adversarial approach. Although relatively few problems have arisen in implementing the agreement, the partnership has provided the basis for dealing with them.

Baldwin Park

Kaiser's urgent need for a new hospital in Southern California provided an opportunity to demonstrate the partnership's new way of working together. Normally, it would take about two years to plan and open a hospital of the size (approximately 240 beds) needed in early 1998 in Baldwin Park. But membership in the area had grown so much that patients had to be sent to non-KP hospitals because beds were not available within the system. To avoid this very expensive option, Kaiser wanted the new facility, which was only a shell with no design or staff, to become operational before the flu season in late fall.

A top-level decision was made to delegate the start-up project to a joint task team made up of a broad cross section of physicians, managers, nurses, technicians, and other employees. Susan Mlot and Anne Comfort from Restructuring Associates, Inc. (RAI) facilitated this project which, as Mlot recalled, at first gave "management a lot of concern because of both the financial and time pressures."

The team was given a "clean sheet of paper" and urged to use all the principles built into the partnership to design a hospital that would create a positive working and health care environment for all parties. The effort, which began in April 1998, involved more than 150 employees, co-led by Leslie Margolin, then Kaiser's senior vice president for hospital and health care operations in Southern California; her medical group partner Gary Lulejian, MD; administrator Richard Rosoff; and union leaders, including SEIU Local 399's Dave Bullock, UNAC's Kathy Sackman, and SEIU Local 535's Priscilla Kania. Employees and managers from other medical centers who were considered leaders within their particular specialties were also members of the team.

These designers were trained in problem solving and consensus decision making and visited GM's Saturn plant in Tennessee and other innovative organizations to assess different models of joint participation and co-management. In addition, they participated in a five-day "Blitz Week" that involved 100 people in intensive discussions about how to design the flow of patient care. Margolin recalls:

> The design team's steering committee figured out the template for how to open the hospital within six months, which seemed impossible. We decided we needed to engage people who knew about how hospital work was done— we hosted a blitz week with all classifications and unions, gave them training on Partnership principles and set them to design the hospital. We challenged them to be creative for what is best for the patient and most productive, efficient, and satisfying for employees. We had doctors and union stewards, people at all levels. They would get to design the hospital, how equipment, staff, patients, would flow. We asked them to think big and bold. They did outstanding work. They broke into teams, and the steering committee met with the teams every night for several hours.

Anne Comfort from RAI recalls:

> After the kick-off, we had a series of subsequent meetings with what we referred to as SWAT teams. These teams were responsible for things like technology selection, vendor contracting and various other areas. A key point of the meetings was that unions would be involved in the decision making in areas where they never previously had any say. These meetings also served to increase people's confidence that this could be done if they worked on it together.

One outcome of the Baldwin Park experience was that individuals who had been opposed to partnership became convinced of its value. "Rick [Rosoff, a key administrator] went through a major transformation from not thinking that the Partnership would be useful to seeing real value in the Partnership," said one union observer. Lulejian, the area medical director, who before this experience only associated unions with people on picket lines, found "tremendous value" in the partnership. "We began to develop trust for each other," said Lulejian. "We also gained an understanding that we had to change the way we traditionally did things. We had to change to work as a team." The partners succeeded in opening an innovative and well-designed hospital, under budget—in a virtually unheard of eight months. The facility focused on patient-centered care. For example, equipment was available at the bedside rather than in specialized areas that required patient transport and coordination. Telemetry units, typically located only in critical care units, were installed in every room, greatly increasing the hospital's flexibility and capacity. Despite a difficult transition after several senior leaders from labor and management left in early 1999, the hospital partnership continued to perform well. Patient satisfaction increased and Baldwin Park ranked below the three other KP hospitals in the area in nursing hours per patient day. In a 2001 interview, medical director for the Southern California Permanente Medical Group Oliver Goldsmith, MD, said: "This is probably the most significant venture we will do inside Kaiser Permanente over the next decade. It will serve as a building block for what lies ahead."

The Optical Laboratory

Another major and early test for the partnership came in early 1998, when a consultant told Kaiser that it could save $800,000 annually by closing its Northern California Optical Laboratory in Berkeley and consolidating its activities into an optical laboratory in Glendale in Southern California.

Northern California's Optical Services consisted of thirty-two retail stores and a manufacturing facility. The eye glasses were made in Berkeley's Optical Lab, which completed more than 350,000 eyeglass jobs a year, which at the time made it the nation's seventh largest optical operation. Its shutdown would have affected dozens of jobs and workers.

Senior management of Optical Services knew this would be the most difficult issue in their upcoming contract negotiations with SEIU Local 535, the union that represented all the hourly workers in the lab. Preston Lasley, president of SEIU local 535, had been on the picket line three times in twenty-two years. "There was a LOT of hostility," he said.

The key decision maker, vice president and regional medical group administrator Tony Gately, had little experience in negotiating with unions and had seen the failure of many prior efforts to get unions to agree to flexibility in work rules. So his initial goal was to negotiate an agreement for an orderly shutdown of the Berkeley lab. "There was a lot of history with labor, and it was not good in Berkeley," he said. "Early on, I was not a proponent of the Partnership. I guess it's because I had been working with labor for 17 years in our traditional labor-management culture. If I had not been at the table, it would have been much easier to just say, 'close it down,' without facing the consequences in a personal way. By being there, I noticed first-hand the pain the closure would cause." As negotiations began, the management team took the expected position: the lab was to be closed and the negotiations should therefore focus on the terms for doing so. With union leaders rejecting this position out of hand, it appeared that the negotiations would quickly reach an impasse.

However, as his chief negotiator, Gately had chosen Diane Easterwood, who believed in the potential of using a problem-solving approach to bargaining. Earlier in her career, Easterwood had worked as a labor relations representative for Kaiser management and had experienced the power of what she called "win-win" approaches in resolving grievances. After leaving Kaiser, she went to work for a health care organization that "was so anti-union" that she chose to leave. "I called Kaiser back and asked if they had any assignments. Tony Gately told me, 'Do I have a job for you! We are thinking about transferring the optical division and we need some labor expertise.'"

As she prepared for negotiations, Easterwood began to question some of the facts and conclusions in the consultant report that estimated $800,000 in savings. So did the union leaders who had been given access to the report. With their traditional approach to negotiations appearing to lead nowhere, both sides requested and were granted permission from their union officers and from Gately to try an interest-based approach. The management and labor negotiators brought in RAI's experienced facilitator Charlie Huggins, and engaged in the training, brainstorming, and related aspects of interest-based negotiations. The first step required the management team to redraft their initial statement, which had read: "Should the Optical Lab be closed or kept open?" After tense discussions and reminders of interest-based principles from the facilitator, the parties agreed to restate the issue as: "How can we contribute to KP's turnaround by improving the performance (financial, service, and quality to members) of the Optical Division?" This left both options on the table—keep the lab open or close it.

After they met separately and identified their key interests, union and management convened together, outlined their interests to each other, and engaged in a process of clarifying each party's interests by having the other side restate them in its own words. This proved to be an eye-opening experience. According to Gately,

> We realized that there was really 80 percent or 90 percent overlap in interests. The differences were all in how we might get there. This was based on the employment security agreement. We had agreed to full employment security, no layoffs, but we could retrain or move people. When we got into the third and fourth days, we began to craft some options. That was when we began to ask, what could solve the problem? The dynamics in the room were changing by then. We had come in on opposite sides of the table, and by this time we were sitting at mixed tables. The relationships were beginning to form.

When the parties began to brainstorm options, they came up with a remarkable list of more than 250 ideas for change and improvement in operations, many of which could reduce costs, increase revenues, and improve quality and service. President of SEIU Local 535 Lasley agreed. "They were really creative," he said. "For the first time, management and union were working together."

Generating ideas proved to be the easiest part. Now they had to be consolidated into a workable number of options and the parties had to agree on criteria for evaluating those options. This proved very challenging. After several more days of intensive, heavily facilitated negotiations, the parties agreed to reorganize operations at the lab in order to incorporate the ideas and options they had generated and to review progress against cost and revenue targets after an eighteen-month trial. If the parties did not agree that progress during this time was adequate, the negotiations could be reopened.

Among other things, the agreement called for an incentive gain-sharing plan based on revenue, quality, and customer satisfaction performance criteria; a change in job design and classification to create a broader utility worker job that would both increase flexibility and lower costs; and a plan to implement the partnership principles and activities in the lab's day-to-day operations. The utility worker job classification represented a major departure from the way jobs were organized in the past. Whereas management saw the change as a major breakthrough, union members greeted it with considerable suspicion and resentment that standards would be degraded by combining several specialty jobs. Implementing the agreement thus required more training and education, especially of the more than 210 front-line unionized employees. Lasley recalled the challenges faced by the union leaders:

> Well, we never had any financial information. So when Kaiser said they were losing money, nobody believed it! All of a sudden, we got the financial data. But we did not know how to read it. So we had to take finance classes. That was a very wise move. You have to know how the business actually works, the intricacies and dynamics.
>
> So for instance, take measures. We have three basic measures we base everything on. The "Re-Do" includes breakage, and work that has to be done over. "Turnaround Time" is how long it takes to get a product back to the local store, once we receive the order. There is a higher cost if the turnaround time is longer, and the member doesn't get the service. And "Net Income." Those were the three "drivers" of the business. So, we set goals: a reasonable turnaround time, a breakage percentage (we compared ours with outside vendors), and net income. We had to meet $800,000 savings and produce more.

Four months into implementation of the reorganization, management reported an 8 percent increase in productivity, reduced turnaround time from 2.7 to 1.7 days, and cost savings that exceeded what could have been realized by closing the lab. As a result of these savings, new equipment to produce polycarbonate lenses was purchased to expand the lab's product offerings, which would likely result in new jobs.

After a full year of operating under the reorganized processes, Gately reported that:

- Net income was up 19 percent and gross revenues were up by 9.8 percent to $5.5 million. Average sales per employee were up 6 percent.
- $250,000 in savings were realized in breakage and rework.
- Turnaround time for customer delivery declined from 2.7 to 1.3 days; overall productivity of the lab increased by 8 percent.
- The incentive plan produced a 2.7 percent payout for employees.

He then summarized his views of the role the partnership had played both in the negotiations and in the day-to-day operations of the lab since 1998:

It is very performance focused. I was impressed, and am still impressed, by how much labor knew about the business. They were never allowed to engage fully in improving the business. . . . They had ideas, but before, they never surfaced, or if they did, they never went anywhere. It was a learning process for me to engage a knowledgeable workforce, and it was possible because management was ready to listen.

The Optical Lab's improved performance record and the partnership there have been sustained over time through three changes in management and labor leaders. Revenues increased 34 percent between 2000 and 2006 and the division exceeded its profit targets in each year, except 2001, when it incurred the costs of opening a new manufacturing facility. (Subsequent to the decision to keep open the Berkeley facility, Kaiser expanded its Berkeley operations and opened a new and larger facility in the same area.) The Optical Laboratory became a widely discussed "success story" in Kaiser Permanente and remains one of the signature achievements of the partnership. It also was the beginning of the transformation of Tony Gately from being a line manager skeptical of working with unions to becoming the leading management spokesman for the partnership.

While the Baldwin Park and Optical Lab projects were among the most visible early uses of the partnership and interest-based processes to address major strategic and operational challenges, other early wins were also realized. In early 2002, the partnership listed about fifty other projects that were initiated in different worksites across the Kaiser system. By 2005, more than 250 partnership projects were in the database. Most achieved cost savings and/or productivity improvements. A call center in San Diego with 500 operators, for example, was often cited for its impressive gains in effectiveness. Lessons from that partnership effort spread to a Fort Worth call center. The Glendale Lab tried out some of the Berkeley-originated ideas and added some of its own, including a department-level incentive program that shared gains produced by reducing spoilage and turn around time of customer orders.

Building the Partnership Infrastructure

Despite Kaiser's financial woes at the time, the partnership began the slow process of building up its infrastructure. The Office of Labor-Management Partnership hired staff to work with joint committees on training, communication, metrics, and administration. Training modules were designed, including an orientation module available for all KP audiences; a module on interest-based problem solving as a foundational skill, which was used to great effect in the Optical Lab case; a module in business understanding to provide workers and their representatives a better base for participating in decision making; and two leadership modules: union partnership representative training and managing in a partnership environment. Recognizing early the need for ongoing evaluation of the partnership, the parties initiated a process of identifying appropriate metrics to capture performance changes. New questions about partnership were added to the organization's employee survey, and annual reports on some metrics were assembled. Kaiser's communications staff built a partnership website, with resources for and information on the LMP, including stories and news about specific partnership projects, ranging from site-specific improvements, training, or cost reduction initiatives to the joint union-management campaign to enact needle-stick protection legislation in California.

The union coalition produced its own newsletter, *Inside Out*, focused on the partnership and broader coalition activities, including organizing successes. In 2002, the partnership continued to report on its activities and projects in a new magazine called *Hank*, named after Henry J. Kaiser.[3] All the while, the Senior Partnership Committee continued to meet regularly and local union leaders and regional operations managers continued to build relationships.

Notwithstanding all these efforts and successes, however, the partnership remained unknown or inaccessible to most union members. According to a KP employee survey in late 1998, less than 20 percent of union workers in the two California regions knew anything about the partnership. In other regions surveyed in 1999, recognition was lower, in some cases much lower.

Comments from workers in focus groups conducted in 1998 illustrate the problem. "I'm suspicious because if it's been in effect for a year or two, why haven't I heard anything about it?" said one worker. "You can't tell if it's the truth or not, if they don't tell us anything," said another. "I think they should put some kind of monthly publication out to keep us informed."

In 1999, workers were surveyed for the first time about their involvement in the partnership. Although workers in the Northwest region reported levels of involvement close to 40 percent, fewer than 10 percent of workers elsewhere reported any involvement at all.

Beyond Specific Projects

Still, some benefits of successful partnership projects went beyond measurable improvements in productivity or costs. For example, referring to his Baldwin Park experience, Dr. Lulejian stated:

> I think the really important things [we achieved] were qualitative, the way people felt about each other, the ability to set forth processes to have a springboard to do more things. . . . I think we are leagues ahead of every other medical center in what we do, because we incorporate and integrate the activities of the partnership within the operations of the medical group.

Union leaders also benefited from realizing common interests. As one union leader said:

> The unions are very committed to the partnership. The employees have gained from job security, pay increases, job satisfaction, and more control over their work environment [through participation in joint workplace/work environment improvement efforts]. The nurses think this will result in improvement for the patients. . . . The results unions want are the same things management wants: basically a reduction in workplace problems and improvement in the "People Pulse" survey [a regular survey of employee attitudes]. KP has been an excellent employer in terms of wages, benefits, and working conditions, so this Partnership can only lead to better results for the unions.

But for any partnership to be sustained, it must continue to change the way workers and supervisors on the front lines do their work on a day-to-day basis. "While we accomplished some significant foundation building in 2001, the partnership has yet to achieve breakthrough changes in the way most employees and units work," said one Labor-Management Partnership Office staff member in late 2001. "Our aim this year is to engage many more employees and managers in jointly examining, restructuring, and improving work processes in their own areas."

Summary: Importance of "Early Wins"

The Kaiser partnership met a threshold test stressed by theories of organizational change: it achieved some early wins to build confidence and support needed to carry on. Indeed, the Baldwin Park and Optical Laboratory cases would become part of the partnership folklore—stories recounted often by partnership supporters to illustrate the value of working together in new ways. However, as the following chapters show, progress beyond this promising start would not be smooth nor linear, but instead a series of uneven steps, often punctuated by unanticipated crises that then helped renew commitment to the partnership path.

CHAPTER 5

Slow Diffusion

Given some early successes such as Baldwin Park, the partnership began to face perhaps inevitable growing pains. Despite strong support from top management as well as physician and union leaders, the partnership did not diffuse smoothly or widely throughout the decentralized Kaiser regions or operations over the first decade of its existence. Nor did the parties have great success in transforming the image and identity of the partnership from an effort to improve labor relations and to engage in labor-management problem solving to one in which partnership principles and processes became an integral part of health care delivery at Kaiser.

Just because the senior leaders decided on the new approach did not mean that other management and union leaders would be willing to initiate the difficult shift toward partnership. Few lower-level managers or union representatives were convinced that this should be the way to go about their daily business of delivering health care or representing their interests and constituencies.

By 2002, it was time for a fresh look, especially as coalition leaders saw a number of personnel changes among their counterparts in the executive ranks that made them worry that key champions of partnership were moving on. To address these and other concerns, Kaiser managers and union leaders agreed to hold two "Labor Management Partnership Vision Reaffirmation Retreats," which were held on 21 August and 6 November 2002.

Whereas the first retreat's focus was program wide, across all regions, events in Southern California shortly afterward forced a more specific focus to the second retreat and raised the stakes. About two weeks before the second retreat, Kaiser executives in Southern California became alarmed at new projections predicting a significant decline in new members (customers). This was both a surprise, given that earlier forecasts had predicted growth, and a big problem in that it would produce a $300 million budget gap over the next three years. An emergency management meeting was called to discuss options for dealing with this looming crisis, including cuts in sick leave and wages as well as layoffs and other staffing changes, actions that would require using the emergency "catastrophic" clause in the Partnership Agreement to void the Employment Security (no layoff) agreement. After hearing of these possible responses from a Kaiser executive, union leaders were furious, arguing that management's plan was a clear violation of the letter and spirit of the partnership and its employment security agreement. If the partnership meant anything, this "crisis" should be addressed jointly and within the framework of the partnership agreement, they said. Kaiser managers agreed to bring senior partnership leaders from outside the Southern California region into the discussion which until then, in Kaiser tradition, was focused within the region, and to make the Southern California crisis an issue at the upcoming reaffirmation retreat.

By the time the parties met, backroom negotiations among management and union groups had cooled things down and enabled the parties to reach a tentative agreement. They agreed to address the budget and growth problem jointly and to consider a wide array of options which, by excluding layoffs, would reaffirm commitment to the partnership in practice. The result was the creation of a joint task force in Southern California that generated projected savings of over $100 million per year, more than enough to close a budget gap if the projected membership losses materialized.

This crisis demonstrated that the partnership seemed to be at its best when confronted with a concrete and immediate problem. The parties could rise to the occasion, if they had the motivation to put the partnership principles to work. This cycle—crisis, joint task force, results realized—would be replicated in Ohio in 2004 and on smaller scales in a number of other regions over the next several years.

The Arduous Path of Diffusion

That the path to partnership was arduous was perhaps inevitable, given the complexity of the organizations and the magnitude of the organizational change involved. Indeed, the fact that diffusion of the partnership at Kaiser was slow and did not follow a smooth, incremental expansion path mirrors experiences in other joint labor-management change processes we have studied.

Consider the well-known partnership between Xerox and the union representing its hourly labor force, the Amalgamated Clothing and Textile Workers Union (now part of UNITE/HERE). Within two years of its initiation in 1980, approximately 20 percent of the workforce was actively involved in some type of partnership project or team activity. Both management and union leaders expected that number to rise steadily to over 80 percent of the workforce by 1985. Instead, less than half the workforce was actively involved by 1985, even though both management and labor leaders considered their partnership to be a great success and were crediting it with generating significant performance improvements.[1]

As would later prove true with Kaiser, the Xerox partnership lurched forward in spurts, fueled by what our colleague Joel Cutcher-Gershenfeld termed "pivotal events"; that is, unanticipated challenges, new issues, or crises that required immediate attention and resolution. The process of resolving them often deepened and broadened commitment to the partnership, moving it forward. At Xerox, examples of such pivotal events were a debate over where to open a new factory and how associated union representation issues would be handled, the introduction of new process technology and how jobs would be restructured, and a critical debate over whether to outsource wire harness work or to find ways to do this work competitively within Xerox.[2]

The Kaiser partnership's slow rate of diffusion can be tracked through the results of its "People Pulse" surveys, an employee survey completed periodically in most regions. In 2002, the data showed about 26 percent of the unionized workforce was involved in some form of partnership activity. By 2004, 39 percent indicated they were actively involved in some form of partnership efforts. But since then, this level of involvement has stabilized at Kaiser, similar to the pattern at Xerox. So while Kaiser's diffusion path was slower than its proponents anticipated, it was not inconsistent with experiences of other organizational change and labor-management partnership efforts.

From early on, partnership leaders sought to transform the new labor relations approach into an operating strategy, that is, to change the way Kaiser delivered health care. This goal was a constant theme in planning sessions and was a common refrain in speeches given by both management and union leaders. But it proved to be an enormous challenge to reproduce this commitment through the ranks and across the regions of this highly decentralized organization. To understand why, we draw on theories of organizational change.

Context: A Sense of Urgency

Figure 5.1, which is based on well-established theories of organizational change from the fields of behavioral sciences and labor-management relations,[3] uses the language and strategies Kaiser leaders adopted in implementing the partnership.

As seen in the Southern California budget crisis, a sense of urgency is needed to motivate acceptance of any major organizational change. But it is not enough for the leaders at the top levels of the partnership to experience urgency; similar pressures have to be felt directly by managers and labor leaders at the front lines. Creating such a sense of urgency was very difficult in an organization as decentralized as Kaiser—top levels of national or regional management had few means by which to make Kaiser's broader challenges salient. Progress in diffusing partnership therefore depended crucially on people seizing the opportunities afforded by the emergence of local crises.

Two Kaiser examples—in Ohio and in Northern California—illustrate this process. In response to sharp declines in enrollment, key leaders from the Ohio partnership met during the summer of 2003 to develop a comprehensive plan to reduce costs. Prior to this crisis-driven effort, most managers in the region had assumed that partnership was "just another short-lived

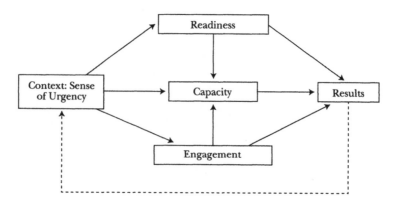

Figure 5.1. Heuristic model of LMP

initiative from California" that would soon blow over. But by mid-2002, it became apparent that significant restructuring and downsizing would be needed to match a precipitous decline in membership (from more than 200,000 members to about 145,000). As was true in Southern California, union leaders in Ohio worried that management was poised to act unilaterally rather than in partnership. After considerable back-and-forth discussion, the parties got to work. Management, physician leaders, and labor leaders set a target of achieving $24 million in cost reductions by 2006. Focusing on the work of their ambulatory units, they assembled an Ambulatory Redesign Group that identified more than 140 improvement ideas, ranging from small savings to very ambitious reorganization of departments.

It took several months of intensive negotiations, intervention by top-level partnership leaders, including Peter diCicco, and intensive involvement of physicians, managers, and employees in individual clinics and offices, but a plan, with targets and timetables, was eventually formulated and accepted. By June 2004, the joint effort had produced an estimated $13 million in savings, more than half way to achieving the target of $24 million by 2006. One of the key achievements of this effort was to get physicians more directly engaged in the Ohio region partnership. It was not philosophical conversion; they saw that change was essential to their livelihood and recognized their voice was needed in the project teams if for no other reason than to protect their interests. As a result of the physicians' involvement, the Ohio region began referring to their partnership as the Labor-Management Physician Partnership (LMPP).

A similar "wake-up call" occurred in Northern California's Napa/Solano service area, which, contrary to expectations, saw member (customer) enrollment fall precipitously. In 2002, its clinics had exceeded their budgets by $10 million, a deficit that would grow to $15 million in 2003 if losses continued at the same pace. In response, a special project was launched, conducted as a stand-alone activity, benefiting from the good working relations between management and labor but not integrated formally into the governance of the area partnership. Management and labor leaders agreed to a plan that would reduce costs on the clinic side of the Napa/Solano service area by $10 million by the end of the second year. The plan included a freeze on hiring and schedule changes to reduce overtime and the need for call-ins on short notice. The plan also called for savings in supplies and other non-labor costs.

Although some of these could have been implemented without further employee input, the parties believed that the greatest savings would come from having the changes discussed and adapted by employees and local managers and physicians to fit the needs of their particular units. Three months into this consultation effort, it became clear to the steering committee that the suggestions coming from the departmental committees were insufficient. Top managers and union leaders took a new approach, calling for stronger and more direct action, rather than waiting for cost-saving ideas from below. They again decided that all openings would be frozen. This time, to deal with possible imbalances in staffing that hiring freezes often produce, a team consisting of the chief steward, top administrators, and the physician-in-charge met daily at 6:30 a.m. to reallocate workers across departments. The result was that a $10 million cost reduction target was met and local-level committees continued to work on options to reduce costs within their units.

Readiness

Joint responses to specific cost or budget crises such as these occurred in other settings, with similar results. The partnership worked best when faced with a clear problem of sufficient magnitude and immediacy. But urgency alone is not sufficient: the parties must also be willing to engage in a partnership mode. Such "readiness" is a function of the history of labor-management relations in the worksite, the commitment and vision of key sponsors, and the extent to which managers and union leaders are held accountable for results.

Given Kaiser's decentralized nature, it is not surprising that the climate and history of relations between labor, management, and physicians varied considerably across locations and regions. This variation affected the success of the partnership and its rate of diffusion. Positive relations provided a platform to take up partnership projects, whereas settings with highly adversarial or arm's-length labor-management-physician histories found it difficult or even impossible to make the partnership work. In most cases physicians were not interested in working with labor representatives unless a clear crisis was evident that would affect their work. Typically, physicians saw the partnership as a labor-relations issue, not something they needed or wanted to engage. This attitude reinforced the views of workers and local union leaders that physicians were aloof and authoritarian in style. Recognizing that such adversarial tensions needed to be addressed, partnership leaders initiated a "readiness" program in 2004, identifying settings where adversarial tensions had persisted and assigning facilitators to work with the parties in those settings. The Los Angeles Medical Center case illustrates how difficult this task could be.

A history of hostile labor-management relations at the Los Angeles Medical Center had generated a series of problems, including high absenteeism and grievance rates, disputes around staffing issues, and racial tensions. Given the hostilities and distrust built up over the years both between management and labor leaders and across several factions within the unions that split members along racial lines, some referred to this location as "the jungle." Some union members wore "stickers" on their uniforms, demanding better work schedules and work-life balance. In such a context, it was not surprising that some managers and union leaders distrusted efforts to engage in partnership activities. But mounting tensions and a desire to turn around the labor-management relationship led to an agreement to have two experienced facilitators work with labor and management leaders on the Issue Resolution Process.

The facilitators convened several meetings in the summer and early fall of 2004. Each party brought a number of issues to the table. Labor representatives were concerned about lack of management support and involvement in some of the department-level teams and councils that had been created and about unilateral decision-making styles of managers in other units. Management wanted the union leadership to demonstrate a good-faith commitment to partnership as opposed to traditional labor relations by publicly repudiating and halting the sticker campaign. The union leaders indicated that although they did not support the sticker tactic, they could not control those using it. If they were to ask their members to desist, the union leaders said they would need to show evidence of management's goodwill and commitment to changing what they saw as bad management behavior, such as making decisions unilaterally, without working in partnership with union leaders or consulting employees.

Faced with a stalemate, the facilitators concluded that the unit was not ready to engage in the type of problem solving required for the Issue Resolution Process to go forward and they withdrew. By terminating their services, the facilitators sent a clear message to both union and management leaders: "Unless you are willing and able to engage in a good-faith effort to address the root causes of the adversarial tensions in your relationship, we are all wasting time and resources in trying to jumpstart partnership initiatives." That message triggered a response—but not at the local level. Rather, regional management and labor leaders intervened and began a slow process of working with local leaders to address the causes of the tensions at the Los

Angeles Medical Center. Though some departmental teams were in place and a joint workplace safety program got started, a year later, the majority of units still were unable or unwilling to initiate partnership projects. This and other examples illustrate a challenge facing not just Kaiser and its union partners, but management and labor leaders in other organizations too: A legacy and persistence of adversarial relations makes the journey to partnership challenging, and explains why diffusion does not take a steady incremental path.

Shared Vision

In addition to the history and nature of the relationship, another factor in readiness is vision. It is common for organizational change models to emphasize the importance of having a shared vision among leaders. The initial vision for the partnership was very ambitious, both in terms of the scope and the depth of joint decision making, consultation, and information sharing the parties expected to achieve and in integrating partnership principles into the operations and processes used to carry out Kaiser's mission of delivering health care services. However, it often takes time to see how these broad principles can be applied to specific problems and settings. Disconnects in the parties' understanding can cause frustration and strain the partnership. Take, for example, the case of a joint marketing initiative, in which union leaders felt management failed to include them early in the planning or strategy-development process.

"They do most of the planning, if not all, and handle most of the initial contacts without letting us know," said one union leader. "Then they come and tell us they are having problems . . . and tell us who should call whom and what we should say, and by when. . . . We've told management that we're not interested in the piecemeal assistance they are looking for from us." Needless to say, that particular "joint" marketing effort fizzled without producing significant results.

The vision for the partnership varied considerably across regions and facilities. In the Northwest region, labor and management leaders worked hard to develop a shared vision of partnership as an operating strategy. Management and labor engaged in a significant consultation before major decisions were made and they indicated that they expected their subordinates to lead in a similar way. "[I made] a formal declaration that my labor partner is an equal, that there should be shared decision-making, strategy, and accountability," said Cynthia Finter, president of Kaiser's Northwest region in 2004. "[Then I got] the medical group and dental group leaders to share in this." Neither side wanted to go quite as far as the co-management model they had observed at Saturn, she said, "but we have to approach [co-management] or maybe even engage in it to learn what the limits are. Further, this vision has been backed up with clear direction for managers: 'You will partner.'"

The challenges of formulating a shared vision can be seen in another pivotal event that occurred at the Northwest Region's only hospital, Sunnyside Medical Center. In the fall of 2003, several unions in the facility conducted a solidarity action focused on problems in the environmental services (EVS) department. Workers were beginning to lose patience with the lack of progress in following through on a joint staffing project. They felt that management had fallen back into a unilateral decision-making pattern. Regional management felt the solidarity action violated an informal "no surprises" rule. Around the same time, there was an incident in the Emergency Department where a nurse was, in the view of some labor representatives, unfairly disciplined. Relationships could easily have deteriorated further at this point. Instead, upper level management continued to show support for the partnership. The manager in the troubled EVS department went on leave and left the organization a few months later. Perhaps more important, the Sunnyside CEO was assigned a full-time labor partner and, in early 2004, was replaced with someone more committed to the partnership. Slowly but surely, with these leadership changes and with strong urging of top regional management and union leaders, middle managers and facility-based union representatives moved forward in implementing the partnership.

This progress toward a shared vision continued as long as the region continued to perform well and the regional president remained in her position. But after she was replaced in 2006, the rocky process of developing a shared vision had to begin anew with the new leaders (there was also a change in the medical group director). The point is that for partnership to work there has to be a working accord between the key leaders and if individuals holding these key positions change, then the trust-building process must start over again.

Some Northwest managers viewed the change in top management as an opportunity to re-establish a balance of power that they felt had shifted too far. One manager presented the situation in these terms (referring to unions as "institutional labor," a phrase that was like fingernails on a chalk board to union leaders):

> [The partnership] in this region seemed to centralize power with the institutional union labor leaders at the top of the organization. The partnership was designed to involve front-line employees. Under the previous regional leadership, [higher level] labor leaders got powerful, which disempowered the front-line stewards. . . . There was a rumor that the union had a list of managers it targeted to get rid of in the restructuring. I don't know whether this is true or not, . . . but it added fuel to the paranoia that labor had too much power.

Not surprisingly, union leaders in the region, some of whom were pulling back from partnership efforts, did not take kindly to this view that partnership was only about the front lines and should not also mean greater involvement by full-time union officials. Union leaders clearly felt frustrated by what they perceived as a management backlash and a diminished role, both at the strategic level and at the local level in facilities where local managers were not supportive of the partnership. At the same time, the region continued joint efforts to move forward with broadening front-line involvement, particularly in the hospital, where the supportive CEO hired in 2004 remained in place. Despite his different approach on the ground, the new regional president affirmed both his "zest" for the partnership and his interest in working with the union leadership, particularly if it could produce real performance improvements.

In summary, partnership in the Northwest region had gone from a showcase to considerable turmoil. The parties were in a struggle over establishing a new, shared vision for the partnership in the face of declining regional performance brought on by serious cost and competitiveness problems and leadership changes in management. Adding to these tensions, union leaders and managers who had bought into the partnership had to contend with peers who were more skeptical of it. Despite this turmoil at the top, in 2007 many front-line workers began to experience the partnership in a concrete way for the first time as the region began steady implementation of unit-based teams first in the hospital and then throughout the region. The concept of unit-based teams had emerged from the 2005 national negotiations as the major priority for the parties in making the partnership operational: that is, improving the delivery of health care.

At least the Northwest region was open to partnership. In Southern California, leaders did not want anything that would approach "co-management" for delivering health care. Because that region contained twelve service areas, each of which was rather autonomous, partnership reflected different visions in different locations. The decentralized nature of Kaiser and the many constituencies within the union coalition meant that the traditions of regional and even specific medical unit autonomy made it impossible for a single shared vision for partnership to spread throughout the organization.

In most cases, the formulation of the vision also lacked specificity. The most concrete formulation of this vision was this model:

Performance = Security + Governance + Rewards[4]

expressed in training materials and in strategy discussions, which posited that performance (efficiency, flexibility, and quality) would improve if the workforce had more security (of employment, income), voice (involvement in decision-making), and rewards (pay for skill and for performance). The model possessed the great merit of identifying crucial prerequisites for employee commitment. But while commitment was a necessary condition for high performance, it was hardly sufficient. To translate commitment into effective performance, employees (and managers) also needed new skills; they needed to be mobilized around shared performance goals; and their efforts needed to be effectively coordinated and supported by better organizational and technical systems. However, the model guiding the partnership did not have anything to say about these factors.

It is instructive to compare this model to the one used at the New United Motors Manufacturing, Inc. (NUMMI). At NUMMI, the labor-management partnership was seen as a coherent part within the Toyota production system and the broader management philosophies and practices enabling that system. In other words, NUMMI had an operational focus from the outset. The partnership was an answer to the question "What form of labor-management relations can best support both business goals—productivity, quality, flexibility—and labor goals—workers' dignity and security?"[5]

At Southwest Airlines, a similar operational focus helped shape the development of more than two decades of consistent growth and positive labor-management relations. The central focus was and continues to be on how to structure employment relations and maintain a workplace culture that supports coordination among different occupational groups and personnel to achieve rapid turnarounds of planes as they land and take off.[6] Contrast the Southwest vision with that of the original architects of the Kaiser partnership, who saw performance as essentially a matter of worker motivation.

As we note in later chapters, finding a path that would take the partnership from a labor relations strategy to an operating strategy was not easy. It became a central focus of the 2005 collective bargaining negotiations, when the negotiators chose to place priority on the development of unit-based teams.

Accountability

To a considerable extent, the readiness of local leaders to engage in partnership depends on whether they feel they are accountable for the successful implementation of a partnership approach. Such accountability was difficult to ensure at Kaiser.

In some medical centers, mid-level managers understood that their senior managers expected them to partner. Northwest region president Cynthia Finter flatly told her management team, "You will partner." In some instances, managers who found they could not adapt left voluntarily. Similarly, union stewards needed to be held accountable for the partnership behavior. "Some of the managers have stepped down and they're no longer working at Kaiser," summarized one union leader. "And some of the stewards were encouraged very strongly to conform or to step away."

In late 2003 and into 2004, the Office of Labor-Management Partnership surveyed labor and management leaders of facility or service area partnership councils in five regions on the status of the partnership in their locations. Figure 5.2 presents the results of a series of questions about the extent to which the management reward system took into account a manager's performance in the partnership. There was considerable variation across the regions and across the type of rewards (promotions, salary increases, and bonuses). The two regions with the reputation of being most "advanced" in terms of partnership at the time, Northwest and Colorado, showed the greatest use of partnership as part of performance appraisals. Overall, these results suggest a growing level of managerial accountability for partnership, at least in the locations with sufficient levels of partnership activity to fill out the survey.

Unfortunately, in many Kaiser units and departments, managers were not being held accountable, which was a constant source of frustration for union leaders in their dealings with managers. When 375 union coalition delegates met in spring of 2005 to prepare for bargaining, they had a rare opportunity to question Leslie Margolin, then Kaiser's senior vice president for Operations and chief negotiator, about the partnership and about Kaiser more

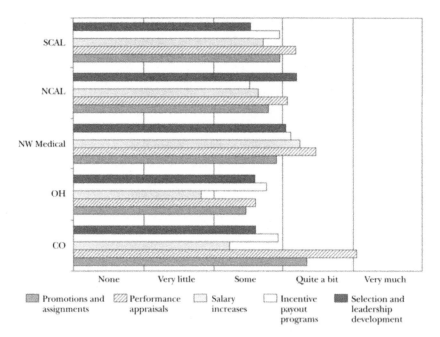

Figure 5.2. Are managers held accountable for supporting the partnership?

Source: LMP implementation tool.

generally. Following a speech to the delegates that earned her a standing ovation, she took questions. For the next ten minutes, she was peppered with tough questions about management, physician, and HR staff accountability. In essence, she was asked, *"When is Kaiser going to deal with this?"* She recognized that there was variation in support for the partnership, a concern she had made a personal priority and which she said Kaiser took seriously, replacing or moving some managers "who don't get it . . ." Margolin continued to be pressed until Peter diCicco intervened, *"Ok, I think she's gotten this message. Are there questions on other issues?"* But questions on accountability continued.

Kaiser's efforts to improve workplace safety, which was identified as a partnership priority as early as 2003, illustrate both the importance and the difficulties associated with holding managers accountable. In 2003, Kaiser had more than 20,000 workers' compensation claims and about 1,000 employees off work on any given day. By 2005, annual workers' compensation costs had risen to the point where they exceeded $500 million. Improving safety posed a difficult challenge, largely because of the dispersed distribution of injuries, more than 50 percent of which happened in departments that had only one injury in a given quarter. It was thus very difficult to target interventions and resources in a way that would have significant, system-wide effects.

Accidents were due to various sources. For example, obesity had increased dramatically and overweight people were more likely to be sick. A San Diego survey showed at least one emergency department admission per week for a patient over 350 pounds. Lifting them was a major source of injury among nurses, especially among the more senior ones. In the meantime, the average age of nurses kept climbing—in 2007 the average age of nurses in California was forty-four.

Safety was also often jeopardized by poor workplace and work process design. For example, many computer work stations had poorly positioned keyboards that could generate repetitive strain injuries. As for work process, one union leader attributed the "terrible safety record" at the EVS department of one hospital to management pressure to "get the job done." A union leader reports on what it took to turn around this department:

> We had a manager who decided we should use the "team" system, where each person handles just one type of cleaning all the time. We had people doing nothing but mop all night. Others did nothing but bathrooms or lifting trash and linen baskets for the entire shift. We had one 45-year-old woman [who did] nothing but lift trash and linen bags all night long. Eventually her back gave out. They sent her for retraining to become a florist. She was sure she was coming back to the medical center to work as a florist in the gift shop. But no, there was no job for her here. So she ended up in a little florist store in town, working for minimum wages, no benefits—three kids with no health coverage at all. Eventually, we forced management to shift to a "zone" system, where people took responsibility for all the cleaning in a whole area. But for five months, management refused to spend the $250,000 required for the new equipment. Finally, management put in a new administrator—and the whole thing turned around in an instant: no more injuries.

Before the partnership, Kaiser had undertaken various workplace safety efforts. A "Quality Circle" (QC) program that allowed teams to add a half hour to the lunch period for QC activities died when access and productivity pressures intensified. A "work practice observation program" was created to get workers to watch each other and help them stay alert to safety issues, but the unions refused to participate when it appeared that managers were using the program punitively.

More programs were initiated under the partnership. One focused on work groups with high injury rates, promoting the creation of labor-management teams that used partnership tools to help identify and eliminate safety hazards. Another "self-help" education and hazard identification program was started in an effort to broaden participation of workers in injury prevention. A "lift team initiative" was introduced in hospitals, which required specially trained technicians to assist patient care staff in transferring heavy patients.

Such programs were typically organized by a hierarchy of labor-management safety committees. Chairs of department-level teams would constitute the medical center team, and chairs of the latter would constitute a regional team, headed by the management and labor co-chairs of the regional labor-management council. All of these oversight groups would typically meet monthly. This was a sizable investment of personnel and time, but the problems were often so numerous and complex that even this investment left efforts to reduce the injury rate floundering in most parts of Kaiser.

A key factor was that workplace safety (WPS) had low visibility in the management control system. This made it very difficult to free up the financial resources to hire staff specialists, to support the safety teams and committees, to backfill for workers attending training sessions, or to purchase new equipment. "The way I see it, workplace safety requires a major culture change, but management has not seriously committed to making that change happen," said one manager involved in the safety initiative. "We put WPS under the partnership and then rolled the partnership out as a parallel structure. As a result, neither the partnership nor WPS have been integrated into management's daily concerns. They are dressing on the side of the salad."

Recognizing the problem, in 2004, the Kaiser board of directors elevated the workplace safety initiative to an organization-wide priority and linked executive compensation to progress on this issue. This step gave the initiative considerable impetus and broader support across the regions, hospitals, and clinics and led to the initiation of a new "Comprehensive Safety Program" modeled after what was seen as a benchmark program at DuPont Corporation. It called for engagement of management-labor partners from the bottom to the top of the Kaiser and union coalition organizations. This initiative has produced significant progress: although injury rates remained largely stuck in the first years of the joint WPS efforts, KP's program-wide average "accepted claim" injury rate was reduced by 46 percent between 2001 and 2007. Over the same period in California, there was a 46 percent reduction in workers' compensation claims related specifically to patient-handling injuries (patient lifting, transferring, moving). In addition to the improvement this meant in workers lives, there were also bottom line benefits for Kaiser. In 2007, KP reduced its workers' compensation balance sheet reserves by more than $125 million; though some of this was due to legislative reforms in California, Kaiser's accountants agreed that the joint injury prevention/workplace safety programs should also be credited. Safety—and a partnership approach to addressing it—had finally become an operating strategy with clear accountabilities and demonstrated results for both the workforce and Kaiser's bottom line.

For the partnership to succeed, accountability was necessary not just from Kaiser management, but from its physicians as well as union leaders. Holding management, labor, and physician leaders, as well as labor and management, accountable for supporting, implementing, and achieving results with the partnership has been a challenge in this highly decentralized organization.

In the Fontana Medical Center, for example, a labor-management team worked hard to develop a strategy for improving patient access, only to have it scuttled at the last moment when a union steward said he could not agree to the required changes in work processes. Kaiser managers often complained that one union representative would commit to something, only to come back later and say he or she did not have authority to commit or to be contradicted by another representative from the same union or, more often, a different union.

In Fresno, the Service Employees International Union (SEIU) was holding its stewards accountable for all their union representation responsibilities, including partnership, just as mid- and lower-level managers were being held accountable by Kaiser. "We had some shop stewards who were not participating, who were not meeting the requirements of the [union's governing board]," said a chief steward in Fresno. "They had an opportunity to come and either reaffirm or give reasons for why they weren't attending meetings and giving good representation and they were either voted back in or asked to step down."

Physician accountability was equally important but hard to achieve in some regions. One nurse anesthetist summarized the situation thus: "The concept of partnership is stellar, but in practice, it's been a struggle. As nurse anesthetists, we work very closely with physicians, but the physicians are not required to take partnership training and are not held accountable for their partnership behavior. It is as if one leg of the three-legged partnership stool is missing. The department is always out of balance."

Engaging physicians would remain an ongoing challenge. As we discuss in more detail in chapter 8, top-level physician leaders of the Permanente Federation expressed strong support for the partnership, whereas regional leaders varied in their support. Some were supportive from the outset, while others were openly disdainful. Regardless of the leadership support, front-line physicians resisted taking time away from their patients to engage in partnership training and projects. Most only got involved when a crisis affecting their work motivated them to do so, as in the Ohio and Napa/Solano cases. The physician culture and professional values, their economic incentives, and their considerable independence and power made them reluctant to take time away from what they defined as their jobs: caring for patients.

Capacity

Urgency and readiness refer to motivation. But effective partnership also requires capacity: do the parties have the skills, knowledge, time, and resources to engage in partnership activities and still ensure that their work is done? The extent to which this capacity had been created varied considerably.

This can be seen from the data obtained in an Implementation Survey conducted in 2003 and 2004 by the Office of Labor-Management Partnership (OLMP). The results indicated that while *LMP Orientation* training had reached at least a majority of employees, stewards, and managers in all regions, training on specific partnership processes, such as interest-based problem solving and issue resolution, was more variable across regions, though it had reached a majority of stewards and managers in most regions.

Training on *Corrective Action*, a problem-solving approach to discipline, and training on basic union and management partnership leadership skills were even more variable. As suggested above, physician participation in training was very limited, ranging from essentially non-existent for *Partnership Leadership*, *Corrective Action*, and *Issue Resolution*, to a high of just 32 percent for *LMP Orientation* in Northern California. Physicians were reluctant or unable to take the time to engage in training for generic LMP processes.

Since the partnership's inception, most of the training focused on educating managers and labor leaders about partnership principles and processes. Despite this training, many front-line workers were either unprepared to participate on an equal footing with management or perceived themselves that way. One medical director described the problem:

> We put these well-intentioned people with high-school educations, etc., into a room of people with MBAs and talk about [improving the delivery of health care] and it was humiliating to them, because, you know, two or three days of training is not enough. . . . So, there was so much naïveté built into our thinking about this. It is a real issue. [We say], "Come to the table and sit next to a CFO or CEO and have these conversations." It's a set up for tension. Somebody's time is being wasted, or everybody's.

Although this comment may reflect the medical director's limited appreciation for the skills and knowledge of front-line workers, the issue was a real one. Lower-level union leaders tasked with the job of supporting workers on partnership committees often reported that workers lacked self-confidence and sometimes lacked the knowledge base they needed. Most partnership training was initially focused on how to participate in partnership processes, rather than on health care delivery or patient care processes.

Capacity also relates to "staff" support. From the earliest days of partnership, there has been a specialized staff to support the partnership, along with resources to fund that staff. As part of the 2000 national agreement, the parties negotiated the Kaiser Permanente Labor-Management Trust Fund to pay partnership-related expenses. In the first year of the contract, employees contributed five cents per hour per employee to the Trust, an amount that rose by one cent each year of the contract and was explicitly designated as a diversion of wages. Kaiser also made separate and substantial contributions to the Trust. The 2005 national contract provided for steady state contributions of nine cents per hour per employee. The Trust funded the OLMP and also covered the coalition's partnership-related costs. (The unions funded "union-only," including bargaining related, coalition expenses.) Both the OLMP and coalition staff grew considerably over the years, from around 20 in 1998 primarily located in the central OLMP in Oakland, to more than over 150 professionals by 2006, most of whom were dispersed throughout the Kaiser regions. Some staffed the full range of partnership projects, while others worked in more specialized program areas (workplace safety, workforce development, and HealthConnect for instance), or support specific functions (education, communication, and metrics). Although the parties invested considerable resources in this support structure, which was among the largest in the history of labor-management partnerships in the nation, some leaders argued that it was insufficient, given the size of the workforce, complexity of the organization, and challenges in making the partnership work.

Backfill

A key dimension of capacity is "backfill," or having personnel to replace employees while they are engaged in partnership activities. Given all the forums and committees that the partnership has spawned and given the union operating guideline that a formally designated union representative (usually a steward) be present at all joint meetings, the need for backfill frequently arose. In some instances the first hurdle was finding the resources to pay for the replacement; resources that had to come out of the regions' operating budgets, not the Trust.

Furthermore, it was important to ensure that absences or backfill replacements would not affect the quality of patient care. "When a steward is participating, it is very difficult to backfill, because patients feel uncomfortable interacting with [a temporary replacement] in the delivery of services," said one business agent. "Then there's a pushback from colleagues who wonder why the steward was allowed to go to a meeting and ended up creating an extra workload for them."

Workers serving in a representative capacity had additional challenges, both in picking up the loose ends in the department and in ensuring that colleagues were briefed about the work of the committee. "I find it very difficult to walk into the departments and get a chance to actually talk with the staff," said one steward. "They are just so busy with patients. It gets very difficult to have those small group discussions with them about what the partnership has done and is working on, what are our goals for the year or next year, and how we see us getting there."

This issue created significant disconnects between stewards and other labor participants in partnership activities and their coworkers. For instance, although participants in the Joint Staffing Committees at Sunnyside Medical Center in the Northwest expressed considerable satisfaction with the process, their non-participating coworkers were not so sure. In a survey done in units that had undergone a Joint Staffing process, non-participants made suggestions on how to improve the process such as: "Regular meetings to better inform staff . . . of how the project is going"; "Get more people involved"; "More communication with everyone on what is going on." Committee representatives felt they had made serious efforts to communicate back, but their peers were still unhappy.

Management and labor leaders in the Northern California region made a conscious effort to address the backfill issue and made considerable progress. A 2002 survey of stewards in a large local union in the region found that a majority (61 percent) did not find it hard to get away from their regular jobs to perform their partnership duties.

By 2006, some regions were making efforts to relax the requirement that each union have its own representative at all meetings relevant to jointly sponsored projects or other partnership activities. The view was that this relaxation was now possible and acceptable in settings where a high level of trust had developed among unions and between labor and management leaders. As the partnership moved more into operational issues and involved front-line teams, this became the only practical way of proceeding without holding up the change process.

Engagement

Besides motivation and capacity, partnership requires employees to have opportunities to actually engage in partnership activities, to be meaningfully and effectively involved in partnership processes, and to identify problems and implement solutions. Given sufficient urgency, readiness, and capacity, successful engagement depends on having appropriate structures and processes for partnership interactions to take place, as well as skillful leadership of joint labor-management activities.

One of the partnership's chief early accomplishments was building a joint governance infrastructure at various levels. In the early years, this governance was done at the national level through the National Labor-Management Partnership Strategy Group and its precursors—the National Partnership Council and the Senior Partnership Council. Over time, however, partnership steering committees or councils were established in virtually all regions, as well as at many facilities and, in some cases, even at the departmental level.

While some regions were still working on putting this infrastructure in place, others were moving past the parallel structures and integrating labor directly into business and operation committees at both the regional and facility levels. For example:

- Southern California, the largest region, had a regional council, along with service area councils. Though it was slower to put in place facility-level structures, Baldwin Park was one facility that had a robust steering committee, fostering the creation of department-based teams throughout the Medical Center.
- Ohio and Georgia also put regional partnership councils in place in 2004, whereas the Northwest region disbanded its regional council and instead, integrated all mid-level managers with stewards and labor representatives into the regional Medical Operations Leadership Team. This integrative approach also was extended into some facilities.

Despite the extensive development of joint structures, at least at mid- to upper levels of the organization, problems remained. In some cases, the partnership structures at different levels were not integrated, especially in the complex Southern California region, where the membership of the regional partnership council did not include representatives from the Service Area councils. This made it difficult to ensure an ongoing flow of information across these bodies. Instead, regional and service area council members met occasionally to coordinate their activities around specific issues such as workplace safety.

Similar problems existed at the local level, where there was a lack of coordination across department-based teams within a medical center. This was the case in the Joint Staffing effort at Sunnyside Medical Center in the Northwest. Because the facility-wide oversight committee failed to function, it did not provide an adequate structure for dealing with inter-departmental issues. Some facilities were more proactive in addressing this issue. Fresno, for example, brought both departmental and project teams together in its monthly partnership meetings.

Partnership structures that were parallel to regular operational management structures tended to reinforce the idea of partnership as a labor relations "program," not an operational strategy for delivering health care. This was an impression that partnership leaders had been trying to change since the partnership's inception.

Summary: Many Small Gains . . . But Not an Overall Transformation

Where partnership principles and processes became an integral part of health care delivery at Kaiser, they clearly generated significant economic payoffs and, as discussed in chapter 11, fostered increased worker satisfaction with their jobs, with Kaiser, and with their union. Yet the parties were eager to go beyond episodic interventions and specific success stories to achieve a more systemic transformation in health care delivery. To do so, however, a new approach, and indeed a new model of organizational change, was needed, one that focused on front-line activities and that could be facilitated by top-level support. How to get this to happen became a central theme in the negotiation of the second Kaiser Permanente national agreement in 2005, discussed in the next chapter.

CHAPTER 6

Negotiating in Partnership:
The 2000 and 2005 National Negotiations

A major question facing labor and management is the relationship between a partnership and their collective bargaining processes. Do contract negotiations proceed as usual? Do partnership activities go into some sort of holding pattern? Do the parties go to the other extreme and find that formal contract renegotiations are no longer needed? In short, how do these two different processes co-exist and influence each other?

We consider such questions by analyzing the parties' experiences and the new ground they broke in negotiating two national labor agreements during the first decade of the Kaiser partnership's existence. Their experience provides a clearer picture of the role collective bargaining can and is likely to play if partnership strategies are pursued by other organizations. We present detailed accounts of the 2000 and 2005 negotiations, with greater emphasis on the 2005 negotiations, which our research team was able to observe directly. Negotiating a labor agreement is a highly intense, personal, and sometimes emotional process that can have a profound effect on the participants and their relationships. As our research team sat in on the 2005 negotiations—in formal sessions, union and management caucuses, private meetings, and in the bars, dining rooms, and hallways where much of the informal work of the negotiations took place—we were able to witness the intense and focused engagement of the key competitive and organizational issues facing Kaiser and the top concerns of the workforce. We left with a new appreciation for the importance of contract negotiations in bringing together a large array of interests and providing a forum for joint decision making.

Health care executives, labor leaders, and policy makers also have to ask a more profound question: Does collective bargaining add value to the health care system, and if so, how? This issue is especially sensitive for the health care industry, for which cost control and quality improvement are high priorities.

The 2000 Negotiations

To Kaiser's CEO Dr. David Lawrence, there had to be a better way than the traditional rituals of collective bargaining. "Labor dumps all over the company that employs them and the company dumps all over the union and tells the world what lousy, unproductive people they are," said Lawrence of the typical approach. "And the consumer sitting out there says, 'What in the world is going on with this organization in the long run?'"

The 2000 negotiations would be a major, early-stage test of whether or not the parties could use partnership principles in this traditionally more adversarial process. Seeking a different approach, the parties designed their 2000 negotiation process around the principles of interest-based negotiations (IBN) involving a relatively new, more problem-solving approach to negotiations.[1] Though they wanted these negotiations to be consistent with the principles underlying their three-year-old partnership, they encountered significant opposition to the decision to try such an approach, especially given the prospect of negotiating a single national (as opposed to multiple local) agreement.

When the partnership agreement initially was signed, the parties had agreed to keep partnership activities separate from collective bargaining. Union leaders felt that to do otherwise would risk losing local union support for partnership activities. It is standard when starting joint labor-management efforts to begin with a proviso that says, "None of the changes that will be implemented will infringe on or modify terms and conditions of existing collective bargaining agreements." Such a proviso helps gain support of both management and labor leaders who are skeptical of joint efforts and fear those efforts will erode hard-won gains or managerial control. Yet partnerships face a dilemma: If they want to tackle the critical issues facing the business and the workforce, they have to find an appropriate and effective way of integrating their joint efforts with the collective bargaining process and the provisions of their labor agreements. The first test of a partnership is often whether it can demonstrate that the new principles make it possible to negotiate an agreement that sets the stage for implementing key program initiatives and that these joint efforts can in turn advance the relationship to the next phase in the change process.

The Northwest Region Strike

It did not take long for the partnership to experience a pivotal event that focused on whether bargaining over a new contract was to remain separate and apart from the partnership. For the first year, separation was the rule. But a 1997 strike in Portland, OR, in Kaiser's Northwest region, forced the parties to consider whether their partnership could withstand a traditional negotiation, particularly one involving a threatened or actual strike. When an SEIU local struck in Portland, the stakes were high, recalls diCicco. "The nurses (members of AFT) then started a supportive sympathy effort and some of them participated in a sit-down activity," he said. "When ten or twelve nurses honored the picket lines, management threatened to fire them. If management followed through, this would have been an all out war. I went up to Portland to help the local negotiate a settlement . . . , working hand in hand with Dick Barnaby [then president of Kaiser Foundation Health Plans and Hospitals] to avoid this." By showing how vulnerable the partnership could be to local conflicts, Portland convinced partnership leaders that a new approach was needed. Otherwise, disputes that remained unsettled could quickly escalate. Effective issue resolution procedures are thus critical to the success of partnerships. But how do the parties achieve this goal?

Designing a Framework and Process for National Negotiations

Various local unions, which had gained experience working together in negotiating the initial partnership agreement, were inclined to propose that everyone negotiate together and create a single national agreement, with supplements to deal with specific local issues. (Such agreements are common, for instance, in the automobile industry.) Kaiser officials initially strongly opposed this approach, fearing that a single common contract deadline would greatly increase union bargaining power by affording unions the opportunity of threatening a system-wide work stoppage. The challenge was to develop an approach that would address the need for more coordination in a way that either avoided a common expiration date for all contracts or otherwise addressed management's concerns.

A joint task force created to explore this question initially proposed to consolidate bargaining and negotiate a single national master agreement, but without a common expiration date. The coalition, which favored this idea, knew that a common expiration date was a "show stopper" for Kaiser. Even so, the Kaiser Permanente Partnership Group (KPPG) rejected this recommendation. Some said the main reason was concern that units in labor market areas outside of California would be unable to pay higher "national" rates. At least one KPPG leader felt that the basic groundwork had not been laid with top leaders; that is, the task force had not consulted top leaders to learn their concerns and whether this proposal addressed them.

The rejection of this proposal created a crisis that could have threatened the partnership. Some union leaders, who had been led to believe that the proposal "would fly," felt that their management counterparts on the joint task force had been "sandbagged." It took top-level negotiations within the KPPG, along with advice from outside experts and assistance from Restructuring Associates, Inc. (RAI) facilitator John Stepp to develop a modified approach that was consistent with the task force's recommendation for a single national level negotiations structure, and which also had process and safeguards that were agreeable to KPPG leaders. The resulting design called for various "gates" in the process, enabling either party to opt out of national negotiations if they were not moving in a constructive fashion. In addition, the plan called for a commitment to maintain regional differentials, as well as extensive training in interest-based negotiations techniques for all participants.

Thus began what would turn out to be the single largest experiment with interest-based negotiations processes conducted to date in U.S. labor-management relations, involving nearly 400 union and management representatives and more than 20 neutral facilitators. Expert negotiators from the outside looking at this arrangement, which included eight international unions with twenty-six locals, were very skeptical. By centralizing the bargaining and using IBN, the parties had "bitten off more than they could chew," said one staff member from the AFL-CIO in Washington. He felt they "were headed for trouble, and it was best to stay as far away from these negotiations as possible."

The process began in April 2000 with extensive training in the concepts and tools of IBN. The basic premise of IBN is that the results of bargaining will be much more satisfactory if the parties are able to avoid, to the extent possible, the taking of positions as is typical in most bargaining processes. That is, the union starts out with an opening position, demanding, for example, a 10 percent wage increase; management's opening position is zero; and then a process of back and forth compromises eventually produces an agreement somewhere between the opening positions. The emphasis in IBN is on having the parties outline their goals and concerns, that is, their interests. This then sets the stage for the development of options for meeting these interests. The tool of brainstorming is frequently used for this purpose. Facilitation is important and can be provided either by consultants or by designated members of the bargaining teams.

To jumpstart IBN in the 2000 negotiations seven decentralized bargaining task groups (BTGs) were established to address wages, benefits, work-life balance, performance and workforce development, quality and service, employee health and safety, and work organization and innovation. These task groups, which were each assisted by facilitators from RAI and Federal Mediation Conciliation Service (FMCS), reported their recommendations to a joint, centralized Common Issues Committee (CIC), co-chaired by diCicco and Kaiser senior vice president Leslie Margolin. The CIC then determined which issues and recommendations needed to be forwarded to the local tables and which applied uniformly across the system and therefore needed to be negotiated centrally by the CIC.

According to one veteran labor relations manager who participated in the joint task force that designed the process, the emphasis was to be on brainstorming options, not on the traditional back-and-forth of proposals and counter-proposals. "We jointly identified and agreed to broad subject matters and structured joint teams around each subject. The task groups were charged with identifying the issues related to their topic and, in an interest-based manner, recommending solutions that met the interests of both sides."

Illustrative of this constructive process is the experience of one subcommittee within the BTG, which addressed performance and workforce development. This group consisted of about twelve people, including a person from hospital operations, a vice president from one of the nursing unions, and other management and union leaders with direct experience and responsibility for the issues within this group's mandate. The schedule involved meeting for three consecutive days every other week. During the intervening period, committee members reflected on what had happened, consulted with constituents, and accomplished behind-the-scenes liaison work and needed data collection. Rather than encouraging the use of specific language, CIC guidelines urged the BTGs to produce guidelines and statements embodying concepts and principles.

When facilitators from RAI and FMCS intervened, especially when the parties were stuck, they asked them to go back to the fundamentals of IBN, to identify interests and generate new options. The facilitators also recorded interests and options on flip charts, prepared notes, and, during the evening after each day's session, produced a summary to help launch the next morning's session.

By early July 2000, the BTGs were ready to report back to the CIC. Approximately 300 people from the BTGs assembled in one room, with all members of KPPG on hand. Each BTG presented its work in a scene that was energizing. According to one participant, everyone came away from the session on a real "high."

The final stages of the process involved several twists and turns. With a September 1 target for completing its work in national bargaining so that the various local unions could then take up issues specific to their units, the CIC in mid-August began what turned out to be a nine-day marathon session to resolve all of the outstanding issues. This "end game" phase resembled traditional bargaining in many respects. As observed by one representative, it was "shaking the trees one more time." Considerable time was required to deal with all the equity issues across the regions and local unions. As the September 1 deadline approached and it became clear that the task of codifying the results of the marathon session would not be finished, several of the large unions said that they would not proceed with their local negotiations until they received appropriate guidance from the CIC (especially with respect to the resolution of financial items).

This required the CIC to reconvene in early September with about ten participants, compared to about forty during the marathon session in August. This part of the end game phase also came to resemble traditional bargaining. After six twenty-hour sessions, agreement was reached in principle, thereby providing the guidance that several local unions needed. Although there was some fine-tuning of economic items at the local level, locals had to accept or reject the full, final package when it was sent back to them. By late September, the agreements were ready for submission to the members, who ratified the national agreement and local contracts by an astonishing 93 percent margin.

The strong support for the recommended agreement validated the design of the process: all of the union and regions were represented on the CIC and the timetable allowed for the final terms to be vetted and fine tuned based on input from the locals.

Leading and Facilitating IBN Processes

This kind of complex negotiations required a mix of both traditional bargaining and interest-based leadership and facilitation skills. The credibility Peter diCicco brought to the process as an experienced and tough negotiator (he led one of GE's most militant union locals) was decisive in gaining initial buy-in from union leaders. DiCicco played a key role on the union side in managing the many pressures that could easily have brought matters to an impasse. "People had to put some of their interests aside for the common good, which you don't see every day," said one union leader. "They had to make sacrifices and deliver 'messages' to their members about the value of solidarity and equity across occupational groups and unions." Some leaders of larger locals, who initially felt they could do just as well for their members by going back to the format of separate local negotiations, played "hardball" toward the end of bargaining and threatened to pull out of the effort to reach a national agreement. "If we had not had the three years of experience with the coalition working together under Pete's leadership, we never would have reached agreement," said one observer. "Pete had the confidence of this large group of individualists and he knew how to keep them focused on the objective of reaching a master agreement. He knew how to spell out the advantages of working together and when a leader went the other way, Pete stepped back and let some of the other leaders who were committed to going forward apply a little collegial arm-twisting."

Similarly, the management side also needed a leader who had respect both from the Kaiser Foundation Health Plan and Hospitals and from the Permanente Medical Groups. That role was served by Margolin, who—besides being a member of the KPPG—brought labor law, negotiations, and executive experience to the negotiations. Margolin was instrumental on the management side, working closely with diCicco to guide an extraordinarily complicated process. At several points in the process, she was asked to attend union meetings to explain management proposals and to answer questions. A federal mediator described the bridge role played by Margolin:

> Leslie enjoyed complete trust with the union leadership and when she said that management had "emptied its pockets," they believed her. In many ways, her toughest job was keeping her management colleagues on the same page. Often when she would return from a union meeting, she would find her teammates embroiled in tense discussion and in the process of backing away from

compromise positions that they had put on the table. She really had her work cut out for her in managing closure and achieving consensus on the part of the management group.

Many union and management leaders also acknowledged the importance of training and facilitation to the success of national negotiations. Because of their earlier work, the RAI staff knew the parties well and were able to keep them on a mutual interest agenda. "I think we did a good job of training people for the process," said Judith Saunders, the head of labor relations at the national level of Kaiser. "The problem is that it is not a process that you can learn in a classroom setting and apply perfectly. It takes a concentrated effort and commitment on the part of all of the participants to understand and focus on interests and not revert to traditional positions. It also requires knowledgeable facilitators, skilled at managing when and how to allow the parties to deviate. It highlighted that the profession could use even more facilitators with expertise in this area."

The final agreement called for a five-year contract with across-the-board wage increases between 4 percent and 6 percent for each of the five years of the agreement (RNs received higher increases because of labor shortages). The pact also created performance targets that could produce payments of 1 percent, 2 percent, and 3 percent in the last three years of the contract, as well as numerous specific changes in practices designed to improve business systems, quality of patient care, and work processes. Pension and benefits were also improved. Furthermore, as in the original partnership agreement, employment security was pledged—not simply security in a particular "job," but retraining and redeploying of workers if necessary. The agreement also created a new trust fund financed at five cents per hour diverted from employee wage increases (after the first year) to support training and other efforts needed to diffuse the partnership throughout the organization.

In return, Kaiser gained, among other things, five years of labor peace— a major achievement given the record of numerous strikes during the preceding decade. "The obvious benefits to both parties first have to do with the value of stability, in economic terms and dislocation terms, for individuals and for entities," said Dr. Lawrence. "We have created a framework that allows for productive relationships and labor-management peace and stability for a period of time. So we're not rehashing conditions of work, conditions of employment, economics, every period. That has enormous benefit to the labor members, because there is a certainty now, there is predictability. And it has great benefit to us. The cost of instability is high for both parties. And it has economic implications. It has reputational implications."

The positive feelings expressed by Lawrence and others directly involved in the negotiations were not, to say the least, completely shared by all top Kaiser executives and physician leaders. Some felt left out of the process; others felt they were either uninformed or misinformed about the actual costs of the agreement. This discontent would surface with considerable force when the parties returned to the bargaining table in 2005. Despite such feelings, the 2000 negotiations strengthened relationships among members of the coalition and between key union and management participants. These stronger bonds then reinforced the partnership by giving these parties the confidence and mutual trust needed to implement the goals of the partnership and to deal with day-to-day frustrations, conflicts, and more serious crises to come.

The 2005 Negotiations

Don't be intimidated by management experts. Management has chosen to put on its negotiating team "content experts"—people who are specialists and know a lot about specific issues. This is good and we should respect their knowledge and use it but not be intimidated by it or be afraid to ask questions or challenge it. You see the broad picture; they will see only their narrow specialization. So don't be afraid to raise questions and don't let them control the discussion around their narrow interpretation.

Peter diCicco, briefing 2005 union negotiators on the task before them

Union leaders like [Sal] Rosselli have to get elected—they have to show their members they are listening to them and have an aggressive approach. That should be kept in mind when listening to Rosselli and when thinking about why the unions do surveys of their members and management doesn't. Management has a hierarchical structure and unions do not.

Judith Saunders, KP's National Director of Labor Relations
Comments made in a management caucus after a speech to
negotiators by Sal Rosselli, president of SEIU's United Healthcare Workers-West

By early 2004, with the 2000 contract due to expire in 2005, it was time for Kaiser executives and union leaders to decide again whether to negotiate a single national labor agreement or to revert to separate negotiations for each local contract. The 2005 negotiations would become another pivotal event in the evolution of the partnership.

Management Preparations for Bargaining: Another National Contract?

Management first needed to decide whether to negotiate another national agreement. In 2005, as it had been in 2000, this was a difficult and contentious issue within management circles. This decision, as well as others needed to guide and instruct the management negotiators, fell to the Kaiser Permanente Partnership Group (KPPG). Some regional KPPG leaders were hesitant to approve another national process. They stressed the important differences in their economic and market situations. There also was some uncertainty and disagreement over what the partnership had achieved since 2000. It took four monthly KPPG meetings and many conversations with members of the Regional Presidents' Group (RPG) and other Kaiser executives before a decision was made to proceed with national bargaining.

At one such meeting in July 2004, Margolin—who was asked by her management colleagues to again lead the management negotiating team—made a detailed presentation outlining the major achievements of the partnership since 2000, citing results of 140 specific improvement projects tracked by the Office of Labor-Management Partnership. She reviewed gains in Kaiser revenue, membership, workplace safety, employee satisfaction, and patient satisfaction over the life of the partnership and outlined gains obtained as a result of the 2000 contract, especially the sustained period of labor peace it had generated.

A spirited discussion ensued over whether wage increases were warranted. "Some on the management team thought we should have cutbacks in benefits," said Margolin. "On wages, some were at zero and others were at [an increase to match the expected rate of increases in consumer prices]. Most thought that any increases ought to be in equity adjustments. So there were a number of different positions and I thought it would be unrealistic to push for a parameter. It was totally unrealistic in a year we made $1.6 billion to believe a zero settlement was possible. And it wasn't what we did for all others—our executive team had a 3 percent salary pool and we all got bonuses up at our maximums because of our performance."

A "group think" dynamic was developing, Margolin continued. With some in management calling for wage hikes of less than 2 percent, "George [Halvorson, CEO on the Health Plan side] said, 'If we do this to them, we have to do it for ourselves . . .' Very quickly, people began to change their tune to say, Well, maybe we could go for performance-based bonuses or increases."

Such different points of view were a harbinger of things to come, reflecting Kaiser's decentralized and dispersed authority and power structure.

Margolin chose not to press the KPPG for specific wage guidelines or parameters at this early stage of the process, as would be standard practice in management preparations for a traditional negotiations process. Such a bottom line parameter would only come later in the process, after more data on market comparisons and comparable wage settlements were collected.

But the KPPG did express a clear interest in *not* putting more money into the fringe benefit package, especially into the defined benefit pension plan, because data suggested that this benefit was already above the market and Kaiser tended to retain senior people. KPPG members were more interested in benefits that would help recruit and retain new employees, especially in hard-to-fill positions.

The Union Coalition Prepares for Bargaining

Discussion within the union coalition over whether to pursue another national agreement was more informal and considerably less controversial. There was a shared sense that returning to the national table was the right thing to do, though early on the question was raised about whether all local contracts should have a common expiration date. The coalition steering committee, made up of leaders of each local union or their designees, held a series of meetings and conducted two wide-ranging surveys that canvassed rank–and-file members for views on their jobs, their unions, the partnership, and issues of concern at their workplaces.

The unions coalesced around two overarching goals for the bargaining: strengthening the partnership, and achieving greater standardization of pay and benefits for all Kaiser workers—a goal that was in sharp contrast to the management goal of maintaining regional and occupational differences.

In early March 2005, about 375 delegates from twenty-nine local unions came together to review background data and to prepare further for national negotiations. Our research team's first impression upon seeing the group assembled in the ballroom of a Los Angeles hotel was how it mirrored the remarkably diverse Kaiser workforce. Over half the delegates were women, about a quarter were African American or Latino, and participants reflected the full spectrum of the workforce, from nurses and technicians to service employees. Over the next two days we observed perhaps the most remarkable union pre-bargaining conference we have ever attended. Most such gatherings resemble pep rallies designed to build solidarity among the various local union and rank-and-file groups and to signal to the negotiating team the intensity of feelings about different bargaining issues. Although this meeting clearly served that purpose, the tone, rhetoric, and even the range of people present were different than the norm.

Leaders from each international union spoke and conveyed their sense of priorities. Data from the survey were presented and discussed, and outside researchers (our team) summarized lessons from the partnership to date. Discussion groups at each table reported their sense of the state of the partnership and the concerns of their rank-and-file peers. The most frequently mentioned issues included retirement, health care and other benefits, workforce planning, staffing and backfill, and attendance-related issues.

Significantly, all of these deliberations took place with the leaders of the management negotiating team present. Kaiser's chief financial officer gave an overview of the state of the business and projections for the future and Margolin gave an impassioned speech on the importance of the upcoming negotiations. The audience gave her a standing ovation after she finished. In a very emotional moment, Peter diCicco gave tribute to his former management partner, Tony Gately, who at the time was losing his battle with cancer.

Unlike at other pre-bargaining sessions we have attended, the anti-management rhetoric often heard at such sessions was absent, though each speaker spoke with passion and conviction about the need to make progress for their constituents in the negotiations. There were certainly criticisms of management—Margolin, for example, heard many comments about the lack of commitment to the partnership by many middle managers and physicians. But the tone remained respectful, both toward individual managers and toward Kaiser as an employer and health care provider. This clearly was shaping up to be a different kind of negotiations.

The presence of Margolin at a key union meeting during the preparation phase for the 2005 negotiations attested to the impact of the partnership; namely, a partial breaking down of the walls that are erected during bargaining to insulate the constituents and principals from the thinking of the other party. Not to make too fine a point: the openness of the preparation phase on the union side represented a significant departure from the norm and although the participation of diCicco at the KPPG level represented an important innovation, the deliberations within management during this phase were not as transparent as those on the union side.

The Context

Collective bargaining negotiations do not occur in a vacuum. The state of the nation's health care system, and Kaiser's role and future as an integrated health care insurer and provider, weighed heavily on the parties as they prepared for bargaining. Also looming in the background was a potential development in the national labor movement. The threat and then the actual split of the AFL-CIO, which involved several unions in the Kaiser Coalition, was especially ominous because the July 2005 decision date for whether one or more of the coalition unions would leave the Federation coincided with the final months of contract negotiations between Kaiser and the coalition.

One of the central issues pushing SEIU and other unions to join what came to be known as the Change to Win Federation was overlapping union jurisdictions. SEIU and its partners argued that the AFL-CIO should force union consolidation along industry lines, a move that would have serious repercussions for the Kaiser union coalition. SEIU had aspired to be the dominant union in health care and believed that members of unions with small health care memberships would be better off affiliating with it. SEIU also had been undergoing internal change, realigning and consolidating its own local unions along industry lines in order to strengthen its power with employers. For example, in 2004, SEIU consolidated its Southern and Northern California health care locals into a single, new union organization—the United Healthcare Workers-West (UHW). This development provided an opportunity for Sal Rosselli—former leader of the Northern California local and the first president of UHW—to demonstrate, particularly to the members of the formerly separate Southern California local, that the merger created greater bargaining power and contributed to standardizing the terms and conditions of employment for its health care industry members. Such changes within SEIU created unease among leaders of the other coalition unions.

The California Nurses Association (CNA), the largest union of Kaiser employees, which has opted to remain outside of and opposed to the partnership, bargained its own contract in 2004. CNA and the United Nurses Association of California (UNAC), the coalition union representing nurses in Southern California, had been embroiled in an inter-union jurisdictional battle during 2004 that was resolved only through intense negotiation and mediation. The threat of further efforts by CNA to raid existing nursing units represented by coalition unions and to publicly criticize the coalition was also part of the context in which Kaiser's 2005 negotiations occurred.

The parties clearly wanted to use these negotiations finally to engage and answer the question of how to transform what—despite the refrains of partnership leaders—continued to be viewed primarily as a partnership focused on improving labor-management relations and solving periodic crises that focused on the operational task of improving health care delivery. For this reason, the makeup of the negotiating teams involved more people from frontline operations, especially on the management side, many of whom had little experience in the "rough and tumble" of traditional negotiations.

Table 6.1 presents results of a survey of the priorities labor and management negotiators attached to different bargaining issues, and shows that the parties carried a mix of common and conflicting interests into the negotiations. Although labor and management negotiators each assigned a high priority to increasing each other's accountability to the partnership and to improving Kaiser's delivery of high-quality health care, this was not their only priority. Both also brought an interest-based perspective to the negotiations. Ninety-four percent of union representatives and 91 percent of management representatives assigned a high priority to addressing the interests and needs of *both* Kaiser and the workforce. Nearly 90 percent of labor and management representatives also shared the goal of increasing trust and respect for each other in negotiations. Both labor and management (92 percent and 85 percent, respectively) gave a high priority to using the negotiations process to strengthen the partnership.

Table 6.1. Union and Management Bargaining Priorities

We are interested in how important a priority you attached to each of the following issues in national negotiations. How important to you was it that these negotiations . . . (percent top or high priority)

	Union	Management
Strengthened and advanced the Partnership	92	85
Reflected different market conditions in different regions	45	78
Increased respect and trust between labor and management	90	89
Increased labor's accountability for organizational performance	70	95
Reduced wage differentials in different regions	86	11
Reflected KP's projected revenue and intensified competition	73	85
Shared KP's financial successes in recent years	85	46
Used Partnership problem solving and interest based principles	89	72
Addressed both KP and workforce interests	94	91
Increased management's accountability for the Partnership	97	70

Source: Post Negotiation Survey.

Labor and management representatives also disagreed on important goals for these negotiations. For management, future market and financial conditions and recognizing differences in market conditions across regions were significantly higher priorities than for union leaders, for whom reducing differentials across regions and sharing in Kaiser's financial successes were higher priorities. To use two well-known terms from bargaining theory,[2] the process involved some issues that were "integrative" (the parties shared a number of common interests) and some that were "distributive" in nature (the parties held divergent or conflicting interests).

Bargaining Begins

The official kick-off of bargaining began at a dinner meeting of the CIC in February 2005, involving about forty senior management and labor leaders. The co-chairs diCicco and Margolin opened the meeting with short motivational speeches, thanking the participants for agreeing to serve on the CIC. They said the 2005 negotiations would take a great deal of time and energy but that the work was very important to Kaiser, to the workforce, to the partnership, and even to the future of health care in the United States. They both expressed the hope that everyone would focus on labor and management's common interests in making the transition from a labor-management partnership to a health care partnership. Although no one was ready at this point to suggest how to do so, it was a clear priority for most of the leaders at that initial meeting to focus the partnership on the task of improving the health care delivery process.

One of the contentious issues emerged right away. It revolved around whether there would be a single common expiration date for local contracts. Rosselli of UHW-SEIU had indicated that agreeing to a single expiration date for all contracts was a threshold issue for moving forward with national bargaining. This was a sensitive issue for top Kaiser management, which in 2000 had worried that agreeing to national bargaining would make Kaiser vulnerable to the possibility of an organization-wide strike if negotiations broke down.

Various side conversations took place during the course of the CIC meeting over how to handle this issue. A first step toward a resolution of the issue came when the parties agreed that the issue should be narrowed to include only SEIU locals and contracts, which already had a near de facto common expiration date. After considerable discussion, the issue was resolved with an informal understanding that the parties would bargain all their local contracts at the same time, immediately after national negotiations were completed. Some expiration dates for SEIU local contracts were altered as part of this agreement.

Another issue looming heavily on the minds of the negotiators was the effect of the pending split of the AFL-CIO on bargaining. Several ideas were discussed for minimizing the risks to bargaining, including postponing negotiations for a year to speeding negotiations up so that they would be completed before the convention. Ultimately, the parties chose neither of these options. Instead, coalition leaders made personal commitments, privately and publicly, that they would hold the coalition together throughout the bargaining, regardless of what transpired at the national level.

Phase 1: The Bargaining Task Groups at Work

> I was really struck at how this seemed like a chapter in the novel of the partnership. There were references—often at crucial times and from important people—in the Benefits BTG, for example, and in the presentations to the fact of being partners, specifically, the idea that this relationship created different expectations, as in "Because we're partners, we're going to do this differently than we otherwise would." Beyond these statements, many of the members of the BTGs came to this task after having worked closely together in their regions as part of the partnership. There was a really strong sense of continuity between this process and the partnership more generally.
>
> Research team member's notes, reflections on the BTGs

As in 2000, bargaining had two distinct phases. In the first phase, eight BTGs met for a total of fifteen days over the course of four months. Each BTG was charged with developing a set of written recommendations that the CIC would take as a starting point in the second, more intense phase of bargaining. Each BTG had about four CIC members, who provided leadership as well as continuity and connection between the two phases of bargaining. Also as in 2000, each BTG had one facilitator from RAI and one from FMCS. This time they were supported by a scribe to take detailed notes, as well as by a joint labor-management data team on call to the BTGs to provide needed information and analyses.

The BTGs met five times in three-day sessions. The first session was devoted to training participants in IBN concepts and processes. Many participants in 2005 bargaining had at least some experience with this model, either from the 2000 negotiations or from other partnership activities where

Table 6.2. Satisfaction with BTG's Negotiations Process (percent)

How satisfied or dissatisfied are you with each of the following aspects of your BTG's negotiations process?

	Very satisfied	Satisfied	Neither satisfied nor dissatisfied	Dissatisfied	Very dissatisfied
Your ability to express your interests on key issues	56	38	3	2	0
The level of trust established with union members of your BTG	42	49	7	1	0
The level of trust established with management members of your BTG	42	44	12	2	1
The scheduling of the BTG meetings (number of meetings, timing, etc.)	18	44	19	16	3
How the union coalition used caucuses	34	45	15	6	1
How the management team used caucuses	33	48	18	1	0
Your ability to keep your constituents or colleagues informed about BTG deliberations	21	53	19	6	1
Your ability to influence the final recommendations of your BTG	38	44	14	4	1

Source: Post Negotiation Survey.
Note: There were 193 respondents in total.

they had been schooled in interest-based problem solving and consensus decision making.

Tables 6.2 and 6.3 summarize a survey of BTG participants conducted shortly after this phase of negotiations was completed. With one exception, BTG members expressed positive views regarding the process of these "side tables." Respondents were less enthusiastic about the scheduling and time commitment required for the work of the BTGs. Because most of the management and union participants held positions where it was not feasible to have replacements, they had to juggle the responsibilities of their regular work with the added demands of BTG meetings and follow-up work that was required between meetings.

Table 6.3. Use of and Interest in Interest-Based Negotiations (percent)

How would you rate your BTG on the use of IBN and your overall satisfaction with the process?

	Extensive use of IBN (% extensive or very extensive)	Satisfaction with the process (% satisfied or very satisfied)
Attendance	95	90
Benefits	35	58
Performance based pay	89	65
Performance improvement	90	80
Service quality	96	100
Scope of practice	84	96
Work life balance	100	100
Workforce development	86	81

Source: Post Negotiations Survey.

Overall, the BTGs used IBN techniques extensively and effectively. The results indicate that interest-based processes dominated traditional negotiations in seven of the eight BTGs. Table 6.3 reports satisfaction levels of 80 percent or more among members of the seven BTGs in which IBN techniques dominated, compared to a 35 percent satisfaction level among members of the BTG (Benefits) in which more traditional positional processes dominated.

Our observational data are largely consistent with the survey data but provide a richer account of the dynamics observed within and across the groups. To illustrate these dynamics, we focus on three BTGs with different mixtures of common and conflicting interests.

The Performance Improvement BTG

This BTG was charged with addressing the critical and broadly shared objective of developing a plan to focus the partnership on improving the delivery of health care services. Group members agreed that partnership principles, such as teamwork, had not fully diffused to front-line physicians, managers, nurses, and other employees in their day-to-day work and they shared a determination to address this challenge. This BTG included a mix of front-line employees, a physician, budget experts, regional managers, and union leaders. After training sessions, the BTG identified data needs and benchmarking examples of effective team-based organizations and then analyzed materials and data collected from these examples, along with data on a number of prior successes and failures of teamwork within the partnership. A long list of issues that needed to be addressed to make decentralized teams work at Kaiser was then generated through a brainstorming process. Next, subgroups worked on specific issues, such as the problem of backfill and accountability. In the final phase, each subgroup reported its recommendations to the full BTG for discussion and a consensus vote.

The result of this process was a detailed plan for introducing unit-based teams throughout Kaiser. By centering the partnership on unit-based teams duplicative structures would be eliminated and "all the stakeholders would be in the same room," working on the common agenda to deliver high-quality medical care on a cost-effective basis. The themes of engagement, accountability, and measurement would be central in the operation of the teams.

Other recommendations included consolidation of the partnership and business structures, affirmation of joint accountability and engagement in work redesign, development of metrics, creation of guidelines for backfill, and design of a mechanism for the transfer of best practices. To implement this last recommendation the BTG asked each region to inventory successful practices and to post them on a national website. Ninety percent of the members in this BTG indicated they made extensive use of IBN processes and 80 percent indicated they were satisfied with the process.

The Attendance BTG

The need for this BTG stemmed from a significant problem of employee absenteeism in some regions. In some instances, most employees were using all of their allotted sick days. Some said this had become an "entitlement," rather than an "insurance policy." This issue was extremely important for management. Many saw it as a make-or-break issue for the partnership's survival. Though he was not present at negotiations, one regional medical director gave his representatives on the BTG clear instructions that he wanted to push for refashioning of the sick-leave program to, among other things, pare down the number of sick days an employee could take.

Throughout negotiations, this issue involved significant intra-organizational bargaining, especially among management representatives, as they juggled their commitments to the directors back in their respective regions against their commitments to fashioning an attendance program through an interest-based process. Conversely, labor representatives worried that management would insist on drastic attendance changes that would devastate morale and fail to deal with the underlying forces driving attendance problems, which they saw as high stress in the health care work environment and management's arbitrary decisions in granting personal leave. Specifically, union leaders worried that management would revert to the practice of combining vacation time and sick leave. Although the parties' interests and analyses of the problem going into bargaining differed significantly, the group ended up proposing an entirely new attendance policy that both sides felt would reduce absenteeism. Key elements of this policy included increased flexibility in the use of life balance days so that employees would not rely on sick time when time off was needed for other reasons; the creation of a sick leave bank for long-term illnesses; and provision for an annual cash-out of unused sick leave as an incentive to decrease the casual use of sick days.

As table 6.2 indicates, 90 percent of the participants in this BTG were satisfied with the process used to reach their agreement and 95 percent indicated they made extensive use of interest-based processes. "We knocked it out of the park," said one group member. "Our goal was to come up with an alternative. We did this."

The Benefits BTG

This group was also charged with addressing high priority and contentious issues. Union members were determined to avoid any benefit reductions. They wanted to improve the dental plan and eliminate a number of cross-regional and cross-occupational differences in pension benefits. (These differences reflected the history of KP—as regions outside of California were acquired, they brought existing pension plans with them.) Management members of the BTG were instructed by CIC leaders to avoid any increases in defined pension plans but, if the line could be held on the defined benefit plan, to consider inaugurating a defined contribution pension plan. As the data in figure 6.3 indicate, the process was more traditional in this BTG than in any of the others. Only 35 percent indicated extensive use of IBN processes. Substantial time was spent in caucuses and progress was slow. The day before the scheduled end of the BTG process, the parties still had not resolved major issues. In an effort to make progress, BTG members agreed to meet for dinner, during which several participants spoke in highly emotional terms, accusing their counterparts of not listening to them and not hearing their interests or their determination to represent the concerns of their constituents. This dinner discussion provided the cathartic release of tensions that was needed to allow the parties to accelerate progress on the last day and to reach a consensus set of recommendations.

A rather traditional process was used the last day to resolve their differences. Co-leaders of the group agreed that proposals would be presented in their entirety prior to any discussion, with the two sides caucusing extensively to process and debate proposals and to shape counter-proposals. Once agreement on the broad outlines of a recommendation was achieved, the parties delegated smaller sub-groups to translate them into specific proposals and language. Not surprising, the participants in this BTG rated their process as much more distributive or traditional and were significantly less satisfied (58 percent) with their process for generating agreement than were participants in the other BTGs.

The contrasting dynamics of these three BTGs illustrate the strengths and limits of IBN tools for dealing with common/shared and conflicting interests. The Performance Improvement Group—similar to the other five BTGs that worked on problems of shared interest—made substantial use of IBN processes and generated recommendations that would eventually become the most prominent post-contract partnership initiative: the formation of joint labor-management unit-based teams throughout the organization. In the Attendance BTG, labor and management representatives came to the group with strong and conflicting positions and constituency expectations. It took a creative reframing of the issues and skilled facilitation and trust-building experiences to transform the negotiations into a more interest-based process. Ultimately, a solution emerged that was unforeseen coming into negotiations. But the same regional director who had given his representatives in the negotiations very specific recommendations around a new sick-leave policy strongly resisted the solution fashioned by the BTG. This demonstrates not only that IBN can be used to transform a positional or highly distributive issue into one where those at the table are convinced they have identified a mutually acceptable or beneficial solution, but that novel solutions might require additional negotiations when leaders with veto power resist them. This raises the challenge of how to deal in negotiations with parties on both sides who are not at the table and not involved in the interest-based process. The partial answer that the parties fashioned was for key members of the CIC to be in close touch on a daily basis with the important decision makers who were not at the table.

The Benefits BTG demonstrated more than any of the others the limits of IBN when parties enter with strong positions on economic agenda items, see significant long-term issues at stake, and are subject to close monitoring and control by superiors and/or constituents outside those at the negotiating table. In this case, IBN played a limited role.

The contrast between the different outcomes for the Attendance and Benefits BTGs deserves some comment because both faced contentious agendas. At the heart of the IBN process is the generation of options. The subject of attendance and absenteeism lends itself to the development of a variety of solutions whereas tackling benefit questions involves possible program changes with big implications for precedence and resources. Issues that require tradeoffs are better handled in the traditional bargaining, which usually takes place at the main table as the deadline approaches.

The Sticker Saga

Most collective bargaining negotiations involve at least one incident or event when tensions that have been building as the parties deal with tough issues finally explode. Although the triggering event often seems trivial to an outside observer, it has deep symbolic meaning and can have such significant political ramifications for one or both parties that if not resolved, it can derail the entire process. Such an incident erupted during BTG deliberations over a union coalition plan to have their members post "stickers" at their workplace, urging support for their bargaining objectives. The original wording of the sticker was, *"THRIVE in 2005. A new union contract."* Some managers became concerned that these stickers sent a message that was too militant and too pro-union and inconsistent with the spirit of partnership in which negotiations were being carried out. Others were also concerned that the stickers would be displayed in places where patients could see them, thus conveying a negative message about morale at Kaiser or that allowing stickers to be displayed would set a legal precedent that would make it difficult to prevent similar workplace displays by unions in the future.

What started as a management concern escalated into a full-fledged conflict. Part of the reason reflected a simple communications malfunction. Coalition leaders promised to get management leaders a copy of the stickers before they were to be printed but for some reason, this did not happen in time for management to provide feedback on the words used. When managers did voice their concerns over the initial language, they were told it was too late, that the stickers had been printed and some were already being shipped to local union offices. Moreover, some within the coalition felt that what and how unions communicated with their members was none of management's business. "Did they forget we are a union?" said one union staff member. "If this were a 'normal' negotiation, I'd have our members walking around with picket signs calling for a fair contract. They seem to forget that we have a responsibility to actually represent our members."

For two days during the BTG process, leaders met in many off-line meetings to deal with what came to be called "the great sticker saga." The process by which the parties worked through this saga offers a window into the negotiating skills of the parties involved, and the high levels of trust they had for each other. At 5:45 p.m. of the second day of the sticker saga, Margolin briefed her management CIC colleagues on the day's efforts to resolve the issue, adding that diCicco would join this meeting shortly to explain why the stickers were important to the unions. DiCicco described how unions would normally communicate with their members in contract negotiations through gatherings, leaflets, buttons, and rallying the troops. This was a necessary part of the negotiations process to demonstrate the union was working hard on the members' behalf; that was why the sticker had to say "union," not partnership.

Kaiser's Northern California region president Mary Ann Thode politely but directly told diCicco that although she understood what he was saying, she just could not sell this to her Northern California colleagues, who opposed the stickers. But her people would be okay if the stickers read, "partnership union contract" or had the partnership logo on it.

DiCicco neither agreed nor disagreed. He said he would talk to his union leaders, though he did not expect them to like the idea. Then another management leader raised a concern about the word "new," to which diCicco responded that use of the word "new" was perfectly normal—they were negotiating a new contract, which did not mean the old one was bad. This second issue was effectively put to rest when Tony Wagner, management VP for labor-management partnership and diCicco's partner, said he understood the concern about use of the word "'new,' but we should not load Pete up with several issues. Let's focus just on the bigger concern expressed by Mary Ann and see what we can do with it."

After the meeting, diCicco gathered his union steering committee. He was very agitated about all this, but took the issue to the group that gathered around him in the back of the hall where union delegates were having dinner. He outlined the compromise: the language of the stickers would not be changed but the stickers would bear logos of both the partnership and the coalition. After explaining the situation, he essentially asked his union colleagues to "give him this one," to which they reluctantly agreed after voicing their shared frustration and anger.

Phase 2: Common Issues Committee Negotiations

After the BTGs completed their work, the Common Issues Committee (CIC) met for two weeks of negotiations. The goal was to complete negotiations of the contract in the first week, leaving a week for drafting contract language and tying up loose ends before the coalition's union delegates were scheduled to convene to review the agreement. Initially, the problem-solving, deliberative manner of the BTGs carried over to this phase, which used a standard procedure: the co-leaders from each BTG presented their recommendations, followed by discussion, then a sense-of-the-meeting poll and, finally, a consensus vote.

Renegotiating Attendance Recommendations

Toward the end of the first week, the co-leaders decided to take up the recommendations of the Attendance BTG. Building consensus for the attendance proposals had required overcoming significant opposition from one of the medical directors, who instructed his representatives on the CIC to propose his preferred alternative, which was to cut sick leave from fifteen to eight days per year in return for a 2 percent wage increase. The management representatives on the CIC, who were reluctant to put this new proposal forward so late in the negotiating process, decided after considerable discussion to work with the BTG recommendations rather than risk a breakdown in trust with their union counterparts by appearing to back away from IBN principles and processes. But it took intensive internal and high-level management negotiations and a sidebar deal that shared the risks and costs of the proposed approach to achieve the acquiescence of this medical director. The crucial selling point was that if the "cash out" provision did not reduce absenteeism, then the union leadership would reengage the subject at some point within the first year.

The time required to resolve this issue not only put the CIC far behind schedule, but it left labor representatives resentful of the time and attention they had devoted to an issue of such importance to management. As a result, the first week of the CIC negotiations ended without consideration of the economic package.

Deadline Bargaining

One week before the deadline, negotiations moved from California to Atlanta, GA, for five days. Although initially these days were planned as a time to draft the final agreement, the economic package had yet to be negotiated. Indeed, the final days took the form of traditional deadline bargaining, with high drama, emotion, and extremely intense internal negotiations within both the management and union organizations.

Day One: Developing Initial Proposals. The first day was spent in separate union and management caucuses, with each side working on opening proposals for the economic package. Margolin tried to prepare the management caucus for what would likely be a more traditional phase of negotiations. "We are under time pressure and now only getting into the guts of the economics," she said. "The interest-based process doesn't lend itself to dealing with this part of it, but we should still hold onto what we've learned. But it's important to remember that [the unions] will get more positional and we will [too.]"

Despite Margolin's speech, many people on the management team appeared unprepared for the switch to more traditional bargaining. Although all of the union officials on the coalition side had extensive experience in bargaining, many on the management side had never been involved in negotiations. Up to this point, they had assumed that bargaining would adhere to interest-based principles from start to finish.

Divisions within the management ranks reflected differences in market conditions across the different regions; similar divisions existed on the union side. Discussion of what to include in the union's opening offer was free-flowing and disorganized, as each participant introduced a particular issue he or she wanted considered. Rather than presenting a realistic first offer, this proposal lumped in everything that the coalition hoped to achieve; everyone treated the coalition's opening on economics as a "wish-list."

Evening Updates: Internal Bargaining at Work. Margolin and other key members of the management team held phone conferences every evening to update the Regional Presidents' Group (RPG) and KPPG on the negotiations. During the first conference call, Margolin reported that although economic proposals had not yet been exchanged, there would likely be a sizable gap between management and union positions. RPG and the KPPG members voiced strong concerns about the potential impact of negotiations on future budget and financial projections and stressed the need to maintain regional differences in across-the-board wage increases. Leaders from Southern California especially made it clear they wanted a less costly settlement than Northern California.

As these phone conversations continued, frustration increased among the management team members. There was clearly no consensus within the group over either what management should initially propose or what management should stick to as its bottom line for the economic package. After the call ended, management members vented their frustrations. "They [top management] just don't get it," said one member. "Here we are trying to get this done and they are still trying to control things without knowing what will work and what is totally unrealistic."

Day Two: A Proposal and Response. Much of second day of the final week was again taken up with separate management and union caucuses. After lunch, management worked on drafting an initial proposal. In mid-afternoon, diCicco asked to see Margolin privately. After about ten minutes, Margolin returned to the management caucus and reported that the coalition was ready to present its offer, one she could only describe as "extreme," totally unrealistic, and way beyond anything anyone in the room expected the union to propose, even as an initial proposal.

When union and management negotiating teams came together in the late afternoon, labor representatives presented their opening proposal. The proposal contained huge requests to deal with wage inequities, called for increases in benefit plans when union member surveys showed members were happy with their benefits across regions, and, overall, presented a plan that added up to a 23 percent increase in the first year. After this, Margolin gave a dramatic speech. She began by saying that she honestly did not know how to respond, that the proposal was: "shocking and stunning and radically different from what the management side had expected." She said it was like union and management were living in separate universes. Labor's proposal, she added, missed the point of an interest-based process in that it did not address the interests of either side because if this proposal were accepted, many regions would immediately go out of business and even California (the strongest region) would eventually suffer. If this was really where labor was in its thinking, she said, "I don't see why we've bothered to engage 400 people over the past five months." She then talked about how she had worked harder on this than anything else in her life and how she did not plan on coming back after Friday if things continued this way. Finally, she said it seemed foolish for management to present its proposal after what they just had heard. The management team then left to caucus.

Reactions to this joint session were profound, with a number of the management representatives visibly upset by the union proposal, making comments such as, "We've been betrayed." On the union side, several vet-eran negotiators were equally surprised by what they viewed as an overly emotional reaction by Margolin to their opening offer. Some thought that she was putting on a show for her team. Others thought this was just a normal start to negotiations over economic issues. "So we're high and they're low," said one union veteran. "What's the big deal? That's bargain-ing, isn't it?"

The joint session, Margolin's speech, and reaction to it provided the ca-thartic and catalytic effect of getting on the table the tension building within each team. It sent a message that a great deal of work had to be done if the parties were to get an agreement by the deadline.

Post-Cathartic Recovery. Early that evening a small group of union and man-agement representatives met and each person talked about their reactions to what had just transpired. Margolin and diCicco decided it was best to take this conversation public and asked their teams to reconvene in a joint session at 10 p.m. Managers talked about how they took the interests of both sides into consideration, whereas labor representatives did not seem to care about those of Kaiser. Management criticized labor for not prioritizing any of the BTG recommendations. Labor talked about what they saw as a breakdown in communication (they were not aware they were supposed to prioritize) and challenged the argument that they did not care about Kaiser as an orga-nization. Most ended their remarks by saying they thought they could still come to an agreement.

Day Three: Management's Initial Proposal. On Wednesday morning, man-agement made a short presentation of its opening proposal to the union. "It was as ridiculous (low) as the union's (high)," said one management negotia-tor. The offer called for three market-based variations in across-the-board increases and small amounts of money to be set aside for equity adjustments and for hard-to-fill positions, as well as some money for a workforce develop-ment fund.

Labor asked lots of questions after the presentation, the most fundamen-tal being why the offer was less than it was in 2000. In a comment that sounded like an ultimatum, one union leader said, "Kaiser took some risks five years ago and it has proved successful. If Kaiser isn't willing to take risks this time around, then we're not willing to take the risk of a long-term con-tract." This comment referred to the fact that although many viewed the economic settlement in 2000 as "generous," the union felt the improvement in operating performance during the intervening years showed that the "investment" had paid off.

When the coalition met in caucus to discuss the management proposal, this same union leader opened by saying, "Now is a time to draw a line in the sand. We need to give them the opportunity to change—to see if the political will is there—and if we need to, we can extend bargaining." For the first time, there was open discussion about possibly walking out of bargaining.

What was happening outside the room during these caucuses was as important as what was happening in the room, as Margolin and a small management team met several times with a small group of union leaders. She then used some of the private information from these sessions to suggest to her full management team what might be possible and acceptable. Margolin's suggested changes to their offer triggered resistance from several management team members, even discernable splits among management present at the table. Discussion also turned to the question that had surfaced in some previous conversations: Should they continue with national bargaining? Margolin pointed out that many of the regions would fare worse if national negotiations broke down and each region went back to separate local negotiations, as had been the case before 2000.

Internal Management Negotiations—Building to a Crisis. That night's phone calls with the RPG and KPPG turned out to be as dramatic and intense as any internal management discussion any of us, researchers and management participants, had ever experienced. Margolin noted that although progress was being made, there were still considerable differences between labor and management proposals and that she needed a clear authorization from top management on the amount of money available to deal with the issues of central concern to the union. The conversation began to heat up as various KPPG members voiced their concerns when told the money already on the table would not be sufficient to get an agreement. Southern California leaders wondered aloud whether they would be better off negotiating separately. Others indicated that they could not see how they could meet their financial goals if they agreed to what the union was proposing. KPPG members suggested changes to the most recent proposal, which were not well received by the members of the management bargaining team, who saw them as second guessing their judgments. At one point, Margolin put the phone on mute and said to her colleagues in the room, "Somebody has to tell them this is not a picnic."

Bargaining team members then pointed out to their management colleagues (and superiors) that they were using their best judgments and that the coalition had modified proposals considerably in the past day. One negotiator put it bluntly:

> You sound as though you don't trust senior, most capable managers you sent to do this job and if that's the case, then we probably shouldn't be here. Either you support this negotiating team or you don't. It's not that we are here to give away the company jewels; we are here to negotiate.

The negotiators' point to their bosses was, essentially, "trust us or replace us."

The phone conversation then turned to an effort to come to terms with specific, unresolved, tough issues. Several KPPG members reiterated their concerns about reaching an agreement that would allow them to meet their budget objectives and to continue to reflect market differences across the regions. Bargaining team members responded by noting they had indeed gotten labor to accept the need for some differentials but that there was no way to move labor off the view that they should at least get what they got in the 2000 contract.

After considerable back-and-forth dialogue, KP CEO George Halvorson summed up the options: go forward as is; negotiate separate contracts with each union; or stay with a national contract, except that the Southern California Medical Group goes it alone. "I've seen organizations with labor unrest and the cost of labor wars is horrible," he said. "They undermine morale. It is also a tough time to argue we are poor. If we are going to argue that, then let's get back to traditional bargaining about work rules, etc. The peace we have had with the partnership has been golden. I sympathize with concerns expressed about absenteeism and quality, but instead, let's think of what we can do with labor and use this as an opportunity to make change." After more heated exchanges, Halvorson asked Margolin, "What do you need to get this done?" After hearing her response, he polled each of the KPPG members to see if they were willing to authorize the amount Margolin thought would be needed and obtained agreement to do so. That allowed Margolin and her bargaining team to go forward into the final stage of negotiations with the resources she believed were needed to reach an agreement.

Push to Agreement. On Thursday, the movement toward a final agreement began in earnest. There was considerable discussion about an outline by diCicco for what he saw as a potential framework for an agreement. At the same time, a number of side conversations were occurring among key management and union leaders, including a critical conversation on Thursday that various people referred to as the "balcony talk," which discussed the allocation of equity adjustment monies across the regions and conditions that would govern a mid-term wage reopener (i.e., negotiations in which the only topics would be wage adjustments for the fourth and fifth years of the agreement).

When union leaders returned to their caucus and presented the results of this side conversation, non-SEIU union leaders exploded. They believed that SEIU was only addressing its own interests, at the expense of the others. This led to long discussions regarding how to rearrange the economic package to address the equity concerns of the other unions. At one point, Margolin cycled back to reiterate that there was no more money available, that management's best offer was now on the table. It was up to the coalition to find ways to allocate it equitably.

Meanwhile, members of the management negotiating team were becoming increasingly upset as they had to endure long periods waiting for the coalition's response to their last offer. Some were threatening to give up and leave. The deadline for calling union delegates—due to arrive the next day for the contract ratification vote—had passed. It was now moving into the middle of Friday night.

A final obstacle to an agreement developed when those drafting language governing equity adjustments ran into a problem with allocating funds to regions outside of California. After several hours of discussion, a breakthrough suggestion was made by one of the union delegates to set up a fund, allowing monies to be allocated by joint labor and management agreement. The drafting team thought this would work. Having overcome this final hurdle, at 3:30 a.m. on Saturday, only hours before the first union delegates would be arriving in Atlanta, the parties declared they had reached a tentative agreement.

The agreement's provisions called for a first-year, across-the-board increase of 5 percent for Northern and Southern California, Colorado, and the Northwest, and 4 percent for the other regions. The second and third years of the agreement called for 4 percent across-the-board increases in California, Colorado, and the Northwest, and 3 percent in other regions. A wage reopener was scheduled for year three to set the across-the-board increases for years four and five of the five-year contract. A targeted 3 percent per year increase was established for performance-sharing improvements, continuing the process and levels negotiated in the 2000 contract. The agreement also called for a workforce development fund, equity adjustment monies, and monies set aside for designated hard-to-fill positions.

From the coalition's standpoint, the settlement achieved some important economic objectives—reducing differentials across regions for people doing the same work, addressing equity issues, avoiding reductions in health or pension benefits (during a time when this was common in bargaining in so many other negotiations around the country), continuing the principle of performance sharing, and creating a trust fund for training. The union delegates who met in Atlanta approved the terms of the new agreement and forwarded it to the membership for ratification. The contract was accepted by a large majority.

Kaiser management was successful in maintaining several key principles and achieving a balance between the centralization and decentralization imperatives: having wages still tied to regional/local market conditions, holding the line on increases to the defined benefit pension program, developing a defined contribution pension program, securing union commitment to creating a flexible benefit program, putting money into hard-to-fill positions, designing a new attendance program, outlining the principles for unit-based teams, and continuing the pay-for-performance program at the same level as in the 2000 contract.

Table 6.4. Satisfaction with National Negotiations Process and Outcomes

Based on your assessment of the process and results of national negotiations, how satisfied or dissatisfied are you that these negotiations . . . (percent very satisfied or satisfied)

	Union	Management
Strengthened and advanced the Partnership	71	61
Reflected different market conditions in different regions	49	27
Increased respect and trust between labor and management	61	60
Increased labor's accountability for organizational performance	64	25
Reduced wage differentials in different regions	62	18
Reflected KP's projected revenue and intensified competition	54	34
Shared KP's financial successes in recent years	65	64
Used Partnership problem solving and interest based principles	68	67
Addressed both KP and workforce interests	72	51
Increased management's accountability for Partnership	46	56

Source: Post Negotiations Survey.

As table 6.4 shows, the post-negotiation survey found that union and management respondents both registered high levels of satisfaction with the impact of the national negotiations on the Labor-Management Partnership (71 percent of union respondents and 62 percent of management respondents), use of problem solving and interest-based principles in negotiations (68 percent of union and 67 percent of management respondents), and the increased respect and trust gained between labor and management (about 60 percent of both union and management respondents).

Significant differences in satisfaction are observed in union and management responses to other questions. Overall, union representatives tended to be more satisfied with the process and the results of national negotiations than management representatives. Specifically, union members expressed more satisfaction regarding the reduction in wage differentials across regions. Management representatives were significantly less satisfied with the extent to which the settlement reflected regional differences (or Kaiser's projected revenue and future competition) and their perception of the extent to which labor was willing to accept accountability for organizational performance. Although the parties were satisfied with the negotiation process, they differed in their satisfaction with the results.

A good deal of the difference in satisfaction with the results can be explained in terms of the different perspectives that management and labor brought to the outcomes that were embodied in the contract. Labor naturally compared the 2005 contract to the previous national negotiation in 2000, and by this measure the latest round could be viewed as a very good agreement. On the other hand, management looking ahead to increased competition and cost pressures was not as confident that all of its concerns had been dealt with in negotiations.

The economic settlement evoked strong reactions among some top Kaiser and coalition leaders. Southern California region medical director Dr. Jeffrey Weisz recounts:

> I was quite concerned that during negotiations, wage rates in Southern California would be escalated to match Northern California's wage structure. My concern was heightened since the Watson Wyatt survey demonstrated that our salary structure was 20 percent above the community. The number one issue in health care today is cost. The contract has a reopener in year 3 and labor will most likely want another salary increase and continue to migrate Southern California wages to match Northern California. We owe our members an affordable product. Now that Medicare reimbursement payment rates

are due to be cut, the organization is concerned about balancing our budget. We are in different markets, have different competitors and must deliver an affordable product. We grew 50,000 members in January, and must be able to deliver an operating margin that allows us to invest in new offices and equipment.

Health and Hospitals' Corporation CEO George Halvorson said:

We ended up pretty near the top of the industry; this doesn't make me uncomfortable as long as it doesn't affect our premiums. I'd rather have well-paid employees, but there has to be a package to make sure they are the most efficient in the industry or it will be untenable. The contract has provisions in it to work together to create efficiencies and better service and a major commitment to deal with absenteeism that wasn't in the earlier contract. So that's the type of issue that needs to be addressed; we can't have the highest pay and high absenteeism.

Now the challenge is to realize the benefits. The deal gives us a structure to help us do good things. So the next challenge is to take advantage of the agreements written into the contract to create the outcomes we want.

How physicians ultimately judge the agreement will be influenced by whether or not the implementation process achieves concrete results. "Right now, they see it as a very expensive settlement," said one leader. "Concerning the partnership, it is very simple: If [physicians] see improvements in attendance and productivity, it will help and if not, it will be the end of the partnership from the physicians' point of view."

UHW president Sal Rosselli called the agreement "perhaps the best contract we've negotiated with Kaiser. The most significant part of the agreement is that we got somewhat away from market-based criteria for wage increases. Having common, across-the-board increases for Colorado, the Northwest, and for Northern and Southern California was really important to us. We eliminated market wage differences in Northern California; in three years all workers will have the Bay Area wage scale. And we made progress in bridging the gap between Northern and Southern California in some of the other adjustments. We now have pretty much the same benefits in all of California."

The commitment to implement unit-based teams as the standard delivery mechanism for performance improvement was also viewed as a major achievement and a step toward transforming the partnership from a labor relations program to a health care delivery-focused partnership. The language of the agreement was very explicit about the parties' determination to make this the standard approach to delivering health care. "Partnership should be the way business is conducted at Kaiser," the agreement said. "Partnership structures should be integrated into existing operational structures of the organization at every level."

Implications for Partnerships

These detailed accounts of negotiating labor agreements in the Kaiser partnership illustrate several key points about what "partnership" means to the future of labor relations.

The very existence of a periodic forum with an explicit deadline and protocol for reaching a decision provided a needed venue for resolving some of the tough issues that can all too often and too easily get put off or not get elevated to the top of an organization for resolution. This had been the case for issues such as attendance and absenteeism, and the question of whether and how to focus the partnership around health care delivery issues. These problems had been raised in discussions at the regional levels and in various partnership forums but needed the pressure of a specific deadline and needed representation from all the constituents in a single place to shape solutions for these issues—agreements that would not just be pieces of paper but would have sufficient power and backing to be implemented. The collective bargaining negotiations provided the needed focus and pressure better than any alternative we can imagine. To borrow a metaphor from Samuel Johnson who once said: "Nothing focuses the mind more than knowing you will be hanged in the morning," in this case the pressure of a deadline, and in traditional bargaining the potential of a strike should an agreement not be reached, provided this focus. All organizations, including health care organizations, face major issues and need some venue to address them and to make tough choices. Collective bargaining can serve this purpose.

No partnership will survive if unions fail to deliver substantial economic gains to their members. The wage increases in the 2000 and 2005 agreements both reflected the market pressures for nurses' salaries and improved the wages of other employees covered under the agreement, perhaps at rates that set new market levels. This is the historic function of unions—to move forward and help employees, particularly lower wage employees, move up the economic ladder. What this means, however, is that in return for higher or even industry-leading wages, the parties have to be able to deliver industry-leading productivity, quality, and other performance-enhancing gains. For partnership to work, especially in the cost-sensitive environment of health care, the parties have to be successful in delivering on a high-wage and high-productivity bargain.

Implementation and follow-through on the ideas and commitments by the parties to unit-based teams, attendance improvements, and other recommendations of the BTGs that were included in the final agreement are critical to the continuity of the partnership and to the ultimate assessment of whether the 2005 negotiations will be recorded as a landmark achievement in labor relations and in health care or as an expensive price to pay for keeping the partnership alive. So is the need to deal with the disparity in perceptions between management and labor representatives with respect to the results of these negotiations. Labor leaders viewed the result as a major move on their part toward greater commitment for using the partnership to drive performance improvement. Management responses to the survey and interviews indicate that they foresaw intense competitive pressures ahead that may in fact require even more from labor leaders, the partnership, and the workforce than their union counterparts might have imagined. We explore how this critical implementation phase played out in the chapters that follow.

The On-Going Mix: IBN and Traditional Negotiations

As in 2000, the parties designed their process using the concepts and tools of IBN. The parties in the 2000 and 2005 negotiations bounded the conflicts by using the modern tools of negotiations and the reservoir of trust and social capital built up from working in partnership to engage the tough issues and find compromises and innovative resolutions that worked for all the parties involved. The sub-committees that met for several months before the main table got to work addressed issues in a problem-solving manner and developed the substantive proposals that created the basis for key parts of the final agreement. Working in the bargaining task groups served to build working rapport and to develop leadership capacity for a large number of union and management participants.

Yet, bargaining a new contract was not without its stumbling blocks, tensions, and traditional bargaining elements. At times it looked as if negotiations were going smoothly: labor and management were engaged in the process, clear about their joint interests and fundamental differences, at the same time generating novel solutions to problems and moving toward an agreement. At other times, a total disintegration of negotiations—and hence the partnership—seemed a real possibility. That both kinds of moments occurred during the course of bargaining illustrate the close connections between these negotiations and the overall labor-management relationship.

The mix of hard bargaining and problem solving that occurred during both the 2000 and 2005 negotiations demonstrates vividly that conflicting interests and responsibilities do not go away in a partnership. Managers are still accountable for controlling costs. Union leaders are still accountable for improving the economic status and working experiences of their members. Workers would lose trust in their representatives and the marketplace, as well as an organization's board of directors, and would conclude that the partnership is not a long-run advantage to the organization if their respective representatives did not vigorously assert their interests. The key in the case of the KP-Coalition partnership is that the parties were able to navigate this complex journey and to deal with all the inherent dilemmas constructively and effectively.

CHAPTER 7

The Union Coalition

Ten years after its founding, the Kaiser union coalition was still together. It weathered countless internal debates over policy and structure; three rounds of bargaining in which internal negotiations were nearly as intense as negotiations across the table with Kaiser management; a break-up of the national federation (AFL-CIO) that left coalition member unions on both sides of the split; and a transition in leadership.

If, as a large body of theory and historical experience suggests, coalitions are inherently unstable, then the fact that the Coalition of Kaiser Permanente Unions survived for at least a decade is in itself noteworthy. Although some coalition leaders had experience with partnerships between their individual unions and other employers, none had ever considered, much less tried, to construct a partnership in coalition with other unions, and certainly nothing approaching the scale and complexity—the number of unions and the number of members—that would be required to deal with Kaiser.

By going down this partnership path, coalition members were entering risky and uncharted terrain. Their efforts would be highly visible among their peers and subject to criticism and potential political backlash should the effort fail. The effort also meant giving up some autonomy in both bargaining and day-to-day labor-management relations.

It is not possible to tell the story of the partnership without telling the story of the coalition and vice versa. The coalition's story—its costs and benefits, what holds it together—provides a window on some of the key challenges facing the U.S. labor movement. This chapter discusses the dynamics of the coalition in four different arenas of activity: organizing, bargaining, partnership, and working in coalition.

The Coalition and Organizing

Growth, or, more accurately, decline, must be at the center of any contemporary discussion of unions and union structures. Although the coalition of Kaiser unions came together first for coordinated collective bargaining and later for labor-management partnership, organizing was also on its agenda from the beginning. According to the AFL-CIO Industrial Union Department's 1995 Strategic Analysis and Campaign Proposal, "Key to both the long-term and short-term goals is a vigorous commitment to organizing worker representation at Kaiser, its contractors and business partners, and ultimately the industry as a whole."

The pursuit of institutional growth, particularly via new organizing, is a key though seldom met challenge for unions involved in labor-management partnerships. Unions have often found themselves in the unsustainable position of working with management to improve organizational performance while battling with management over organizing the remaining non-union facilities. The Amalgamated Clothing and Textile Workers Union (later the Union of Needletrades, Industrial, and Textile Employees [UNITE]), for example, struggled for years with its decision to partner with management in one plant of a Johnson & Johnson subsidiary even as the company actively battled the union in another. Similarly, in the 1970s, the United Automobile Workers (UAW) participated in Quality of Working Life experiments with GM while GM pursued its non-union "Southern Strategy." Over time, the UAW negotiated various provisions with GM to facilitate organizing in the non-union plants. Neutrality and card check agreements, which ease conflicts over new organizing, are now often negotiated in the context of partnerships. But many of these arrangements have proven difficult to enforce and to translate into membership growth.

Organizing Agreements with Kaiser Permanente

When the Industrial Union Department (IUD) first formed a Coordinated Bargaining Committee for Kaiser in 1995, Kaiser's non-physician workforce was about 85 percent unionized, but there were still substantial pockets of unorganized workers, including many in new regions in which Kaiser had just begun to operate.[1] Given the centrality of maintaining or preferably increasing union density within Kaiser, it was important to the unions to negotiate an initial partnership agreement that would protect this key institutional interest. As noted in chapter 4, to achieve this goal, the parties negotiated a "Union Security" clause, the text of which appears below. We mention this agreement again here because of its importance to gaining and, more importantly, maintaining commitment of the coalition unions to the partnership and because it provided the foundation on which the unions based their negotiations for resolving potential inter-union disputes over organizing.

Union Security Section from Partnership Agreement

The parties to this agreement believe that Kaiser Permanente employees should exercise free choice and decide for themselves whether or not they wish to be represented by a labor organization.

Kaiser Permanente has no objection to a union signatory to this agreement becoming the bargaining representative to its people. Where a signatory union becomes involved in organizing KP employees, the employer will maintain a strictly neutral position.

It is the intention of the parties that employees' desire for exclusive bargaining representation be resolved in the most expeditious manner possible. Whenever a majority of employees in a unit the parties agree to be appropriate express clearly and unambiguously the wish to be represented by a signatory union, Kaiser Permanente agrees to recognize that union. An umpire shall be selected who will have the final authority to resolve ambiguities as to majority status and disagreements as to unit appropriateness.

Kaiser Permanente reserves the right to speak out in any appropriate manner when undue provocation is evident in an organizing campaign. Kaiser will encourage subcontractors, vendors, mergers and alliance partners to adopt the same policy regarding the union representation of their employees.

Source: Kaiser Permanente National Labor Agreement, 2000.

Internal Organizing Agreements

Given the multiple unions involved in the coalition, it was important for the coalition to work out guidelines and a process for resolving inter-union disputes about organizing. Specifically, rules were needed about what union would get the sole right to organize a particular unit, a procedure known as "clearance" within organized labor.

The coalition's organizing committee developed an internal union agreement that—although based on the IUD's target clearing procedures, a term for the process of awarding a particular union jurisdiction over a particular organizing target—was further tailored to Kaiser's particular circumstances. Under the agreement, the organizing committee was designated as the decision-making body; decisions were to be made by consensus and disputes would go to a neutral umpire. "Clearance" was awarded for a period of six months, after which it would be subject to review by the committee. Clearance could be lost if a union failed to maintain "substantive" organizing activity.

Beyond these ground rules, the agreement also laid out factors to be considered in awarding targets to particular unions. It gave weight to "the general levels of representation that exist at the inception of the partnership" and to the avoidance of proliferation of units or unions. Other factors to be considered were whether the requesting union represented similar units (occupations) within the market in question, the impact on the bargaining power of the union in its industry and labor markets, the union's likely success in organizing and representing the workforce, and the union's health care purchasing power in the market. This last factor related directly to one explicit goal of the partnership—that is, union assistance in marketing Kaiser as the provider or as an option for union or collectively bargained health care plans. Finally, the target clearance rules divided Kaiser into different types of markets, with implications for which unions might be allowed to organize workers in those markets: Foothold, Toehold, Non-Union, New, and Mergers and Acquisitions. Table 7.1 provides definitions of these markets.

These procedures were used frequently as the unions took full advantage of the organizing opportunities presented by these agreements. As of early 2005, there were approximately sixteen target clearance disputes, most of which were resolved by the organizing committee. The first of several disputes the committee was unable to resolve began in 1998 between the Union of American Physicians and Dentists (UAPD)—a new affiliate of American Federation of State, County and Municipal Employees (AFSCME)—and Service Employees International Union (SEIU) over organizing optometrists in Southern California. The neutral umpire (Kenneth Young) found that the target clearance rules were confusing but supported SEIU's position. He also recommended that the coalition review and clarify the language regarding

Table 7.1. Market Categories and Definitions

Market category	Definition	Implication for targeting
Foothold	At least 1,000 KP workers organized	Presumption that no new unions allowed. Only Factor 1 applies.
Toehold	<1,000 KP workers organized	Both sets of factors apply.
Non-Union	Current KP market that is not organized	Both sets of factors apply.
New	Newly acquired non-union markets	Treated like non-union market. IUD to decide when they become available for target claims.
Mergers and acquisitions	Self explanatory	Depending on the type (union vs. non-union in new vs. current markets), placed in one of the other categories or considered on a case by case basis.

Source: Coalition of Kaiser Permanente Unions.

the time limits on clearances and the process by which they would be ended or extended, language which was the main source of the conflict between the two unions. After the organizing committee met and made these clarifications, AFSCME, this time via its affiliate and coalition/partnership member (United Nurses Associations of California [UNAC]), obtained clearance and successfully organized the optometrists.

The same umpire issued a second decision in February 2004 in a dispute between SEIU and the United Food and Commercial Workers (UFCW) over a new group of psychological social workers at Kaiser's facility in Bakersfield in Southern California and a very small group of health educators, also in Bakersfield. The umpire concluded that this issue was beyond his jurisdiction because neither union had sought target clearance. Rather, the unions argued that their bargaining agreements with Kaiser gave them the right to organize these workers. On a second issue, he ruled in favor of SEIU, which had sought and obtained a clearance for a variety of professional titles, including health educators in Southern California. Young ruled for SEIU because it had actually conducted a successful card count in 2002 and was in the process of negotiating a first contract.

Perhaps the most interesting dispute involving the umpire came at the end of 2004. Kaiser had decided to build a new medical center in the Portland area of its Northwest region, where the partnership was deeply embedded and where labor was heavily involved in operational management bodies. Given the advanced level of partnership in the region, coalition union members and Kaiser agreed to plan and design the hospital in partnership. The question, however, was what union should speak for and represent the future employees and potential union members—the Oregon Federation of Nurses and Health Professionals (OFNHP), which represented most Kaiser RNs in the region, or the Oregon Nurses Association (ONA), also a coalition member. The latter represented only 70 Kaiser RNs, but more than 10,000 RNs working for other employers in the state.

The first issue confronting the umpire was whether the arbitration was timely, as no workers/members had yet been hired. Young found that, given the joint planning process, the dispute was timely. At that point in the hearing, ONA caucused and gave up its claim. The umpire directed the organizing committee to award OFNHP the clearance for six months to pursue an accretion agreement with Kaiser. The plan for the new hospital was placed on hold when the Northwest region faced financial problems.

In sum, the target clearance process seems to have gone smoothly, with all but four clearance requests involving conflict between at least two unions being settled by the committee itself. Nor do the conflicts that went through this process seem to have engendered long-term bitterness on the part of the "losing" party. Margaret Peisert, associate director of the coalition summed up the results:

> We had a few little blowups along the way, but for the most part, . . . I think [the internal organizing agreement] was a factor in bringing people together, you didn't have that barrier of competition for these Kaiser members. It was important, it freed them up, it put that behind them. Markets were cleared, and people were out organizing.

However, as discussed in the section on managing inter-union relations, things did not go as well with organizing disputes with non-coalition unions. One of these, discussed in chapter 3, concerned the Communications Workers of America (CWA), which organized a Kaiser Call Center in 2004, despite strong opposition from SEIU. At the time, SEIU had recently begun its campaign to better align union structures with industries and thus opposed this entry of another union into the Kaiser jurisdiction. To demonstrate its seriousness, SEIU opposed CWA joining the coalition, effectively blocking its entry. Although CWA succeeded in achieving recognition for the workers, the unit was later decertified, leaving the workers without union representation.

Other organizing disputes outside the coalition and therefore outside the target clearance process involving the California Nurses Association (CNA) caused significant turmoil within the coalition. One such incident involved

SEIU, AFSCME, and CNA. In December 2003, SEIU signed an organizing pact with CNA whereby, "SEIU will support campaigns by RNs to join CNA, and CNA will support campaigns by professional, licensed, certified and other health care workers to join SEIU."[2] Representatives of other Kaiser unions were angry that SEIU had not consulted or even informed them ahead of the public announcement about the CNA agreement. They felt that SEIU appeared to be making common cause with CNA. Most affected in this regard was UNAC, which represented RNs in Kaiser facilities and in other health care providers in Southern California. Indeed, CNA began raiding UNAC units in early 2004, shortly after reaching its agreement with SEIU. CNA also made some unsuccessful organizing forays into Kaiser regions outside of California after the 2005 agreement was settled.

For many in the coalition, the SEIU agreement with CNA and CNA's subsequent raiding was a pivotal moment in coalition history. There were suspicions, which SEIU denied, that it had put CNA up to the raid or was somehow complicit in it. Eventually, with the intervention of AFL-CIO secretary-treasurer Richard Trumka, as well as SEIU and coalition leaders and several top Kaiser managers, the parties were able to reach an agreement regarding jurisdictions and a process to avoid future raiding. Although the episode soured relations between UNAC and SEIU and helped to heighten concerns about SEIU's intentions, the coalition had survived a very difficult and potentially catastrophic episode, demonstrating considerable resilience in the process.

Membership Growth and Organizing Outcomes

As the Kaiser unions pursued an active and often successful organizing agenda, much of it took place in what were then newly acquired, non-union markets. For instance, from the earliest days of coordinated bargaining discussions, AFSCME, AFT, and the Office and Professional Employees International Union (OPEIU) worked to organize Kaiser's new facilities of Community Health Plan (CHP)—the HMO that Kaiser had purchased—in the Northeast,[3] while SEIU successfully organized employees in Kansas City, a non-union market. However, in the face of continued financial difficulties, Kaiser terminated both of these operations.

The growth in coalition membership was substantial, increasing from about 55,000 in 1997 to 86,000 in 2006. Table 7.2 lists the growth for each of the original affiliates, as well as 2006 membership for two late joiners to the coalition (Teamsters and United American Nurses). Although the largest

Table 7.2. Membership in Coalition Unions, 1997 and 2006

Union	1997	2006	Increase (%)
American Federation of State, County and Municipal Employees (UNAC)	4,500	9,519	112
American Federation of Teachers	1,238	2,577	108
International Brotherhood of Teamsters	—	317	N/A
International Federation of Professional and Technical Engineers	826	1,133	37
KP Nurse Anesthetists Association	250	300	20
Office and Professional Employees International Union	5,300	10,525	99
Service Employees International Union	29,130	50,033	72
United American Nurses	—	140	N/A
United Food and Commercial Workers	3,332	6,831	105
United Steelworkers of America	2,800	4,663	67
Total	47,376	86,038	81.6

Source: Coalition of Kaiser Permanente Unions.

absolute growth occurred at the largest union in the coalition, SEIU, other unions experienced more substantial growth in percentage terms. At the same time, the larger non-coalition, non-partnership unions also grew. During this same period, CNA increased by nearly 50 percent, from 8,000 to almost 12,000 members. UNITE HERE, representing Kaiser workers in Hawaii, increased a more modest 22 percent, from 1,500 to more than 1,800.

The sources of growth for the member unions included the organization of new units, accretion of already organized workers into existing units, and employment growth in existing units. Although we are unable to say precisely what percentage of the overall growth resulted from each source, approximately 7,400 workers were successfully organized across twenty-nine campaigns carried out during the partnership, constituting about 20 percent of the coalition's overall growth. Despite the substantial organizing gains described here, coalition unions were not always successful in their campaigns. According to Kaiser's brief to the National Labor Relations Board (NLRB) in the Dana/Metaldyne cases, for instance, unions failed in five out of twenty-three card check campaigns. This 80 percent success rate is in line with prior research on the outcomes card check agreements [4] These campaigns took place in all regions of the country, including traditionally anti-union states such as Georgia, and involved many different occupational groups.

The Coalition and Bargaining

The 2000 Negotiations

The successful completion of bargaining in 2000 was a pivotal event, strengthening or in some instances creating cohesion for the first time within the coalition. Previously, coordination among the unions had remained relatively loose. The 2000 national agreement represented achievement of the coalition's original goal of coordinated bargaining. "[Bargaining is] much better now," said one union representative in 2001. "National bargaining was messy, and not perfect, but it was very much improved, from our standpoint. [A] minimum number of deals [were] cut behind closed doors."

During negotiations, the unions were able to manage their way through a very complex set of diverse interests within the coalition, such as the ongoing issue of inequities in pay and benefits among and even within regions. Although all coalition members supported increased standardization across these boundaries in principle, reducing these differentials through negotiations was a source of tension. Other tensions arose among coalition unions representing higher skilled occupations in tight labor markets (nurses and some other professional and technical titles), who felt their members should command higher-than-average wage increases; other unions were less sympathetic to these market-based arguments. In fact, Kaiser was also interested in providing supplemental increases for nurses and other hard-to-fill occupations and, with the agreement of at least some of the "non-nursing" unions, the 2000 agreement recognized the different occupational labor market realities.

The president of a large nurses union celebrated the willingness of SEIU to sacrifice money it could have gotten for its own members so the nurses could regain parity with other regions—parity they had lost during the concessionary period. "Look at the contracts," the official said. "The nurses get more, and SEIU and OPEIU [both unions without many nurses or technician members] agreed. . . . They agreed we should get more money for parity, out of money they had already bargained. It was amazing."

As indicated by its 92 percent ratification of the 2000 agreement, the rank-and-file members endorsed the changes that had been made in traditional differentials. In early 2005, 65 percent of members surveyed still reported satisfaction with the 2000 agreement, and 71 percent agreed that they had done better in negotiations since the unions began working together in the coalition.

For all this support, preparation for 2005 bargaining took place in an atmosphere of change and turmoil, some of which was described in chapter 6. SEIU was pushing for change in the AFL-CIO and undergoing considerable internal reorganization, including a merger of the two large, non-professional health care locals in Northern and Southern California into United Healthcare Workers-West (UHW). As part of its goal to centralize and consolidate bargaining, SEIU eventually achieved a master contract for all its Kaiser locals in California. For some members of the coalition, SEIU's insistence to centralize bargaining on its own, separate from the work of the coalition, deepened concerns about SEIU's commitment to the coalition and to national bargaining and created the impression that SEIU was going to be setting the agenda for the coalition.

Although the formal speeches at the March 2005 Union Delegates' conference emphasized the message of unity and solidarity, at the same time there was an undercurrent of tension and cross-union rivalry. Sal Rosselli's speech to the delegates was particularly interesting in this regard. His talk was effectively organized around the stories of three "representative" SEIU members and it highlighted the growth in SEIU's density in the Southern California health care market. Rosselli's presentation also emphasized the need to move toward equalization of wages and benefits across different Kaiser regions and the importance of maintaining unity within the coalition. Other speakers also reinforced the importance of unity, but on the second day, UFCW participants coordinated the wearing of yellow T-shirts to counter SEIU's "purple," its official color. Behind the scenes, many delegates muttered about separate SEIU caucuses that were held throughout the several months of bargaining. After the completion of bargaining in the fall of 2005, coalition executive director Pete diCicco reflected, "SEIU had their own goals and that was a source of some tension. SEIU would go off and meet, caucus separately—then OPEIU and UFCW did the same."

The underlying conflict surfaced briefly in the early stages of negotiations, when UFCW and SEIU clashed over the future of a UFCW bargaining unit in Bakersfield, CA. Bargaining unit members had initiated a decertification drive, which UFCW leaders believed SEIU was encouraging while also recruiting unit members to join. UFCW delegates considered withdrawing from bargaining over this issue, but decided to remain in national bargaining. Eventually, the issue reached the national leadership levels of the two unions. Several weeks later, it was put to rest in an exchange of letters committing both unions to stop local efforts to challenge the other's representation. The resolution of this incident was clearly part of a broader discussion over whether the UFCW would join SEIU in the proposed Change to Win coalition of unions that was in the process of leaving the AFL-CIO. (The fact that UFCW chose to join Change to Win no doubt helped resolve the local issue.) Given the strong potential of this incident to pull the coalition apart, and to do so at a crucial moment (heading into national bargaining), some local leaders and staff members described this episode as pivotal in the coalition's history. On the one hand, the coalition had demonstrated its resilience by surviving a big challenge. On the other hand, trust in SEIU was further undermined among some local union leaders, setting the stage for conflict during bargaining.

Disunity was evident elsewhere within the coalition at about the same time. "The tensions [among the unions] now are evident and they weren't there a year ago," said a regional manager involved in national bargaining. "There's a genuine fear of Sal Rosselli by the non-SEIU locals." He said he could sense increased difficulties in inter-union relations in his regular dealings with the unions in his region, particularly around partnership issues, "They're always uncoordinated but not usually chaotic and recently I've been getting contradictory suggestions. . . . [The unions] might have sent mixed signals in the past, but this is a new level."

Despite all this, as the Bargaining Task Groups (BTGs) worked through the first half of the summer of 2005, there was little evidence of real inter-union tension at the tables and wide satisfaction with the process by all parties. Our survey of the union delegates on the BTGs showed no significant differences in satisfaction between SEIU and other union delegates. Although unity prevailed during this phase of the process, there was still much discussion behind the scenes about events at the national level as well as some complaining about SEIU.

Intra-coalition tensions mounted during the next phase of bargaining, which involved negotiation of economic issues under the pressure of an approaching deadline, took a more positional turn, and involved intensified intra-organizational bargaining. The primary source of conflict among the unions concerned two types of supplemental pay increases sought by the coalition. One reflected the outcome of years of decentralized bargaining: wage differences for similar jobs and titles from one facility to another, both across regions and even within regions. In particular, reflecting labor market conditions and union strength, Northern California's wage rates were the highest in Kaiser. For instance, according to Kaiser's 2005 wage surveys (which were conducted primarily to compare Kaiser's compensation with their competitors within a region), the weighted average RN hourly wages were highest in Northern California (a hospital-based region).[5] Average weighted wages for Southern California's RNs (also a hospital-based region) were 85 percent of those in Northern California, while those in the Northwest (with one hospital) and Ohio (no hospital) were 73 percent and 60 percent of Northern California, respectively. There were also inter-city differences. Reducing these differentials through pay supplements was an important goal of the coalition during the 2005 negotiations. However, Kaiser had neither the money, or so it argued, nor the will to meet these demands. The other type of pay supplement gave higher increases for occupations, especially RNs, in tight labor markets. These "hard-to-fill" positions, as Kaiser called them, reflected the shortages of workers with either the available skills or the willingness to work for the wages and working conditions offered within the U.S. health care system.

For the newly merged mega-local UHW in California, the goal of moving their Southern California members into Northern California pay rates was key to proving the value of the merger to members. Some within the coalition felt that SEIU was pursuing this goal to the detriment of other equity concerns, such as pay differentials *within* Southern California (between San Diego and Los Angeles) and substantial worker contributions to health insurance in the newer, Eastern regions of the organization. "SEIU/UHW tried to stop bringing the San Diego rates up to LA levels for all the locals," said one coalition staff person. "Kaiser offered to fix those inequities in the first year. That was on the table. But UHW used that money to move Southern California to Northern California rates, [even though] there's no business case for it. . . . It's appalling, because the employer offered to fix it."

Many others in the coalition felt strongly that the decision to put money toward reducing the pay gap between Northern and Southern California, rather than toward resolving internal inequities within Southern California, was an important step in achieving the coalition's goal of reducing, or eventually eliminating, differentials among regions.

Some even credited SEIU/UHW with sacrificing money for a broader fix to the equity problems confronting non-SEIU locals in California and beyond. As Pete diCicco put it,

The fact of the matter is that SEIU has 60% of the total membership and so they have to lead this thing. It's the political reality. We have to respond to SEIU's interest and they have an obligation to help the smaller unions—and we saw it, particularly with these latter final pieces—they are giving up money in the bank to fund these other issues.

A staff member from SEIU/UHW summed up the relations within the coalition after bargaining:

At the end, a lot of people outside the Change to Win coalition came up to me and thanked us for help in getting what they need, and some others weren't so gracious. In the future, the coalition will probably be strained until everyone realizes we are serious about having one health care union, but we aren't going to go about raiding them. There are enough others out there to organize. We did this before and operated separately and that definitely didn't work and we have clearly done better with the Coalition.

Some representatives of the large nurses unions in Southern California and the Northwest were particularly unhappy with the settlement. Although these nurses unions did get additional money for their members, they felt those supplements should have been even greater. "Now many are asking, 'Could we have done better on our own?' It's a fair question. The jury is still out," said one nurse leader. "[The] wages are mediocre for nurses and extraordinary for non-nurses. . . . The nurses are tired of the ego-centric behavior of SEIU."

Despite the tensions, the post-bargaining survey indicated overall support for both the internal coalition dynamics and the bargaining outcome, with 69 percent of union and 55 percent of management feeling that the negotiations would have a positive impact on the coalition's internal cohesion. In the open-ended comments section, only five respondents complained about SEIU's dominance of the negotiations, suggesting it was not the most salient issue for most negotiators and delegates. In sum, it seems clear that in general the unions had done better in bargaining than they would have on their own. There was little if any dissent from that view coming out of 2000 bargaining. In 2005, the majority of coalition leaders and staff still held that view. There was, however, a significant minority—mostly in the unions representing nurses—who were questioning whether their members had benefited as greatly from the coalition as others had.

The Coalition and the Partnership: Four Key Challenges

In addition to the fundamental issue of organizing and growth discussed above, the past twenty-five years of union involvement in partnerships with management has identified four key challenges that these arrangements create for unions. Most of these challenges have been experienced by unions partnered individually with management at the local level. The next section describes how the coalition attempted to overcome these challenges.

Balancing Traditional and New Roles

The first and perhaps most fundamental challenge is assuring an appropriate balance between the time and resources devoted to partnership activities and those devoted to traditional representation via collective bargaining and grievance handling. This is closely related to the political risk of getting too close to management at the expense of being a strong, independent advocate for member interests, a risk that invites political opposition and membership backlash. For example, the local union leadership at Saturn was unseated by an opposition caucus that, among other things, pointed to the large amount of time the officers were spending on co-managing the business instead of on the more traditional responsibility of representing individuals.

From the beginning, the Kaiser coalition was wary of the disconnect that can develop between leaders and members in a labor-management partnership. As Peter diCicco constantly emphasized, the key to avoiding this disconnect was to make it clear to all that partnership was not just "labor-management cooperation." In his view, partnership was a different and more effective way to represent members and to break new ground outside of the legal or mandatory scope of issues that current labor law requires management to negotiate. DiCicco was credible in communicating this view of partnership partly because he and others who helped form the coalition were not ideologically pre-disposed to building a partnership. They had been willing to consider and had actually begun to pursue the alternative strategy of mounting an aggressive corporate campaign against Kaiser. The fact that diCicco and the other coalition leaders had "proven" their ability to engage in militant actions in the past (and presumably were willing to do so again, if necessary) proved critical to building and maintaining respect and support across the many unions participating in the coalition.

As noted in chapter 2, diCicco often used his "outside the NLRB Box" diagram (refer to figure 2.1) to illustrate his view that a labor-management partnership can serve to expand worker and union influence into issues that are off-limits in traditional bargaining relationships. Under NLRB rules, a clear line is drawn between rights reserved to management's discretion and management's obligation to negotiate with the union. Unions have a legal right to negotiate only over wages, hours, and working conditions. In an effective partnership, however, this legal line of demarcation becomes blurred, if not eliminated. At Kaiser, for example, the coalition's executive director sat on the top management coordinating committee (the KPPG) and attended meetings of the Kaiser board of directors. Coalition leaders at regional and facility levels also sat on management operating committees or councils where the full range of business issues were discussed and decisions were made. As a result, unions were able to influence issues that were outside the scope of mandatory bargaining but which were of central concern to workers, especially drivers of patient care quality, such as staffing ratios, coordination of care, training, access, and time with the patient.

Another key difference is that union leaders are engaged in decision-making discussions early in the process, rather than being informed after the fact and then left with the option of negotiating over the effects of the decision. This expanded scope of influence is not without its difficulties and consequences. The trade-off is that union leaders must not only respect confidentiality requirements regarding proprietary information (though there are rarely problems with this), they must also accept responsibility for the decisions and be held accountable for supporting them through implementation. A prime example at Kaiser was the challenge of working to reduce unacceptable levels of absenteeism. Although union leaders had to step up to this issue, they could not afford to be viewed as just another arm of management, blaming their own members for the problem.

While pursuing partnership, the unions also maintained their commitment to representation in the traditional realms of bargaining and grievances. As already seen, for example, they mobilized considerable resources for collective bargaining in 2000 and 2005. Further, labor and management developed alternative problem-solving processes as a key part of the partnership: Issue Resolution is an interest-based process that can be used for a wide array of workplace problems, whereas Corrective Action is an alternative to the traditional disciplinary system. Despite the development of these processes, workers continued to have access to the traditional grievance procedure. The coalition conducted a phone survey of 1,000 coalition union

Table 7.3. Member Attitudes toward Balancing Roles, 2005 (percent)

	Agree or strongly agree
Union good at balancing partnership and traditional roles (*N*=1,412)	68
Partnership helps unions represent workers (*N*=1,473)	73
	Satisfied or very satisfied
Satisfaction with union in dealing with grievances (*N*=1,291)	75

Source: Coalition of Kaiser Permanente Unions.

members in early 2005. As shown in table 7.3, the survey results confirmed that most members were not concerned about the partnership undermining traditional representation. Two-thirds to three-fourths of respondents agreed that: (a) their union did a good job in balancing partnership with traditional roles; (b) the partnership helped unions represent workers; and (c) they were satisfied with their union.

Union Leadership Skills and Capacity

A second key challenge for unions and their leaders engaged in partnerships with management is the acquisition of new skills and organizational capacities needed to engage management on issues of business strategy, operations, finance, and other areas of business decision making not normally open or necessarily familiar to unions. The coalition dealt with these skill and human resource challenges in a variety of ways. Beginning with the agreement bargained in 2000, the labor-management trust, which funds the partnership, paid the coalition's partnership related expenses. Significant financial resources were available to the coalition to develop skills and pay for personnel, especially compared to other labor-management partnerships. The coalition staff grew substantially over the years, to more than twenty in 2005. These staff members were typically paired with managerial employees to co-lead partnership activities in regions and national partnership programs (e.g., workplace safety) and provide support in particular functional areas (e.g., communications). Despite the growth of staff support, many coalition staff and leaders argued that the resources remained insufficient, given the scale of the Kaiser effort:

We have not grasped how large KP is, never dedicated enough resources. . . . The Labor-Management Partnership Trust has $20 million a year to spend,

[but] only spent $13-$15 million last year [2004] and sent money back to regions. . . . We have 400 facilitators for 150,000 employees and $8 billion in
revenues. (Coalition staff)

Although some may argue, as the staff member above did, that the resources
remained inadequate, they were in fact vastly larger than those available for
any other labor-management partnership of which we are aware. For instance, the SEIU Local 1199/New York hospital partnership's budget, for
about the same number of workers, is about five million dollars. Ultimately,
the frustration may have been less with the total resources available and
more with how they were used or with the failure to involve more workers on
the front lines.

Local union staff were also heavily involved in partnership work. Local
leaders reported that on average, half the time they spent servicing Kaiser
employees was spent on partnership activity. Some local unions were able to
use partnership resources to hire "labor liaisons," who worked full time on
partnership activities at the local level, attending partnership meetings,
working with stewards, recruiting members to participate, and maintaining
communication within the union about the partnership. In addition, Kaiser
sometimes covered the cost of replacement for front-line workers involved in
partnership activities.

Problems with this backfill practice—specifically the extremely uneven
and limited way it was implemented—were, in theory, addressed in the
2005 agreement.[6] The agreement called for the development of a "comprehensive" approach to the backfill problem, including (1) a systematic analysis
of the gap between current staffing levels and staffing levels that would enable workers to take time away from work to engage in partnership activities,
training, and more traditional contract administration without stressing both
the department and the individuals, and (2) budgeting in order to fill that
gap. In fact, with the lack of a system to do the "gap analysis," tight budgets
throughout the Kaiser regions, and the focus on unit-based teams, this area
of the contract was weakly implemented, at least nationally, in the first two
years of the contract. As before, some regions and some facilities invested
more fully in backfill.

At the time that agreement was negotiated, local leaders and coalition
staff were reporting that locals were stretched quite thin as they attempted
to balance supporting the partnership with their responsibilities for representing their members in other ways. As one local leader in Southern California put it, this effort "wears the staff out. The local [union] Kaiser staff are

working like dogs. . . . We go back to the local and say we need more help and the reaction is, 'This was supposed to make life easier.' But it doesn't for field staff. They have to find all the reps for all the committees and make sure it's going right."

A coalition staff member agreed, "We did not anticipate the amount of resources necessary to engage in the partnership. We underestimated our capacity and resources. The locals are set up along traditional lines, for organizing and handling grievances. It is difficult to balance partnership with the day-to-day work in the union. . . . [We should be] shifting more resources to facilities so we can help the rank-and-file where they work to build the partnership. [Workers] need support and assistance."

An obvious solution to the problem of staff resources was to involve union members in the partnership, but staffing and backfill were central problems in terms of deepening the level of member involvement. Another concern was whether staff and members had the skills they needed to participate with confidence in joint partnership committees. Training modules in a variety of new skills, including process skills (interest-based problem solving, consensus decision making) and business literacy were developed through the partnership and delivered to union staff and members as they participated in partnership projects. In addition, the coalition worked with external consultants from Cornell University's ILR School to develop a focused Union Partnership Representative Training aimed at helping union representatives work through the typical dilemmas presented by the partnership. In 2005, union leaders reported that, on average, between one-third and one-half of their members had availed themselves of these various training opportunities. Training continued to be a source of concern to some local leaders and coalition staff.

Although widespread agreement existed among the staff and local leaders that the unions had not yet solved the human resource problems that are typical of unions involved in partnerships, there was considerable evidence from the coalition's 2005 survey that membership involvement in the partnership had had a significant positive impact on attitudes toward the union.

Table 7.4 shows that satisfaction with the union both in general and in specific areas, such as grievances, dues, and leadership, was considerably higher among members who were involved in the partnership than those who were not. Similarly, members who were involved in the partnership were much more likely to report that the unions in their workplace worked well together and that workers did better in negotiations after the unions started

Table 7.4. Partnership Involvement and Attitudes toward the Union, 2005 (percent)

	Very/somewhat involved in partnership (N=920)	Not involved/ would like to be (N=214)	Not involved/don't want to be (N=350)
Satisfaction with the union (satisfied or very satisfied)	77.5	59.8	66.0
Satisfaction with how the union deals with grievances	70.6	55.1	50.6
Leaders demonstrate good leadership ability (agree or strongly agree)	63.5	42.5	46.0
Union does a good job communicating	61.9	45.3	47.4
Union listens to what I have to say	64.1	44.4	51.5
I feel committed to the union	72.0	60.7	53.4
Union dues are well spent	50.4	29.9	34.0
Union is positive force for quality care	73.8	62.1	58.0
Unions in my workplace work well together	68.9	48.6	52.5
Kaiser workers have done better in negotiations since the unions began working together	68.8	52.8	53.4
Union participation (answering "always" or "often")	43.3	24.8	15.4

Source: Coalition of Kaiser Permanente Unions.

working together. The results for union commitment were not quite so strong—workers who were involved in the partnership reported higher levels of union commitment, but workers who wanted to be involved, but were not, also felt much more commitment than did members who did not want to be involved, suggesting a mix of selection and participation effects. That is, workers who were more committed to the union in the first place were more likely to report that they participated in the partnership. Of particular interest is that workers involved in the partnership reported much higher rates of union participation (defined as "things like attending meetings, reading union publications, and voting in union elections").

Conflict and Cooperation

A third key challenge for unions is balancing conflict and cooperation in their relations with management. Partnership has a complex impact on the sources of power that can be mobilized. On the one hand, when union involvement in decision making embeds the union in the operational systems of the company, it can lead to greater leverage and bargaining power. On the other hand, union leaders need to bargain hard when interests diverge. Many union leaders question whether solidarity among workers can be built in the absence of regular conflict with the employer.

Combining problem solving with hard bargaining approaches often requires education of both management and union leaders. Managers tend to equate partnership with cooperation and are surprised when union leaders revert to more traditional bargaining behaviors or use solidarity building tactics (such as wearing union stickers) when conflicts arise. As mentioned in chapter 2, the CNA was concerned that the partnership would stifle the unions' ability to engage public criticism of Kaiser and would thus trade off class-wide solidarity for potential organization-specific advantages. That concern was shared by workers and union members within the coalition.

At Kaiser, some local leaders were well aware of these tensions and expressed concern about their ability to build solidarity as adversarial relations became a distant memory or even a non-memory for most members. "We're more accustomed to fighting," said a local leader in the Northwest region, "and don't know how to work within partnership. How do we build the union in that context? There are . . . not many models for that. Without the fight, it makes workers question [whether] they need the union." A local leader from Southern California noted another problem: "About half our members are new since 2000. They have no concept of the past, the relationship, the endless battling, the working conditions. No idea. They don't know and they don't want to know anything about the contract. So there's a real cultural divide among the members between old and new."

The survey data provide mixed evidence around these concerns. The coalition member surveys included a question about militancy (see table 7.5).

Table 7.5. Member Views of Union Militancy, 1998 and 2005 (percent)

Your union is:	1998	2005	Change
too militant	9	11	+2
about right	45	54	+9
not militant enough	47	36	−11

Source: Coalition of Kaiser Permanente Unions.

Despite the centrality of partnership to the unions' collective strategy, there was a substantial decline in the percentage of respondents reporting that the union was not militant enough (see table 7.5). Interestingly, the survey results also indicated that lower seniority members held significantly more positive views of, but also participated less in, the union. Perhaps both the hopes and fears of union leaders were coming true—newer hires without the experience of conflict appreciated the partnership approach and the greater scope of union participation and the reduced conflict while also being less inclined to support the union through their own involvement.

Managing Inter-Union Relationships

A final set of challenges is the need to manage relationships among the national and local unions. The participation of multiple unions in a partnership program creates considerable difficulty in this regard. In our prior research, we have found that the existence of multiple unions was a significant negative predictor of the survival of participation programs.[7] In the case of AT&T's labor-management partnership, the two unions involved, Communications Workers of American and International Brotherhood of Electrical Workers, had different organizational cultures. Conflict between the two unions was often as contentious as conflict between the unions and the company. Similarly, the Minneapolis multi-employer health care partnership involved different local unions from different national affiliates and conflict among those unions contributed to the decline of that effort.

The local leader surveys provide some information on leader views of the impact of partnership on their relations with other unions. Local leaders were asked to rate the impact on the relationships from 1 ("worsened a great deal") to 5 ("improved a great deal"). (See table 7.6 for the results.) As might be expected, local leaders saw the greatest impact on relations among locals within the coalition, and between locals and their national unions. In both cases, however, local leaders reported improvements in the relationships. This is quite a different result than seen in the Saturn case, where partnership at the local level at times severely strained relations with the national UAW. It may be that in some ways, the coalition substituted for the national union in the Kaiser relationship. Throughout interviews, for instance, we noted some frustration from local leaders concerning the resources available from the coalition for partnership activities. The contrast between the Saturn and the KP cases regarding national-local union conflict may also result from differences in centralization, both in the two industries and with the unions involved.

Table 7.6. How Well Do Coalition Unions Work with Other Unions?

Partnership impact on how well:	Mean
local unions in the coalition work together	4.47
the local works with other KP unions in the region that are not in the coalition	3.36
the local works with other non-KP unions in the area	3.36
the local works with the national union	3.79

Source: Coalition of Kaiser Permanente Unions.
Note: 1 = worsened a great deal; 5 = improved a great deal; *N* = 15.

It is important to note that in early 2008, open, public warfare broke out between SEIU/UHW and its leader, Sal Rosselli, and the national SEIU and its president, Andy Stern. Although the conflict had many dimensions, one strong root of this conflict was the push by the national union for greater centralization particularly in bargaining and relationships with employers, centralization explicitly modeled on the "CIO" unions like the UAW. Not surprisingly, Rosselli, a strong local leader, began to push back when his local's autonomy was threatened. One of Rosselli's accusations against Stern was that he was too willing to create alliances and partnerships with employers in order to facilitate new organizing that compromised the representation of member interests. It is essential to recognize that this criticism was focused on deals with employers other than Kaiser; neither side in the internal SEIU battle suggested the Kaiser partnership was inappropriate. Nonetheless, the battle pulled SEIU/UHW's attention away from the partnership at a crucial moment and at times spilled over into internal coalition politics.

One important barrier to the unions working together was the substantial difference in union culture across these organizations. For instance, one local leader pointed to the difficulties unions had in working together when one union was more staff-oriented and the other more member-oriented. Some leaders discussed difficulties working with unions that had a large percentage of their membership outside of Kaiser or outside of health care. Others discussed the differences between unions with differing levels of highly educated members in professional jobs.

Coalition unions worked hard to improve and formalize relations among local unions in some regions and facilities. The most formalized institution for cross-union cooperation at the facility level was the steward council, involving regular meetings of stewards from the various unions that represented workers at the facility. These councils shared information, planned for partnership meetings, and in some cases, conducted solidarity actions. In most Kaiser regions, locals also moved toward monthly inter-union meetings among key local leaders to discuss strategy, plan, coordinate activities, and share information. For instance, coalition staff in Colorado reported holding monthly strategy meetings lasting two to three hours, with about a dozen people from two unions focusing on strategies and priorities. According to coalition staff, "It's the single best coalition structure for communication and solidarity to move unions and interests forward."

In Ohio, the local units gathered monthly to report activity and raise issues. Coalition staff and local leaders felt both these region-wide bodies and the facility-level stewards councils, where they existed, were significant improvements over the pre-coalition days. Of course, these efforts did not extend beyond the coalition. This was especially true in Northern California, where nurses were represented by CNA.

A coalition is, by definition, a voluntary association of autonomous parties that can be expected to continue to work together as long as each member can achieve better results than by acting alone.[8] Working in coalition is even more difficult for organizations with elected leadership, because it is not clear if members will credit their elected leaders or the shared leadership of the coalition for successes or failures. We next delineate the centrifugal forces pulling the coalition apart and some factors that have held it together.

Resources. Building the coalition required considerable resources. The member unions invested and continued to invest significant money and time in the coalition. From the founding of the coalition through 1999, the AFL-CIO also provided financial resources and, under the auspices of the IUD, a neutral place to begin the conversation. This combination of initial seed funding from the Federation with small but increasing contributions from participating unions can be a model for future efforts where labor is confronted with one or more large employers in which multiple unions currently represent employees in different locations or different occupations or where multiple unions are engaged in or prepared to invest resources in future organizing efforts.

Leadership. The coalition survived the transition from Peter diCicco, who led it for the first eight years, to John August, who took over in 2006. Holding together a diverse internal coalition while simultaneously building respect, trust, and influence with management partners were two separate, difficult balancing acts. Chapter 8 discusses specific leaders of the Kaiser Coalition and considers the challenges involved in leading partnerships.

Opportunities for Creating Relationships. The intense conflicts generated by intra-organizational bargaining have been detailed both in this chapter and in chapter 6. Less discussed have been the opportunities for interaction and bonding created by bargaining. Indeed, some coalition leaders explicitly identified the 2000 bargaining as the real "coming together" of the coalition, when for the first time, leaders worked together over a sustained period of time on the difficult but constructive and successful "project" of creating a new national agreement.

Partnership provided an on-going forum for intra-organizational conflicts, but more important, an opportunity for sustained interaction and relationship building through regular meetings and project work. Although the academic literature discusses the contributions of labor-management partnerships in creating social capital across labor-management boundaries, and the Kaiser partnership was certainly successful on that score, it also created formal and informal opportunities across union boundaries, at least for those local and national union leaders engaged regularly in the partnership.

Distribution of Power. The uneven distribution of power among the member unions may under certain circumstances have improved cohesion, even though its first-order effect had the potential to weaken cohesion. Smaller unions were often tempted to assume the largest coalition partner, in this case SEIU, was advancing its own interests at the expense of the coalition's; but one of our interviewees, a national level leader from a non-SEIU coalition union, argued that the coalition may have been strengthened by having one major player rather than a mix of more equal minor players:

> [There are a] couple of laws of this type of inter-union deal: First, the relative weight of different unions is always on the table, [it's] the starting point, and getting folks to weigh it in the same way is crucial. Facts can be denied or accepted by folks, so a union . . . can close its eyes to the fact that success depends on SEIU . . . and not accept this as a fact of life. In this case [the formation of the coalition], folks got over this hump, in large part because SEIU didn't make this hard. Second, when you don't have a big dog, it is hard to do, or if the big dog doesn't want to be accommodating to the others, it is hard to do.

In short, the "big dog" needs to hold back and to help others; but the "little dogs" need to acknowledge that there is a big dog. Our interviews suggest that most, though definitely not all, of the other players in the coalition felt that the "big dog" had been reasonably accommodating to the interests of the smaller unions.

Although SEIU has been reasonably accommodating thus far, it is less clear whether this trend will continue. SEIU leaders at the local and international levels made no secret of their view that there should be fewer unions in the health care industry and the coalition is, as one SEIU leader put it, "an expensive and time consuming alternative to a single voice." SEIU, in 2008, is caught in the ironic position of wielding its considerable power to reinforce and sustain a structure it views as the second best alternative.

At the same time, it is clear that many occupational groups, particularly more professionalized ones, have a strong desire to have their own organizations that reflect their occupational cultures and their particular interests. It is perhaps possible that those needs and interests could be accommodated within a larger structure, as has been the case of skilled trades workers in manufacturing unions. However, many members would be dismayed by the prospect of losing their own organizations and the considerable autonomy afforded those local unions by their internationals and at least some nurse union leaders were highly critical of SEIU's representation of nurses. Some criticize SEIU as being undemocratic and too willing to make deals with employers that compromise worker interests. Other criticism was more specific, for example, that SEIU nurse contracts were below industry standards. A CNA flyer argued that SEIU's contract at a Reno, Nevada hospital "gave RNs less pay, much higher health insurance premiums, and less staffing protections than all the other non-SEIU RN union contracts with [the] same hospital chain."[9] This is not to overlook the vested interests that many union leaders have in holding on to their titles and status that come from being at the top of their organizations.

Ultimately, the strongest internal challenge to the coalition's survival will likely be the strategic choices made by SEIU. That is why the internal conflict within SEIU in early 2008 was so unsettling. That conflict had been further exacerbated by simultaneous clashes between CNA and the national SEIU. CNA had aggressively come after nurse units organized or organizing with SEIU (none in Kaiser facilities). In Las Vegas, CNA had challenged existing SEIU representation of nurses in a number of hospitals, and in Ohio, it disrupted an organizing campaign at the Catholic hospital system. One of the substantive issues on which CNA has criticized SEIU was its willingness to partner with employers. CNA's position in 2008 echoed its criticism of the original Kaiser partnership deal: "CNA/NNOC believes that our registered nurse members and patients fundamentally have different interests than the healthcare corporations that, under our current system, prioritize profits over patients. As a result, we do not partner or make private deals with them. . . ."[10] Significantly, neither UHW nor the national SEIU showed any signs of retreat in their commitment to the Kaiser partnership or the coalition, even in the context of this intense offensive by CNA.

Just because it has survived for a decade does not assure the future of the coalition. Increasingly, coalition leaders are being challenged to further melt away union boundaries as the partnership seeks to implement cross-functional (and therefore cross-union) teams on the front lines of health care delivery. If coalition members are paid industry leading wages and benefits, they are going to be expected to return industry leading levels of productivity and service quality. At a minimum, this requires reducing absenteeism rates in many facilities. If Kaiser is to take full advantage of new electronic medical record technologies, new jobs that cut across traditional occupational and union jurisdictions will need to be created. If Kaiser is to meet successfully the new lower cost competitors and the growing demand for lower cost insurance products, new organizational divisions with equivalent new working arrangements may be required. Thus, the next decade is likely to pose new but equally daunting challenges to the coalition as were experienced in its first ten years of existence.

In some ways, these are generic challenges facing modern labor movements. If the coalition is able to meet them successfully, then it can continue to serve as a learning laboratory for the rest of the U.S. labor movement. If not, it could foreshadow its further decline.

Forever Linked: The Coalition and the Partnership

The story of the Kaiser union coalition is inextricably linked to the story of the partnership: it is hard to imagine one without the other. It is clear that both the partnership and the coalition have led to positive outcomes for the union institutions and their members, especially in the arenas of organizing and bargaining. At the same time, partnership itself creates challenges for unions, which have been well documented in the academic literature on partnerships. These include the balancing of new and traditional roles, strategies, and tactics; the development of new skills and capacity; and the managing of inter-union relationships. The Kaiser coalition has handled these challenges well and appears to have kept or even increased the commitment and loyalty of union members. At the same time, conflict within the labor movement more broadly as well as among and within institutional members of the coalition is a source of ongoing instability.

CHAPTER 8

Leading in Partnership

To make this learning laboratory, and thus the partnership itself, succeed would require not just any, but a special kind of leadership. This chapter examines what it takes to lead a partnership—and what leading in partnership at Kaiser Permanente (KP) suggests about the type of leadership needed in modern, decentralized, and networked organizations, particularly in a health care setting.

The very phrase, "leading in partnership," may sound like an oxymoron as most people equate leadership with characteristics, behaviors, and actions of *individuals*. Isn't leadership the job of the CEO in an organization? Indeed, for more than a decade, countless business books and case studies have put the "transformational" visionary CEO on a pedestal, attributing turnarounds at companies such as IBM to Lou Gerstner and General Electric's aggressive pursuit of shareholder value to Jack Welch. Second thoughts and more critical views of leadership have been offered in the wake of the falls from grace of CEOs once lauded for such vision and achievements. Others have argued that the business press is too quick to attribute the success of a large enterprise to the CEO. In fact, it takes leadership contributions and efforts from all levels of an organization to achieve a turnaround, much less a sustained pattern of good performance.

Criticisms of the view of the CEO as *the* leader who single-handedly shapes or reshapes the culture and transforms an organization have led to the concept of "distributed" leadership, which focuses on values and actions of leaders operating at all levels of an organization, from executive suites to the front lines.[1] One approach to distributed leadership being taught at the MIT Leadership Center views leadership as distributed across many players, levels, and disciplines within and across organizations, wherever information, expertise, vision, new ideas, and ways of working are situated.[2] In this chapter, we use the concept of distributed leadership to describe how managers, labor representatives, and physicians at all levels of the organization are struggling to transform Kaiser Permanente from a traditional and bifurcated structure that identifies labor-management partnership mainly as a labor relations program to an organization that makes partnership the signature, defining strategy for transforming its organizational culture and delivering health care.

As already noted, Kaiser's decentralized structure, in which power and authority is shared among health care managers and physicians, makes the need to practice distributed leadership critical. Adding a labor-management partnership further increases the importance of *shared* leadership because, by definition and intent, labor and management partners share authority and responsibility for leading what is, in essence, a continuous change process. When leadership is shared in this way, it is even more essential that the values and priorities of those sharing power be aligned and that they are working toward common objectives. Having such an alignment on priorities and task objectives was found to be a key driver of manufacturing performance among co-team leaders at Saturn. In his study of that partnership, Rubinstein showed that management and union partners at the first level of "management" who were well aligned in their priorities and in the understanding of their roles achieved significantly higher levels and better rates of improvement in quality than those who were not.[3] This does not mean that disagreements and conflicts disappear; on the contrary, the greater the interdependence and power sharing among different parties, the more likely it is that differences or conflicts that are kept under the surface in more hierarchical power structures will be put on the table and require resolution. For decentralized organizations that want to benefit from distributed leadership, negotiations and conflict resolution thus become essential leadership skills. In short, transforming an organization to build a sustainable partnership requires managers and union leaders at all levels of the organization to learn to lead as partners.

We will illustrate the leadership styles and contributions at Kaiser by drawing on some of the pivotal events discussed in prior chapters and other crises that periodically arose. Such events can challenge the continuity of the partnership but if addressed directly and resolved effectively, they can also strengthen commitment to the partnership and advance the transformation process.

Shared Leadership at the Start: The Decision to Try Partnership

Recall the dramatic shifts in strategies and the choices that had to be made by both Kaiser and union leaders to initiate the partnership. Kaiser was losing more than $250 million at the time and was being advised by McKinsey to break itself up and take other steps to better match the cost structures of competing HMOs. CEO David Lawrence could have followed that advice and abandoned Kaiser's historic commitment to being an integrated health care provider and insurer and an employee- and union-friendly employer, knowing how that would be received by the unions that were such an important part of his customer (member) base. Or he could have explored an alternative with the union leaders, who had themselves been escalating their pressure tactics on Kaiser.

Similarly, Peter diCicco and the leaders of the unions had to decide between partnership and an all-out corporate campaign. The latter was familiar ground and it would build solidarity among the constituent unions and members who were frustrated and angry with Kaiser's hardball tactics. The partnership path was less well trodden by labor; it was not clear that Kaiser was interested; and most of all, it would be controversial and entail significant political risks for union leaders should it fail.

The idea of working with labor was personally attractive to Lawrence. He was supported especially by one director on his board, who was having positive experiences from a labor-management partnership in his own company. On the labor side, it would not be good public relations or good for the future of the labor movement to go to war with Kaiser, the nation's biggest and most unionized health care employer. When the nation's top mediator, John Calhoun Wells, agreed to arrange and facilitate a top-level meeting in Dallas between Kaiser management and labor leaders, it showed that even before the partnership was in its formal incubation period, it was already relying on the leadership and negotiating skills of multiple parties.

Wells felt he needed to become personally acquainted with Lawrence before hosting the joint meeting (he knew SEIU's John Sweeney from previous mediations and labor management interactions). Wells recalls forming an easy and personal bond with Lawrence:

Lawrence immediately impressed me as a down-to-earth, practical yet visionary man with good values. In fact we traced our common roots back to the
same area of Kentucky. He confided in me that he wanted to lead Kaiser in a
more positive direction but labor needed to be a help, not a hindrance, if they
were to hold the integrated structure together and make it work in the newly
competitive world of health care. So I knew it was worth the effort to bring
[Lawrence] together with Sweeney and colleagues.

This leadership encounter had two possible outcomes: war or partnership.
Because of a long history of mutual respect, strong incentives on the part of
both parties to work together, and wise but non-intrusive facilitation by a
mediator and mediation agency both parties trusted—the context was set
for choosing the partnership option. Wells continues:

I didn't have to do much at that meeting other than get it started with a little
speech pointing out how important it was for both parties to explore the question of whether or how they might work together. They hardly needed to be
reminded that they were the biggest unionized health care organization in
the country and that the country would need them to work together to help
solve the growing health care crisis the country was facing. They took it from
there, starting with the impassioned speech by David Lawrence and the rein-
forcing comments by Sweeney and diCicco. From there, we worked with the
labor relations staff at Kaiser and the union coalition to craft the initial partnership agreement.

This episode, as seen through the eyes of the key leaders, illustrates the
best features of distributed and shared leadership in labor-management relations. Each of these leaders played a key role in founding the partnership.
From the start, the partnership required shared leadership and an indica-
tion that values and priorities were aligned enough to work together. A skilled
and trusted third-party facilitator helped initiate and structure the dialogue,
thereby reducing the risks associated with the meeting for both groups. Had
Wells felt, based on his preliminary conversations, that prospects for a productive discussion were dim, he would not have brought the parties together
or he could have offered more active facilitation or mediation. The vision for
the partnership may not have been clear, but the willingness to work together to create a shared vision proved critical.

But leadership at the top of both management and labor, facilitated by a
skilled neutral, though necessary to initiate this partnership, was far from

sufficient. The next step required follow-through by management and labor professionals throughout their organizations.

Transforming Kaiser's Management Culture

Kaiser's management culture and structure were, and in many respects still are, not conducive to leading in partnership. Regions guard their autonomy from the central office. Management is structured along both functional and geographic lines, with labor relations being a specialized unit separate from line operations. Medical care is delivered by physicians organized into their own separate federation. The Kaiser and Permanente sides of Kaiser Permanente had, in the years prior to the partnership, grown apart to the point that Lawrence worried that the entire organization was getting "balkanized." The McKinsey report calling for Kaiser Permanente to be split up resonated with some managers and physicians who were convinced they could do better on their own.

Into that context was introduced this new initiative called a labor-management partnership. The first inclination of most managers was that this was just another labor relations program that they could leave to the specialists and maybe to national leaders and top executives in Oakland headquarters far removed from front-line work in the regions. If this partnership "thing" helped reduce labor conflict and improve relationships among top leaders, fine. But many managers and physicians did not think it should affect how they did their work.

How did the partnership penetrate this management culture and structure? Slowly and partially, and most frequently only through more direct experiences, many of which replicated the Dallas meeting of top leaders at more decentralized levels of Kaiser and the coalition.

A vivid example of this was the negotiations that led to the restructuring of the Optical Laboratory, described in chapter 4. Tony Gately, the vice president in charge of Optical Services in Northern California, had been a line manager for more than twenty years. He was highly skeptical of unions, but he stayed one step removed from dealing with them, leaving direct contact to labor relations staff. However, due to his experience in negotiating the restructuring of the Optical Laboratory, Gately went from a skeptic to a strong believer in the partnership. Remember, Gately had originally instructed his bargaining team to negotiate the lab's closing. But having heard about some of the early accomplishments of the partnership, he had an open mind about options for solving the lab's financial problems. Though past failures to get more flexibility from labor had led him to believe that closure was the only viable option, Gately decided, after consulting with his superiors, to explore whether interest-based bargaining could be helpful in their upcoming negotiations.

Gately went on to become one of the leading proponents of the partnership, appearing in an interest-based negotiations' training video and eventually becoming the management co-leader for the partnership. His years as an operating executive gave him credibility with his management peers and his quiet but determined and straightforward demeanor helped him build trust and credibility with his labor partners. Sadly, Gately died of cancer in 2005, just as national bargaining was beginning.

The key source of Gately's conversion from a skeptical line executive to a partnership proponent and trusted and respected leader was that he saw—in real terms with hard data—how performance improved by working together. Gately said in a 2001 interview that he saw the partnership as "very performance focused. I was impressed by how much labor knew the business. They were never allowed to engage fully in improving the business. They had ideas but they never surfaced or if they did, they never went anywhere. It was a learning process for me to engage a knowledgeable workforce and see what was possible if management was ready to listen."

The power of this story carried forward. Diane Easterwood, the leader of the management negotiating team in the lab restructuring, succeeded Gately as the vice president in charge of the Optical Lab. Preston Lasley, the chief union negotiator in the restructuring, became her union partner when he was elected president of SEIU Local 535, the lab's largest union local. When Easterwood and Lasley accepted new positions in 2005, their successors brought in partnership staff and facilitators to review the history of the lab and its labor relations journey. Understanding the history of what had been accomplished helped them make the leadership transition and continue to work in partnership.

This vignette demonstrates how a gradual back-and-forth and pragmatic learning through constructive negotiations helped shape people who learned how to lead in partnership. Gately would not have come to be such a partnership proponent without the support and skilled negotiations effort of Easterwood, Lasley, and Charles Huggins, an experienced facilitator. They would not have been able to save and restructure the Optical Lab without being able to identify real savings. The partnership would not have been sustainable through the tenure of a second and third generation of leaders unless the lab's performance levels remained high. Such is the nature of distributed and shared leadership in a labor-management partnership.

Leading Management in Partnership: A Perils of Pauline (Leslie) Story

While reviewing a draft of our research team's report on the first five years of the partnership, Leslie Margolin excused herself to take a call on her cell phone. She returned to our meeting several minutes later, looking rather somber. "David Lawrence just told me I wasn't in the running to succeed him as CEO," she explained. "Moreover, he told me that given this, it might be best for me to just leave Kaiser. So I guess [that] in effect, my status just changed from a candidate for CEO to a former Kaiser employee."

This was not the first, nor would it be the last, cliff-hanging like episode in Margolin's time at Kaiser.[4] Why did such a talented and highly acclaimed leader, one who had successfully led the joint effort to open the Baldwin Park Hospital and then led management through its first-ever national negotiations in 2000 and who had gained the genuine respect of her labor partners, run into enough political resistance from her management colleagues to require her to leave the organization? To Margolin's labor partners, the situation raised serious questions about whether Kaiser was truly committed to the partnership. In a 27 February 2002 letter to David Lawrence and other senior Kaiser executives, the coalition steering committee expressed its "very deep concern [that] Permanente has allowed the key executive management leader for Labor-Management Partnership, Leslie Margolin, to take elsewhere her formidable talent and her unique, irreplaceable institutional knowledge of our Partnership. . . . Her departure leaves our Unions without a relationship with anyone at the top executive level who we believe fully understands the vision of the Partnership."

While reaffirming the union's commitment to the vision and goals of the partnership, the union leaders noted their "responsibility to our 68,000 front-line members to ensure that the promise of the Labor-Management Partnership be fulfilled in accordance with the 1997 agreement, the Pathways to Partnership, and the 2000 National Agreement."

Even after Margolin left Kaiser, diCicco did not abandon the issue, reviving it after George Halvorson was named Lawrence's successor. Union leaders were pleased with the appointment. They knew of Halvorson's positive role in working with union leaders in his prior post as chief executive of a Minneapolis hospital. In a private meeting, diCicco briefed the new CEO about the partnership and about the leadership void left by Margolin's departure. After that meeting, diCicco suggested that our research team delay printing what was a nearly final draft of our report on the first five years of the partnership. "There might be an interesting new development to include in the report coming soon," he suggested.

That "interesting development," announced by Halvorson three months after he became CEO, was that Leslie Margolin was returning as a senior vice president for operations in charge of coordinating the work of the regions. The announcement came as Halvorson outlined his view of the key strategic and relationship challenges facing Kaiser and announced the members of his new management team. In a June 2002 memo to senior Kaiser executives, Halvorson explained his move. "Leslie Margolin left us temporarily because she wasn't interested in a career solely in human resources. She will now rejoin us as the team leader for the group of people who serve as presidents of our eight regions. Leslie is a strong team builder, and one of my objectives it to have the regional leadership function as a strong, mutually supportive and synergistic team. When I asked people in our organization who had been our best team building executive, quite a few people mentioned Leslie."

This remarkable sequence of events—a contender for CEO being asked to resign, leaving, then being recruited back into a senior position by the new CEO—illustrates the importance of shared leadership in a partnership. Because of the trust and confidence labor leaders had developed for Margolin, they had taken the extraordinary step of publicly protesting her departure and privately urging her return. Many within Kaiser management welcomed her back wholeheartedly because they shared Halvorson's view that she had both the teambuilding and relationship skills and the clear vision and drive needed to not just make the labor-management partnership work, but to bring together the disparate regions and bridge the bifurcated structure of the Kaiser and Permanente divisions.

Although those who observed Margolin's role in navigating the internal management divisions and gap in labor and management expectations—including management, union, and neutral facilitators alike—lauded her leadership, she was not universally loved within top executive circles. In fact, it may have been her strong advocacy in negotiations and her closeness to the partnership and to her labor counterparts that led her to once again decide to leave Kaiser in 2006. She interpreted a shuffling of roles as a signal that she was once again being moved out of the potential line of succession to CEO when Halvorson chose to retire. To put it directly, Margolin had made some significant enemies in negotiating with her executive counterparts for the resources needed to reach the 2005 bargaining agreement. But like the fate of other prophets in their own country, Margolin gained wide respect from outside observers. Among other achievements, she was named San Francisco Woman of the Year in 2006.

Margolin's departure again created uncertainty about the depth of commitment to partnership at the top of Kaiser's management. In citing the partnership as a top relationship priority in the same memo in which he announced the rehiring of Margolin and by stepping up to resolve the internal management impasse at a crucial stage in the 2005 negotiations, Halvorson carried on his predecessor's support for the partnership. A year after Margolin's second departure, one senior executive noted a lingering ambivalent attitude toward the partnership. "There are members of [the top management team] that have to put the Partnership higher on their priority list. . . . [They] have to feel it matters to them. Sometimes they do and sometimes they don't."

Margolin's experience is also instructive of the fine line management leaders (and as we will see, union leaders) have to walk when leading in partnerships. The on-off career history of its strongest champion in the management structure suggests that being viewed as too much of an advocate for the partnership may be too much of a good thing. Those managers who do not share the same level of commitment or are not as directly and intensively exposed to the partnership will remain skeptical of it and of their peers who promote it. Managing such skeptical "constituents" is an extremely important part of leading in partnership.

Physician Leaders

One of the greatest challenges facing the partnership was to work with physician leaders. Almost by nature, physicians are difficult to engage. But by building on what they often care about most—quality patient care—a successful connection could be made.

Dr. Jay Crosson's—the head of the Permanente Federation—main mission was his patients. When Crosson began at Kaiser thirty years ago, he saw it as just a job. "Then the job morphed into a career and later into a mission," he said. "[My wife, who is a pediatrician, and I] came in the midst of a flu season and worked like dogs. Early on, we recognized that we were responsible for 16,000 babies and we had to take care of them. So when it came down to the normal grievances of people working together, we were all in it together and we had a responsibility to fellow pediatricians and our patients."

Crosson's strong sense of mission and commitment to the values and model of clinical care embedded in Kaiser's culture, history, and strategy was clear. But so, too, would be his commitment to the partnership. Similarly, Dr. Robbie Pearl, president of the Permanente Group in the Northern California region of Kaiser Permanente, was initially uncertain about "how far the partnership will go, but I encourage the rest of the world to go down this path. It opens up more opportunities and even if all we can accomplish is a better relationship among senior leaders, that is worth it and better than the alternative. But I hope we can make this the model of how to provide health care in the nation and for how labor and management relate to each other. That would fulfill my vision for the partnership."

This section examines how physician leaders, such as Crosson and Pearl, who were steeped in the professional norms and culture of the medical profession and subject to the political realities of being elected leaders of a federation of independently minded peers, came to embrace the partnership.

Crosson played an instrumental role in helping fashion agreement over how to bargain a national contract without common expiration dates for local agreements that would risk a national strike. He had been a strong proponent of the partnership and an articulate public spokesman for it. He developed good relationships with key union leaders. This all grew, he recalled, from an early experience with labor relations in 1986 that left a lasting impression that there ought to be a better way for workers, unions, and employers to relate to each other. "We went through a nine-week strike that ended on Christmas Eve," he said. "I was assistant physician-in-chief and had no experience with labor at that time. I came out of that strike with a very strong view that I didn't want the organization to go through this again, with all the animosity and stupidity we saw on both sides."

So Crosson welcomed the partnership. The main benefit of the partnership, he said following the 2000 negotiations, was that it "provid[ed] five years of labor peace." He went on to say that if the partnership could help assure a motivated and satisfied workforce, it could contribute to improved delivery of health care services. By 2007, that hopefulness started to fade. The time for delivering on performance improvements had come, he felt. Unless some clear and substantial progress on issues such as attendance and productivity were forthcoming, his patience as well as the support of other physicians in leadership positions and those on the front lines would erode.

Indeed, interviews with physicians in the Permanente Federation reinforced this pragmatic, bottom-line perspective. Physicians viewed working with labor as a means for carrying out their primary mission of meeting their patients' needs for high quality care in an efficient manner. If the partnership could help with this, it would garner physician support. If it could not, it would still be tolerated for its other benefits—such as achieving and maintaining labor peace and developing good working relationships and problem-solving potential among top labor, management, and physician leaders, as long as it did not interfere with the doctors' work. Clearly, the partnership would be resisted if it became an impediment or infringed on their time and autonomy. "Front-line physicians . . . haven't seen any benefit of the partnership," said Pearl. "They don't see the partnership as having interest in the biggest challenges they face, [which is] attendance, flexibility, and dealing with problem individuals. They don't see it worth investing a lot of time."

Physicians in general (not just at Kaiser) are not known for their teamwork skills. Until recently, medical school education and internships for the most part socialized them to view themselves as individual, highly skilled professionals, deserving autonomy and respect.

Given this view, it was not surprising that it was easy to build commitment and support for the partnership among physicians below the physician leadership level. Physicians balked at participating in "LMP Orientation" training, feeling it diverted them from their core activities. But when labor partners and focused teams stepped forward and worked directly with physicians to solve critical financial and/or clinical care problems in particular cases, physicians became converts to the partnership.

Take the transformation of one powerful and visible physician leader, Dr. Jeffrey Weisz, president of the Southern California Permanente Federation, who illustrates the difficulties, the importance, and the potential of gaining physician support. During the 2005 negotiations, Weisz was outspoken about the need to address the attendance problem. He took a harder stand in rolling back sick leave benefits than was acceptable to either his management or labor colleagues. In a post-negotiation interview, he voiced further skepticism about the prospects for success in working with labor on attendance and other issues. "The union has to commit," he said. "Sick leave is for sick leave and you can't call off at the last minute. Our docs and managers only average four to five days per year. I haven't seen their [union leaders'] commitment. They have to get out there and deliver."

Weisz's initial strategy was to step back and let others take the lead in working with the unions. He asked Dr. Marty Gilbert, his key representative in the 2005 negotiations, to take up this liaison role. But at the same time, he took to heart advice he was getting from colleagues who had worked effectively with labor leaders in other settings, who advised him to meet privately with his key union counterparts, to use his ability to talk frankly about his views, and to see if a level of trust and mutual respect could be developed.

A year later, Weisz's management, physician, and labor partners had all seen a remarkable change in his view of the partnership. When asked to explain the change in his image and reputation, Weisz said half jokingly, "I haven't changed. They did." More seriously, he said he liked the new leaders and "the way they talk about accountability. . . . We speak the same language, [which is] a big plus. They understand [that] unless we can improve our performance, the dollars won't be there for their people. So there's a chance; we are aligned in what we want to get accomplished." In the course of a year, key union leaders had reached out to Weisz at the personal, individual level to begin the process of building a better relationship. His turnaround is a prime illustration of the importance of alignment between the priorities and vision of partners who share leadership responsibilities.

One of those who worked with Weisz, regional union leader Walter Allen, said it was unfair to blame Weisz for all that had happened during bargaining. "There was a bad taste in everyone's mouth," Allen said. "Jeff got a beating in bargaining . . . as if it was all [his] fault. . . . I thought this was unfair—there is no one person who could screw [negotiations] up. The first thing I did [after negotiations were over] was to dash off a blind email to Jeff Weisz, explaining who I was, [that we had] never met before, and saying you need to know that you are not the only one concerned about the attendance issue." Allen continued efforts to build a relationship with Weisz after Allen became the union coalition's lead representative in Southern California. In this case, overcoming the history of low trust and strained relationships took a combination of a change in leadership and a broadening of the range of individuals involved.

So far, this has been a story of how leaders at the top of this region worked together to test whether their goals and priorities were sufficiently aligned to build the personal trust needed for shared leadership to work. But more work was needed to build the same commitment to working and leading in partnership among managers, physicians, and union leaders at lower levels of the regional structures. To do this, Weisz and his counterpart on the hospital management side, Dr. Ben Chu, president of Kaiser's Southern California region, invited Allen to join their leadership council and to speak at their annual meeting of managers and physicians. This was a visible signal to those present that top management and union leaders were serious about working together in new partnership ways.

This story illustrates another important aspect of leading in partnership: that the willingness and ability to cross boundaries and build relationships is essential. That is a key aspect to the Allen-Weisz story and the new energy they brought to the partnership in Southern California. We saw the importance of relationship building among leaders at lower levels of the organization as well. For instance, in Kaiser's Fresno facility, stewards and managers reported improvements in relationships—improvements that enabled real-time problem-solving—through the constant interactions both on partnership committees and through day-to-day partnering ("just doing the work"). "I think we took the time to really listen and understand each other's roles. This is where we were able to really let that barrier down," said a chief steward. "That's what I try to tell the other stewards: Just because they're management doesn't mean they're always wrong."

Leading Labor in a Partnership

Perhaps the most difficult role in a partnership is reserved for labor leaders. U.S. labor leaders lead a schizophrenic life. On the one hand, they are exhorted by the public, political leaders, managers, and even their members to lead in a cooperative, statesman-like fashion. On the other hand, these same leaders live in a world in which labor's very existence is being attacked by some managers and executives and undermined by federal labor law that, by all objective accounts, is outmoded and broken. Labor leaders also function in a political environment in which members are far less interested in cooperation for the sake of cooperation—they vote leaders out or in based on pragmatic, tangible results. How, then, have union leaders adapted to the roles required of them in the partnership?

Leading the Union Coalition and Co-Leading the Partnership

The most visible labor leadership role—executive director of the Coalition of Kaiser Permanente Unions—illustrates how these conflicting pressures can be managed. The person in this role also serves as the labor co-lead for the partnership. For ten years—from the inception of the partnership through the 2005 negotiations—this person was Peter diCicco. By unanimous acclaim, diCicco was an outstanding leader. He carried a lifetime of experience in traditional positional bargaining and in managing contentious internal union politics. He came from the school of hard knocks in labor relations—he was the business agent of one of the most combative local unions at General Electric before becoming an officer of the AFL-CIO Industrial Union Department. Thus, diCicco knew how to "fire up" the troops when necessary, but he found ways to do this that were consistent with the spirit of the partnership. An example was the way he addressed the 200 members of the union negotiating team and bargaining sub-groups during a dinner meeting caucus early in 2005. diCicco wanted to energize the troops and give them confidence and convey some clear messages about their priorities in bargaining. Recall the comment we quoted earlier: "Don't be intimidated by the management experts," he said. "In these negotiations (unlike in 2000), management has chosen to put 'content experts' on the negotiating team, people who are specialists and know a lot about specific issues. This is good and we should respect their knowledge and use it but not be intimidated by it or be afraid to ask questions or challenge it. You see the broad picture; they will see only their narrow specialization. So don't be afraid to raise questions and don't let them control the discussion around their narrow interpretation."

By saying "be confident, don't hesitate to speak up for our interests," diCicco sought to rally the troops without disparaging Kaiser management. One of diCicco's favorite statements was: "labor management partnership is not just labor management cooperation." His "Outside the NLRB Box" diagram (see figure 2.1) illustrated his vision for how a partnership equated to expanded voice, power, and results for union members. At the same time, he developed a high degree of credibility with senior management leaders at Kaiser. He was granted the right to attend the KPPG and meetings of Kaiser's board of directors and was consulted (and in the Margolin case offered unsolicited advice) on senior executive appointments.

Given diCicco's reputation, anyone succeeding him would have large shoes to fill. No internal candidate could be convinced to take the job (several were approached but declined for various reasons), so an extensive and somewhat lengthy external process ensued. Interviews with a cross-section of managers and coalition leaders conducted by John Stepp from Restructuring Associates, Inc. (RAI) suggested that the time was right for someone who could focus on building leadership capacity and support for the partnership among middle and front-line management and union leaders. In July 2006 John August, a veteran union leader who had worked for the Teamsters, SEIU Local 1199, and several other unions was chosen.

August's first major challenge was implementation of the terms of the 2005 agreement. The top two issues involved moving forward with unit-based teams, which we discuss more in the next chapter, and addressing the attendance/absenteeism issue. August recognized that if Kaiser employees were to be paid at the top of the industry, the partnership had to focus on and deliver performance improvements. His analysis of Kaiser's market position was even harsher than comments coming from top Kaiser executives. "Kaiser is the best company in the industry . . . but it is not at the top on quality, not competitive in the new growth markets, and on service, it's ranking is . . . 241 out of 265 in one service area. Kaiser should be in the lead [in health care]. . . . We need to help get it there." August was equally straightforward on the attendance issue. After reviewing data showing that implementation of the 2005 agreement provisions was not generating anything more than very marginal improvements in attendance rates, he mobilized his coalition steering committee colleagues to propose a new experimental approach.

Because of these and other efforts, August developed a high level of credibility with Kaiser executives and other coalition leaders. "[DiCicco] was just the right kind of leader to get us started, to build the union coalition and to build credibility with management," said a high-level Kaiser executive. "He was aggressive and yet gained the confidence and trust of management because he delivered on what he promised. John has a very different style. [He is] more of a listener and then takes action. He's really focused on delivering value on the front lines of the partnership. He is just the right person for this phase of the partnership."

Like Margolin on the management side of the partnership, union leaders had critics within the coalition. Given the democratic and otherwise more overtly political nature of union organizations, such criticism tends to be more vocal and internal conflicts tend to be more open and visible. For example, a number of union coalition leaders felt their experiences and interests were being sacrificed in favor of satisfying the more powerful SEIU. "Sal (Rosselli) is running the coalition," said one coalition leader. "John is doing his bidding."

Union leaders must balance working in partnership with visible and, when necessary, aggressive representation of the separate interests of members and mediation of internal differences. All are crucial to sustaining a partnership and fulfilling other leadership responsibilities.

Leading from Individual Unions

By all accounts Sal Rosselli, who was president of SEIU's United Healthcare Workers-West (UHW) when it was created by the merger of the Northern and Southern California health care locals, was the most powerful union leader in the coalition. This is not surprising as SEIU was the "big dog," representing 60 percent of coalition members. But of the 140,000 members in UHW, only 50,000 were employed at Kaiser. As such, Rosselli stayed a step removed from day-to-day operation of the coalition and the partnership, though he was called upon to make key interventions and negotiate agreements at pivotal moments or crises, both within the coalition and with management leaders. His leadership influence was critical, for example, in resolving the final sticking points in the 2005 negotiations. First, he pressed management negotiators to increase the amount of "equity adjustment" money offered and then he worked out a compromise with other unions over how to distribute these funds across the different work groups. Earlier, Rosselli was the coalition spokesperson at the critical labor-management summit meeting in 2003, when top leaders "reaffirmed" their support for the partnership. Such multiple responsibilities of union leaders at his level required viewing the partnership in a way akin to how it is seen by physician leaders—it must be instrumental to and fit well within the broader strategy for building and expanding the union and managing the relationships with both Kaiser and other health care employers with which the union bargains or is seeking to organize. By nature, this inevitably created some tensions within the coalition and the partnership—tensions that are common to all labor-management partnerships that involve either multiple local unions and/or national union leaders with broader membership responsibilities.

SEIU president Andrew Stern, one of the U.S.'s most visible labor leaders, had an even broader agenda and set of relationships to manage. For Stern, partnership must serve both a substantive and a symbolic role. On substance, it needs to deliver benefits equal to what he sees as the high costs of managing such a complex structure and large undertaking. This must be seen in the context of Stern's clear preference for a simpler arrangement, in which SEIU would represent all health care workers, including all those in the coalition. Although controversial, this is part of Stern's vision for a more streamlined and aggressive labor movement. Yet Stern also has stated his strong support for the partnership as a model for what SEIU and labor in general can do to contribute to solving the nation's health care crisis and to work with employers in a professional, cooperative fashion.

In this way, the partnership has served as a symbol of SEIU's innovative and professional manner, something that can be used in organizing drives in other parts of the health care industry. Moreover, at critical times, Stern has quietly and effectively stepped in to help resolve internal differences, such as the SEIU-UFCW jurisdictional dispute discussed earlier and to reaffirm his personal support for the partnership with top-level Kaiser leaders.

Kathy Sackman heads the United Nurses Associations of California (UNAC), an affiliate of the American Federation of State, County and Municipal Employees (AFSCME), which represents the largest body of nurses (9,500) in the partnership. Sackman became a nurse in 1960 and went to work at the Kaiser-Fontana hospital in 1964. After being forced to work long hours during a Steelworkers strike at that hospital, she recognized the benefits won by the union through that job action and started an organizing effort among the nurses. For years, Sackman continued to work as a nurse and was an officer in the union. In 1986, she moved into the full-time position of executive vice president of UNAC. Although UNAC conducted two strikes against Kaiser, one in the 1970s and one in the early 1980s, UNAC and Sackman maintained an overall good relationship with Kaiser. But this relationship altered substantially as Kaiser re-oriented its labor relations strategy in the 1990s. Like diCicco, Sackman's militant history and her long knowledge of Kaiser provided her safe cover for engaging in partnership.

Given her long tenure at Kaiser and the fact that most of her union's members are Kaiser employees, Sackman has followed a much more hands-on approach than Rosselli. Also, given the size and strategic importance of her members in Kaiser's largest region, she was also among the top echelon of the coalition's local leaders. Like many local leaders, Sackman initially resisted a partnership. "I said to Pete [diCicco], I'm 60 years old, I can't do this, I can't be a part of this," she recalled. "I would sabotage it." At the same time, Sackman knew her members cared a great deal about the quality of patient care and believed that Kaiser's integrated model provided the best platform for preventive care. She saw the partnership as a vehicle for nurse involvement in improving and sustaining that model. Thus, despite her initial misgivings, she put the 1997 partnership agreement up for vote to her members and served on the initial Senior Partnership Council and, later, on the Partnership Strategy Group. She was also involved in the early stages of setting up the Baldwin Park process and was intimately involved in the process that led to the national negotiations in 2000 and 2005. Sackman remains a strong proponent of the partnership and an equally strong and vocal advocate for the nurses she represents both within the coalition and with Kaiser managers and physicians.

Leading in the Middle of a Partnership Hierarchy

As the partnership at Kaiser moved more aggressively to implement unit-based teams and transform the partnership from a labor relations instrument to an operating strategy, the pressures on people at the middle levels of the organization intensified—and their opposition began to surface.

More than twenty years ago, surveys of supervisors involved in employee participation programs conducted by our MIT colleague Janice Klein produced something close to a universal finding for the field of labor-management relations and organizational change. When asked whether employee participation was good, 70 percent of the supervisors agreed it was good for their company; 50 percent agreed it was good for rank-and-file employees, and only 30 percent agreed it was good for them.[5] Middle managers have, by definition, always understood that they are accountable "upwards" to their supervisors. Now, in a partnership, they find themselves also accountable laterally to their union partners and to the people under their supervision. Conversely, union leaders recognize their accountabilities "downward" to their members; now they too are accountable to their management partners and to Kaiser, as an organization expecting performance improvements and improved day-to-day relationships.

Recognizing that middle managers were having difficulties adapting to the partnership, Kaiser management organized a series of supervisor focus group meetings in 2007. In a memo, feedback from these supervisors echoed Klein's data. Among other things:

- Managers need to better understand the tangible benefits of partnership, "what's in it for me." Many managers . . . remain skeptical about the value and see . . . partnership initiatives as "one more thing I have to do."
- There is significant mistrust and skepticism about the value of the partnership. Many managers see it as a labor-driven effort and see the LMP and the unions as one and the same.
- The organization needs to focus on performance and results—especially on how partnership and unit-based teams have helped address performance problems and problem individuals.
- Managers see huge gaps in training and experience—within management ranks as well as between themselves and most stewards and union staff. These are two distinct audiences, and it may be hard to serve them both. They have to clarify roles, performance expectations, and accountabilities in unit-based teams and the parameters and processes for team decision

making. Provide practical (peer) advice, resource links, professional
development tools, etc.
- The focus should be on case studies with lessons in handling well-defined,
real-world problems.

Although some middle managers were skeptical of the value of the partnership, others recognized its benefits to Kaiser as an organization and to the
delivery of health care. But they saw little personal gain and considerable
difficulty in changing their leadership styles. All worried they lacked the resources needed to make partnership work at their level in the organization.

"[Leading in partnership] . . . will make your life very difficult," said one
manager. "you're constantly fighting it, the involvement, it's going to be very
hard for you. . . . If you've always done [your job] as a managerial top-down
type of thing, it's going to be very hard to adapt to the lateral-type of environment. . . . Some have voluntarily left." Another manager noted the need
for transparency and added that partnership can fail at first because it is
hard for managers to lead in this new way. "For managers in particular, it's
very hard for us to stand up in front of a group and say, 'Yes, that was kind of
stupid wasn't it?' or, 'It didn't seem stupid when I did it but now it does.
Thank you for pointing it out.' But you earn credibility when you do," said a
department administrator. "Managers are very well trained that leadership
requires a certain kind of aura of knowledge and expertise and I don't think
we spend enough time acknowledging mistakes. . . . But I don't think you
can do partnership without a lot more transparency and vulnerability. . . .
That's what partners do—they make themselves vulnerable to each other. I
know a lot about what goes on inside [local unions] and what they're struggling with—and they know a lot about budget and strategic issues [that], in
the old days, management never would have shared with them."

Other managers had grown to appreciate the advantages of partnership
as trust develops and they see that employees and stewards have much to
contribute:

[At first] they didn't feel like labor really had the skill set to really do their
[management] job, so then they're teaching them how they do their job. I
think most of them felt it very frustrating and difficult that we had to get
agreement on every little change we wanted to make. That is one of the biggest frustrations. But over time, their trust has been built. They've started to
see it as a partner in a true sense. Somebody who knows how it is every day,
who works on the floor, usually has great ideas about how to improve their job.

So, I think that in the long run, we see it as a great thing. But initially, it's just a big change in how we do our daily work.

A common refrain at first was that partnership appeared to slow things down and take away scarce time from middle managers and, worse, there was little recognition of this fact from higher level managers:

> Initially, I think of it as slowing things down. It takes time to educate. It takes time to have a meeting. And then if I couldn't cover them on the floor, I couldn't have a meeting. But the administration still holds the rest of us to deadlines. I did have some resentment. . . . My deadlines weren't changing. . . . If we did have to go forward because we were past the deadline, immediately, we were attacked, "Well, you didn't partner." Our administration didn't accept "Well, she wasn't available. She got called for a union meeting." "No, that's your problem. You have to fix it. Your core staffing should have been in place."

Supervisors, like their higher management counterparts, also recognized that not all of their union partners were equally prepared or inclined to take up their partnership roles, that they needed to learn how to adjust to different union leadership styles:

> [One] steward probably gave me the most trouble, for she had this idea that after [she came back from] the two-day training, we were going to co-manage together. I kept saying "You have a lot to learn," and then she thought I was elevating myself to a higher level. There was a lot of conflict, and when we didn't co-manage, she was very disappointed.

Referring to another steward, this same supervisor said:

> I worked to get all the information together and to lay it out. "Here's the problem, what do you think, and let's figure it out together." But she didn't want me to come at her with all this information. The response I got was, "You are management, you ought to know what to do."

Like their management counterparts, union stewards had varying views on how deeply they wanted to get involved in what heretofore were management processes and decisions. In the end, one supervisor felt she found a way to work with the differences and the political pressures union leaders face.

I have really struggled, but I feel that we are learning how to be balanced—where the union steward sits politically and has a difficult position that I need to understand. And there have to be boundaries. I think we're learning a lot as we work together.

The steward we have now has been a breath of fresh air. I approach problems by saying I am interested in her thoughts, and she does the same with me. It's a partnership relationship, because we have mutual respect for each other. We're sharing information.

Another supervisor had a similar learning experience several years ago, when a committee she had formed did not work, causing her to try a different approach that did succeed. Initially, she said:

We started with a committee that we called the Labor-Management Partnership Committee. We started with basic ground rules and norms of behavior and the goals that we wanted to accomplish. We sent the members of the new committee to a two-day training session on labor-management partnership and how to form a committee. We met three to four times, but I must say, there was a lot of confusion. The communication was not good, and there was a lot of blaming in the meetings. When we realized we weren't getting things accomplished, and we were not addressing long-standing operational issues like staffing, we made a decision to disband the process. In retrospect, we had made a terrible mistake in deciding that we should involve all four facilities in the same committee and have them at the same meetings. It's clear that a successful partnership involves a lot of delegation and a lot of accountability—and we didn't have enough of either.

Then came a very different process and outcome:

When the cost reduction program got started, we created four separate labor-management work groups, rather than one combined group. This time there was a clear objective and there was something that focused what we came together to do. We also received help from an outside facilitator. The success of this effort is . . . that our department was among the departments that was the most over-budget, like 11 percent, and we were able to turn that around by the end of the year and we actually finished the year about $17,000 below the budget. The experience was fabulous. It was a collaborative effort. The team came up with ideas; some worked, some did not. We tried to maintain accountability for everything we tried.

Middle level union leaders experienced parallel challenges. The democratic structures and values of unions and the political nature of union leadership roles made it critical to find the right balance between engaging in partnership decisions and taking responsibility for their outcomes and advocating members' concerns independent of management actions. In some instances, union leaders needed to rely on their management counterparts to convey bad news:

A good example of how we make connections has to do with the devastating news for many of our members that the hospital opening [in the Northwest region] was going to be put off for a whole year. We tried to educate the members about the budget issues behind this decision. But it got to a point where they were always asking "why is this happening, and why does Kaiser do this or that?" We said, "We can't answer this." So we had the service area manager come. He addressed the group, and did a marvelous job, even though they hit him with some pretty tough questions.

Aside from the generic problem of lacking adequate time to attend to both partnership and other daily responsibilities, finding an optimal balance between advocacy and partnership proved to be one of the most difficult challenges for middle level union leaders. One service area manager provided a good summary statement on how management and union leaders can achieve the balance they need to carry out their other duties, serve their constituents/superiors, and manage relationships with those more skeptical or opposed to partnership:

Management has to do their job with performance management and people's attendance. We have gotten caught in what I would call "the partnership trap." Managers have lost their ability to manage and to hold people accountable. We have to hold people accountable when they don't come to work. But we have to be consistent. And that's the hard part. One department cannot have rigid numbers while another department doesn't have any standards at all. We are coming up with new guidelines to help management set a context, and I think all this will help us going forward. I will be talking to my management team about all this, and yet at the same time, we need to make sure labor knows what we're doing (which they do) and understand why. Because if we don't manage attendance, then people don't come to work, and then we fall short. It affects workplace safety, morale. Management has the responsibility to step up to this problem.

Some middle level managers and union stewards were so conditioned to manage and interact in traditional ways that they could not make the transition to a shared leadership approach. In these cases, higher levels of the management and/or union organizations had to take action to either coach the problematic leaders or move them to a position that would not require them to lead in partnership. For example, in one region a union representative who had been assigned to Kaiser used foul language over the phone to a human resource staff member. This union staff member had previously serviced units in the union that were characterized by very traditional relationships. The medical director got on the phone with the president of the union and this individual was quickly reassigned to another jurisdiction away from Kaiser.

The working relationships that can accompany a partnership can create an organization that is much more open to problem solving. "It is so cool to walk in to a manager and actually speak to him instead of walking in in a defense mode," said a labor liaison. "I'll sit next to him in meetings versus all of us union folks on one side of the table and him on the other. I'll have lunch with him. . . . I can walk into an open door and he can say, 'Hey, I got a little thing here; can you review this and meet with the employee?' It is so much easier."

Such building of relationships among leaders, which improves communications and problem solving, pays dividends in ways that are not always possible to measure or capture in a formal way.

Facilitating a Partnership

Mediation—that is, a process in which a neutral third party assists parties in conflict in reaching a voluntary agreement—has a long and rich tradition in labor-management relations. With the advent of organizational change initiatives and labor-management partnerships and interest-based negotiations, a modified approach to mediation known generally as facilitation has come on the scene. Although mediating and facilitating share many commonalities, compared to mediators, facilitators are more focused on managing group and inter-group processes and refrain from making substantive suggestions for how to resolve differences.

Facilitation played a key role in the partnership right from the beginning. RAI's John Stepp served as the main consultant and facilitator through the first decade of the partnership's existence. He was well prepared for this role, having years of experience in both traditional mediation (he had worked as a mediator at the Federal Mediation and Conciliation Service (FMCS) and in facilitating other labor-management partnerships. He drew on both sets of skills in helping to put in place the basic structure for the 2000 and 2005 negotiations and in mediating conflicts within and between the labor and management organizations that inevitably occurred in negotiations. In 2000, his mediation skills were initially tested when management leaders rejected the idea of carrying out a single national negotiation with common expiration dates for local contracts. It took a number of private discussions with key management leaders for Stepp to learn what concerned these management leaders most about the proposed approach. He then used this understanding to propose a set of design features to deal with management's concerns (largely the fear that national negotiations might produce a national strike or a single "national" wage agreement) while keeping labor leaders from exercising their frustrations with management by walking away from the negotiations (and perhaps the partnership). Having a mix of mediation and facilitation skills, and being able to hold the partnership together in times of crisis long enough to find a solution to the immediate problem, is critical to leading in partnership. Because of his ability to do so, the neutral facilitator was also a key leader of the partnership.

On-Going Challenges: Diffusing and Sustaining Leadership Support

The development of a robust partnership does not take place without key leaders in management and labor taking the initiative to foster the concept and to make it a reality. In the case of KP and the coalition the journey began with a meeting of the minds between Lawrence and diCicco, key leaders of their respective organizations. However, their vision would not have been translated into something organic without the commitment of other leaders. In some cases support for the partnership only occurred after these individuals had experienced the value of the partnership first hand; for example, restructuring the optical lab and participating in national negotiations.

This diffusion or "distribution" of support for the partnership took place both horizontally—the lead doctor for Permanente early on embraced the idea, as well as vertically—as labor leaders from the major unions signed on to the concept. Ultimately, the viability of the partnership rests on the commitment of those in authority at the operating level; for example, for supervisors and stewards to "walk the talk" of the partnership.

The lessons learned from distributed and shared leadership in the Kaiser and other labor-management partnerships have broader lessons for how to manage and lead in today's decentralized and network-like organizational structures and lateral relationships where power is shared across organizational boundaries. Clearly the Kaiser experience illustrates that no single leader, or pair of leaders, at the top or at any level, can assure the success of the partnership or take credit for the transformation of a complex organization. It takes contributions of many leaders working together and sometimes acting individually to solve problems, resolve conflicts, identify and confront challenges and crises, and carry on through periodic frustrations and setbacks. Moreover, sustaining a partnership requires active steps to manage leadership transitions, because few managers or union leaders who take up roles in partnerships have experience with shared leadership across the union-management divide. These are some of the reasons why partnerships have such precarious existences. Making partnerships more resilient requires leadership at yet another level—the societal level where labor policy is constructed and where national labor, management, and government leaders interact and shape the overall climate for labor-management relations. We revisit the key role of leadership at the national level in the last chapter of this volume.

CHAPTER 9

Partnership and HealthConnect

George Halvorson saw an opportunity to lead the nation in electronic health records (EHR) technologies when he joined Kaiser Permanente (KP) as CEO in 2002. In *Epidemic of Care*, a book he co-authored with George J. Isham, Halvorson wrote, "Real improvement in the quality and consistency of care will require the use of automated medical records that give doctors and patients full information about care and care systems right in the exam room. Every other profession makes use of computers to perform these kinds of services. Medicine will soon follow." Halvorson would become the leading champion for moving aggressively to transform Kaiser's health care delivery system through investment in Kaiser's EHR system, HealthConnect.

Given the massive investment (HealthConnect was initially budgeted at about $1.8 billion but is likely to cost several times more, considering actual expenditures to date) and the potential impact of such a major technological change on the workforce, this initiative intersected directly with the partnership. Ample historical and contemporary evidence suggests that work practices and workforce responses to technological changes are crucial both for introducing new technologies and for realizing their potential to contribute to performance. This chapter explores whether the partnership has been and will be a positive, negative, or largely neutral factor in helping realize Halvorson's vision of using information technology (IT) to transform and dramatically improve health care delivery.[1]

Lessons from the Past

What does evidence from prior research suggest about how the workforce and/or the presence of strong unions at Kaiser might influence investment, implementation, and effects of these technologies? Some economic theorists would argue that the presence of unions might deter investments in technology because labor can hold management "over the barrel" once the investment has been made, extracting all of the returns to the sunk investment by demanding higher wages and/or dampening the anticipated benefits from capital substitution by securing wage and employment security agreements for existing workers.[2] An alternative theoretical argument is that the presence of strong unions encourages employers to invest more in technology in order to gain advantage from a high wage/high productivity strategy.[3]

Although economic theory is indeterminate, sociological theory suggests that because technological changes often eliminate some jobs and change the work content and skill requirements of others, workers vulnerable to these changes are likely to fear them. Unions representing such workers thus face the task of either opposing technological change or negotiating adjustment provisions to deal with worker job security concerns.[4] Empirical studies of both manufacturing and information technologies have shown that technological changes have limited (or even zero to negative) payoffs if not complemented by appropriate changes in work processes.[5]

If these lessons from past experiences apply to electronic health records technologies, then the transformation and improvements in health care delivery envisioned by Halvorson will depend heavily on the involvement, training, and acceptance of change by the workforce and on integration of the hardware and software features of the technology with changes in work processes. Specifically, studies suggest three ways to leverage the partnership to make the technology more effective. First, the partnership can ensure that the design and configuration of HealthConnect will go hand-in-hand with work process design.[6] Second, a partnership approach to the project at all stages—configuration, implementation, deployment, ongoing use, and optimization—will guarantee meaningful labor involvement and "ownership" of Kaiser's EHR system.[7] Even if the emergent EHR configuration squares with or improves Kaiser workflows, the performance pay-off will be greater if it is arrived at through partnership, rather than through a top-down mandate. Finally, the partnership can ensure that the benefits of technology do not come at the expense of the workforce. The partnership can ensure that workers whose jobs are altered or eliminated are offered retraining, redeployment, or other opportunities to work with their employer "to make themselves whole" in accordance with the pre-negotiated job security pledge. Workforce planning, when integrated into larger IT and operations strategizing, can ensure that the job and income security agreements are met, enabling union leaders to promote the project at all levels by credibly reminding workers that no one stands to lose.[8]

A Brief Primer on Electronic Health Records

Understanding the partnership's influence on HealthConnect and the ways technology might contribute to Kaiser's bottom line first requires an understanding of an EHR system's properties and capabilities. The two core components of an EHR system are an electronic medical record (EMR) and a personal health record (PHR). If an individual's complete records from a single physician or a single hospital were in electronic form, the result would be an EMR. These data are controlled and used by a medical provider. They are not integrated among providers, so a single patient could have multiple, unconnected EMRs. Some patients might have Web-based access to their health information through a PHR. Data on medications, allergies, immunizations, lab test results, office or hospital visit information can come from one or many sources, including manual entries by patients themselves or information provided by a patient's health plan.

Most of the value added from computerizing paper records stems not from the creation of EMRs or even the PHRs, but from the additional step of integrating all of a patient's information into a single EHR, which includes historical and current information not only from generalists and specialists, and inpatient and outpatient care, but from pharmacies, labs, and radiology. Because it is stored in a shared database, this EHR can be accessed by each of the providers at the point of care. Taking the further step of linking individual patient data to a clinical decision support system can both reduce medical errors and improve the standards of care. For example, by linking the individual patient data to state-of-the-art information on treatments for specific diseases, a primary care physician might be alerted to a potentially dangerous interaction between a drug he or she is about to prescribe and one already prescribed by a specialist or that a particular treatment is no longer considered best practice for certain patient populations, such as smokers, men, or the elderly. The system can also be used to generate reminders that patients are due for a particular test or screening. Finally, the integrated nature of an EHR enables it to include not only health care data, but key health financing information, such as coverage details and billing information. This allows patients to log in to check their progress toward an annual deductible. It also provides front-line workers with up-to-date information on which patients are covered for which treatments, as well as when a patient's coverage is expected to lapse.

HealthConnect is an amalgam of Kaiser-configured software modules developed by Epic Systems Corporation to perform all the tasks described above. The modules can be partitioned into three "suites"—"ambulatory" or outpatient clinical records, hospital or inpatient records, and "practice management," composed of modules for billing, scheduling, and other nonclinical operations. In addition to these suites, HealthConnect includes a personal health record and what it refers to as a set of "SmartTools" (checkoff sheets, drug alerts, patient reminders, etc.) that can be accessed or sent automatically to clinicians, staff, or even patients.

By the end of 2007, Kaiser members across all eight regions could set up personal records accounts through which they could access lab results, medical records, and patient-directed clinical content. They could also make and change appointments, refill prescriptions, review their health plan benefits and accounting information, and exchange secure messages with their providers. Seven of the regions had made the transition from paper-based or regional legacy systems to the HealthConnect practice management suite. Progress was less even on the clinical side. Northern and Southern California lagged behind the other six regions with respect to ambulatory clinical records, in part due to California's focus on its hospitals. None of the four regions with Kaiser-owned hospitals—Northern and Southern California, Hawaii, or the Northwest—had implemented the inpatient clinical records functions. However, all Kaiser-owned hospitals had fully deployed HealthConnect's practice management module.

Kaiser physicians were more likely to have IT at their disposal than other physicians in the country. Figure 9.1 shows the share of U.S. physicians reporting access to health IT for each of seven functions, based on physician responses to the Community Tracking Survey.[9] The survey's results grossly overstated physicians' access to and use of EHR systems, because it was based on a series of seven yes or no questions, which did not assess the integration of the seven functions, nor did they get details on the IT in use.[10] As a result, an affirmative response to the question regarding treatment options arose if a physician surfed the Web looking for information on Lyme disease. Likewise, a physician may have used IT to take notes on patients, but through freeform text, perhaps even with a standard word processor. Even so, as of

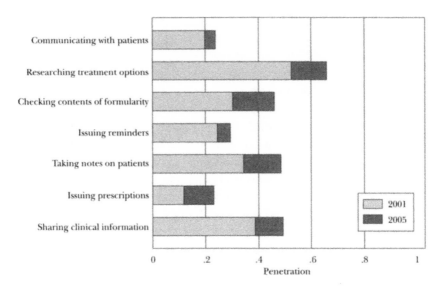

Figure 9.1. National data on physicians' access to individual components of health information technology
Source: Adam Seth Litwin's analysis of Community Tracking Study physician surveys, 2008.

2005, most physicians in the United States were not using computers to facilitate communication with patients and just under half used them to communicate with each other. Despite the low bar for "issuing reminders"—in which a computer may have only been used to print form letters—fewer than 30 percent of physicians could answer affirmatively. The best estimates of EHR diffusion circa 2005 suggest fewer than one in four physicians' offices used the technology,[11] even less for the smaller practices that accounted for 88 percent of all outpatient visits.[12] In contrast, by 2007 all seven of these functions were available to Kaiser physicians, staff, and patients.

Strategic, Organizational, and Employment Contexts

Kaiser wanted more than just to be a national leader in EHR. Kaiser's integrated structure, which combines insurance and care delivery, positions it to reap greater benefits, both financially and clinically, from EHR.[13] Kaiser profits by keeping as much of its per-member per-month premium as it can and loses money on patients with heart disease, cancer, and other acute illnesses. HMOs such as Kaiser are uniquely positioned to benefit from IT that can be used to keep patients healthy and/or detect diseases at an early stage, which explains why Kaiser took action to ensure its physicians had access to EHRs. Kaiser is able to increase its margins when it invests to ensure that women are screened for breast and cervical cancer, men are screened for prostate cancer, and that those at risk for heart attacks are administered inexpensive, effective beta blockers.

EHRs aligned Halvorson's ideas for health care reform with a strategy for moving the organization forward. As a reformer, Halvorson believed that runaway costs and declining quality of care stem from the industry's office-visit orientation, where individual problems are disposed of individually. Through this approach, clinicians generally cannot or do not make use of other information on a particular patient, let alone data on other patients reporting similar symptoms or rates of success or failure with different treatment options. As a result, only 55 percent of patients nationally receive care in compliance with agreed upon best practices.[14] Focusing on only individual patient encounters rather than managing the health of the entire patient population also directs the system toward disease treatment and palliative care, rather than on disease prevention. In fact, caring for those with acute illnesses, many of which are preventable, consumes more than 75 percent of the country's annual health care bill.[15] Halvorson also thought EHR systems could boost efficiency and quality by preventing medical errors. The pay-off could be enormous, because—by one estimate—avoidable medical errors sicken, injure, or kill 1.5 million hospital patients and injure another 530,000 Medicare outpatients each year.[16]

Halvorson also had Kaiser-specific goals in mind for HealthConnect, which hinged on getting real-time, accurate information to front-line workers. For example, Kaiser was leaving millions of dollars per year "on the table" by failing to "refresh" its Medicare patients. That is, Kaiser was not collecting all of the money to which it was entitled because it was not complying with the government's rules for regular re-demonstration of a patient's illness burden, which requires that Medicare patients "check in" with their provider with pre-determined frequency based on their particular condition. With paper records, physicians had no way of determining, at any point in time, the names and phone numbers of all their patients due for the refresh, a problem EHR, in the form of HealthConnect, could correct.

HealthConnect also supported Kaiser's newest products, such as its new line of "skinny" or high-deductible health plans targeted to individuals. The proliferation of these plans, on top of the myriad of traditional options already available, yielded a complicated, inconsistent set of co-payments and deductibles. Revenue from cost sharing had become an important source of income for Kaiser. Front-line staff had to know exactly how far patients were from reaching their deductible and how much a patient's plan would pay for a particular office visit or treatment. Without such information, Kaiser staff relied on their own best guesses or on frequently outdated or even incorrect information provided by the patient.

Bargaining "Effects" Agreement

Union leaders were briefed on Kaiser's initial plans to invest heavily in EHR technologies as early as 2002, even before Halvorson took over as CEO. Because all recognized the major workforce and work process implications of the EHR initiative, Kaiser management readily agreed with the coalition's suggestion that a union staff person with expertise in these technologies be assigned to work full-time as the coalition's representative in the design and planning stages of the initiative. Some regions took the additional step of assigning a union representative to serve as a regional coordinator or point person to represent the coalition in regional design and implementation efforts. As planning moved forward and some early implementation projects were undertaken, the magnitude of the impacts and the need for a general set of guidelines, policies, and adjustment options became apparent. Management and union coalition leaders decided to work these out in a separate national level bargaining process in advance of the 2005 negotiations. The outcome, which became known as the "Effects Agreement," negotiated provisions governing the effects of the technological change on the workforce. (See figure 9.2 for the highlights of the agreement.)

The agreement opened by establishing that HealthConnect was not a technology, but a massive organizational change aimed at transforming the way Kaiser delivered healthcare. It signified a joint commitment to the project and laid out what management anticipated from labor and vice versa. It established union involvement in all stages of the project and committed management to funding national and regional HealthConnect labor coordinators (some were already in place), as well as the training, release, and backfill engendered as a result of the project, for all members of the bargaining unit. The agreement established two other important policies. First, it acknowledged that workers would be displaced by HealthConnect and established Kaiser-funded options for retraining and redeploying those workers. Although not necessarily guaranteed their current job, workers were assured continued employment if they were willing to retrain. Displaced workers could also opt for a severance package rather than retraining. Second,

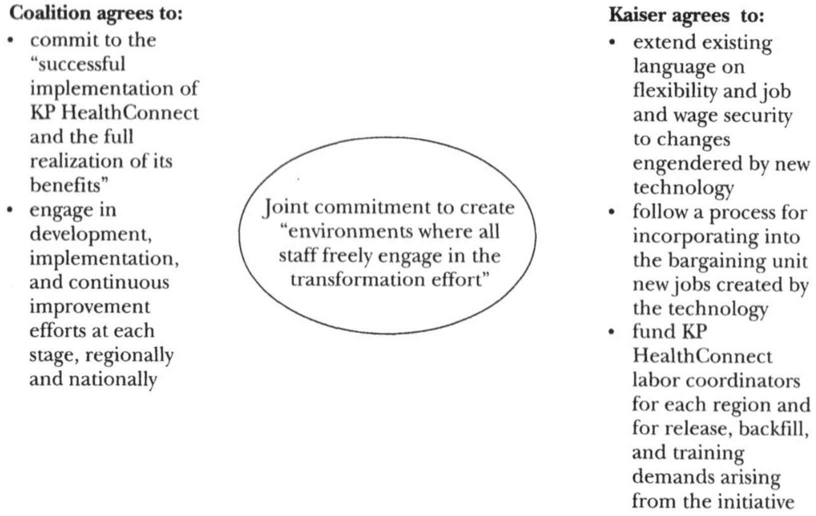

Coalition agrees to:
- commit to the "successful implementation of KP HealthConnect and the full realization of its benefits"
- engage in development, implementation, and continuous improvement efforts at each stage, regionally and nationally

Joint commitment to create "environments where all staff freely engage in the transformation effort"

Kaiser agrees to:
- extend existing language on flexibility and job and wage security to changes engendered by new technology
- follow a process for incorporating into the bargaining unit new jobs created by the technology
- fund KP HealthConnect labor coordinators for each region and for release, backfill, and training demands arising from the initiative

Figure 9.2. Highlights of the KP HealthConnect effects bargaining agreement between Kaiser Permanente and Coalition of Kaiser Permanente Unions
Source: KP HealthConnect Effects Bargain, effective 5 April 2005.

union negotiators bargained successfully for language to incorporate the jobs newly created by HealthConnect in the bargaining unit. Over time, this would both make up for membership losses due to the new technology and bring in more highly skilled positions, such as site support specialists and application coordinators.

By reaching a national level agreement relatively early in the process—albeit after implementation had begun in some regions—the parties removed thorny and potentially divisive issues that would otherwise have had to be addressed in each implementation project. Moreover, in the absence of the coalition and national level partnership, agreements of this nature would have had to be negotiated separately with each local union, some of which had more to fear than others from the effects of the new technology and therefore might have been more inclined to resist its introduction. Instead, with the national agreement, union and management leaders in all Kaiser worksites had a clear protocol and a set of rules for dealing with their workers' employment security concerns. Furthermore, local union leaders and regional labor coordinators were inserted into HealthConnect planning and could represent workers' interests in the technology and the work changes it would necessitate. In exchange for bringing labor into the process, management was assured that the partnership would promote the project at all levels, including asking workers to take on new tasks. By making it possible to negotiate this overall agreement, the partnership provided a clear channel for moving forward with implementation across Kaiser's decentralized structures and varied worksites.

Implementation on the Front Lines

The benefits of the Effects Agreement manifested themselves immediately and frequently. Three examples of the engagement of local union leaders in supporting the implementation process come from Northern California's Central Valley service area. The first example of the partnership helping workers adjust to new job requirements involved the Central Valley's efforts to use HealthConnect's tool for improving "revenue capture"—collecting money owed to Kaiser by patients at the point of service. Although Health-Connect's practice management suite provided the billing information needed to support this function, the medical assistants now being asked to perform it had long been trained that "the member is always right." Reluctant to discuss payment issues, some of these assistants preferred the old practice of billing members by mail, rather than requiring them to pay at the point of service. Management in Central Valley sought the help of union leaders in dealing with this transition, who responded by coaching medical assistants in how to have what became known as "courageous conversations" with patients.

A second example was initiated by local union leaders as they anticipated the stress felt by chart room workers who were about to see their jobs disappear. Many of these workers were reluctant to face this reality, but union leaders worked with them to encourage them to seek out new positions in Kaiser and to work through the partnership to arrange the training and certifications needed to gain access to these jobs. As a result all the workers were able to find alternative jobs at Kaiser.

A third example comes from another Central Valley chart room. The service area had stopped hiring new people for chart room positions that would soon be discontinued, so the retraining of incumbent employees created unmet demand for backfill. The problem was especially acute for more senior positions in the chart room, because fewer workers had ever been trained to do that work. The use of temporary workers was limited by concerns of cost and data privacy and discouraged by the Effects Agreement. Further reliance on overtime would be costly as well. Workers and managers in the chart room developed and implemented two solutions. First, to reduce the use of discretionary leave, managers agreed to provide a free vacation day for every thirty consecutive days worked, which was a much less expensive option than up-front overtime pay. Second, they encouraged workers to undertake training to do the work of the more senior positions in the chart room. Chart room managers agreed that workers would be paid for the training and would be paid at the rates of the senior-level job while doing senior-level work. As one supervisor put it, "They can decide whatever they want in Oakland [at Kaiser headquarters]. We need to actually get through the day." Neither of these steps required a complicated approval process as the net effect was a reduction in spending, not an increase. The local union leaders involved were pleased with this approach and saw it as an application of the Effects Agreement principles to their specific situation; they therefore felt no need to consult or seek approval from higher level union officials.

These examples illustrate both the value and the limits of the Effects Agreement. Though necessary to the success of HealthConnect, the Effects Agreement provided only an umbrella containing protections and protocols that both management and the coalition needed to move ahead with the implementation process. It took involvement and partnership on the front lines to realize the changes in work processes and to cope with the human consequences of technological change necessary to realize the benefits of the new systems.

Accommodating Regional Variation

When the KP HealthConnect initiative was officially unveiled to the public in early 2003, its projected cost was $1.8 billion. This cost ballooned over the next year to $3 billion[17] and continued to rise over the next three and a half years to an undisclosed amount that almost certainly exceeds $5 billion. A significant cause of the higher costs was the need to accommodate local variations in practices.

Recall that the EHR system would generate value by promoting evidence-based medicine on the clinical side and "best practices" for capturing revenue on the business side—in sum, by process standardization. Consequently, the original budget for HealthConnect assumed one, fairly monolithic EHR system that would require only minor adjustments for each region. Kaiser hoped that the partnership would help drive the regions to make this happen by harmonizing regional variations in work practices to conform to those identified as "best practices."

However, all the will of labor and management could not conjure away inter-regional variation. First, regions were at different starting points, organizationally and technologically. For example, the Northwest region had been using Epic's module for outpatient clinical records, whereas Colorado had been using a homegrown system. On the organizational side, the Northwest originally expected to pilot its use of the scheduling functions in a single call center serving just two clinics. However, the involvement of front-line staff made it immediately apparent that all nurses, not just those at the affected clinics, would need to be trained immediately because they were all making appointments in the two affected clinics. Similarly, prior to the introduction of HealthConnect, Northern California had taken steps to broaden the responsibilities of medical assistants to involve them in revenue collection. This meant that all medical assistants would have to be trained in the new revenue capture tools and applications.

Second, regions differed in their "scopes of practice"—which job classifications can do which work—with boundaries established more by state regulations than by union contract rules. As noted in chapter 5, principles for addressing this issue were developed and codified in the 2005 national negotiations, but each location still had to apply these principles to fit their specific situation and state-level regulations.

Third, regions also differed in the services they offered. For example, only the Northwest region offered dentistry. Just three regions owned and operated their own hospitals, and each of the others had idiosyncratic arrangements for delivering inpatient care. Finally, with respect to Hawaii, where there was no partnership, the Oakland headquarters was ill-prepared for the inordinate cost of desktop IT support, cost resulting from employees booking inter-island flights on short notice.

Overall, inter-regional variability in both the software and organizational arrangements to support it led to something closer to eight similar systems rather than one large one. This made it more difficult to exploit scale economies in training and other support structures, because each region had to be given "block grants" for its own efforts. Had the cost overruns stemmed mainly from underestimating outlays for hardware and software, favorable tax rules could have shielded Kaiser from the brunt of poor planning. However, outlays for training and "change management," the very intangibles that the HealthConnect planners did not fully anticipate, must always be expensed up-front.

Moreover, these and other regional variations led to IT systems that were different enough to create serious hurdles to the seamless transfer of information across regions, which was essential to leveraging some of Kaiser's unique organizational attributes. The same decentralized structures and regional variations that slowed the diffusion of the labor-management partnership added costs and slowed the realization of the full potential of these new technologies.

Segregated versus Integrated Approaches

Two examples, one preceding the Effects Agreement and one following it, further illustrate the differences in implementation processes with and without strong partnership involvement.

Consider first the implementation process in Colorado that occurred in 2004, just prior to the negotiation of the Effects Agreement. Even if the impetus for the adoption of HealthConnect came from the headquarters, it could not have been better timed for Colorado—unless it had come a year or two earlier. As mentioned above, the Colorado region had been using a homegrown solution for its outpatient medical records called Clinical Information System (CIS). CIS ran on an obsolete, pre-Windows platform that was in wide use when Colorado first developed the system. IT staff in the region made frequent updates to the system until the point when further updates would require major changes to its core. By the time the region made the decision to stop updating CIS, the system had become unreliable and unbearably slow, particularly in retrieving records of patients with long clinical histories. Forecasts for steep and rapid regional demand growth indicated that CIS could seriously constrain Colorado's competitive success. When plans called for building a new Rock Creek Medical Office in Lafayette, CO, regional managers had to acknowledge the crisis and take action. Colorado did not even own enough of the obsolete IBM PS/2 machines to install at Rock Creek, let alone replace the failing ones already in place. As one doctor quipped, "The only place we could find any of those machines was on eBay." Colorado needed to replace CIS and needed to do it right away.

Colorado's implementation of HealthConnect displayed all the traits one might expect—good and bad—from a technologically driven and time-constrained project. Regional actors were less concerned about how to leverage HealthConnect toward the long-term goals of the region than they were about averting disaster. As a result, regional leadership defined the project as an IT project, not as a program for changing the way Colorado produced and delivered quality health care. Citing the region's previous transition from paper-based records, management leaders framed this implementation as purely "technical"—not organizational or workforce-related—assuming that these latter dimensions would not need to change. Regional leadership on the labor side did not share this view. Taking their cues from coalition leaders, regional representatives from the SEIU and UFCW representing medical assistants, nurses, and other support staff assumed their posts on the fifteen-person regional HealthConnect project team, ready to learn more about how the technology worked and to articulate workers' concerns and suggestions as to how it could be configured to make workers more effective.

But HealthConnect labor coordinators were discouraged by regional operations, human resources, and IT leadership from involving themselves in anything technical. Attempts to contribute to discussions about the new system's design were met with, "We are just switching systems." They were not offered the same consideration—a company credit card for travel-related expenses, a "loaner" laptop computer equipped with software to allow secure, remote access to the system—as others on the planning team. Throughout the process, management cited the "tight budget"' and "tight schedule," even in the face of opposition from the coalition's national leadership. Management discouraged union representatives from concerning themselves with anything other than mobilizing the rank-and-file members around HealthConnect. Union frustration reached such high levels that most other partnership activities came to a halt. According to one regional management leader, "Labor just needed to trust us." The problem was that management had not earned labor's trust.

Management pushed ahead and was able to bring the new system on-line. In about a month management completed what had been assumed would be a year long change-over project. However, technology and organizational strategy were not addressed simultaneously, and the process was neither co-determined nor co-owned. As a result, the needs and interests of many workers had been overlooked and had to be dealt with after the rollout. The workers found that processes they had long believed ineffective and redundant were re-institutionalized in the new system. For example, in some areas, medical assistants did not have "write privileges," that is, the ability to enter data into parts of the medical record they were now expected to update. These problems could be addressed in future releases of the software, but not without considerable short-term inconvenience to members and staff, and possibly, longer term costs from workers not having "co-owned" the HealthConnect initiative in Colorado.

In comparison, the Northwest region had the time and the budget to be methodical and deliberate in its rollout of the practice management suite.

Aside from the two full-time employees budgeted as HealthConnect coordinators, one for each of the two largest unions in the region, the region also budgeted for twenty members of the bargaining unit to be temporarily pulled from their regular jobs to serve as members of the HealthConnect "Flex Team." Flex Team members were the first end users trained, and they traveled around the region coaching their co-workers. They also met regularly as a group to share information about common workflow and worker challenges and common technical issues. Members of this team reported that all advice nurses, not just those in certain clinics, needed to be ready to use the new functionality. Two years later, having long since returned to their regular job roles, these former Flex Team members were still the de facto "go-to" problem solvers in their own clinics and for others in their job classification across the region.

Northwest regional managers saw the process as unduly slow and costly, relative to similar implementations they had worked on in previous jobs. Indeed, the costs were considerable, both in the time and expense of assembling the Flex Team and in securing backfill for them. More generally, managers believed that decisions about core functionality had to be explained and substantiated to a larger number of people, many of whom would not have been part of this process elsewhere. Nonetheless, management leaders saw the long-term, strategic benefits of labor inclusion, particularly the early involvement of eventual end users. They understood that HealthConnect was an investment in more than just Epic's product, but in complicated organizational reforms. As long as regional leadership and Oakland anticipated large, front-loaded outlays and a far-from-immediate return, they could continue to include labor as a full and essential partner in HealthConnect planning and implementation.

Summary and a Look Ahead

The experience in implementing HealthConnect provides a window on the realities and tensions of this labor-management partnership. Kaiser's partnership and its investment in health IT both gained national attention as leaders in their respective technical and employment domains. As top-down change initiatives, both received strong support and resources (although the investment in HealthConnect dwarfed the level of investment in the partnership, a reality often lamented by the coalition leaders), and both were seen as key strategic initiatives. Both, however, experienced more difficulties and took longer than anticipated to diffuse.

The two initiatives did not start off together as part of some common vision or coordinated approach. Instead, it took the Effects Agreement prior to 2005 national negotiations to pave the way for a more coordinated implementation process on the front lines to move forward. At the micro level, the use of partnership principles of labor representation and employee involvement also presented the opportunity to comply with what prior research suggests offers the greatest payoff: an integration of technical and organizational/workforce innovations. As the Colorado and Northwest examples illustrate, however, the realization of this potential varied from location to location. In those situations where prior relationships were good and the partnership strong, the implementation process appears to have gone well. Where the parties had more arm's-length or adversarial relationships, implementation was more difficult and slower.

The full potential for integrating these new technologies and leveraging the partnership to achieve a transformation in health care delivery had not yet been realized. As of late 2007, the regions entered the optimization phase in which workers would move past day-to-day "survival" with HealthConnect to the kind of follow-up training and mentoring that would encourage the transformational use of the system. This would also be the time when gains from complementarity—that is, the joint benefits gained from effectively linking technical and work process/workforce innovations—would begin to manifest themselves. The benefits to HealthConnect derived due to an ongoing partnership being in place may prove to be far greater even than those experienced in the initial implementation process.

The same forces that stressed the partnership in general put particular pressure on HealthConnect, which also faced some additional challenges. First, ballooning budget overruns could be blamed on poor cost accounting in the project's early days. Outlays for training, which can never be capitalized, were more than anticipated, in part, because the project was never envisioned as an ongoing, evolving one. To some extent, this represents a flaw in the original design to integrate the technology and organization strategies. Looking ahead, partnership leaders will need to address this initial flaw by looking for ways to reorganize work to make maximum use of the new technology.

At the same time, as the large California regions move further down the path to paperless outpatient medical records, it is likely to become harder to find positions for displaced chart room workers. Many have very limited skills or will need more training than anticipated, such as intense English language courses. Furthermore, the shortage of staff has prevented Kaiser from meeting its promise to provide backfill for some of the workers in training or otherwise serving the HealthConnect project. Both of these issues may make HealthConnect the object of resentment for overworked staff. These feelings were already apparent in the Northwest region, and will likely dampen or delay the returns to HealthConnect.

Finally, the partnership encountered an unanticipated issue in the IT professionals' general disinterest in unions. Despite management's commitment in negotiating the Effects Agreement and to remain neutral in efforts to organize IT professionals, newly created positions remain entirely non-union. Many blame middle managers in IT and elsewhere for discouraging unionism and the partnership to would-be union members. This behavior, inconsistent with the rhetoric of Kaiser leadership, weakens the power of the HealthConnect Effects Agreement. If Kaiser appears to be abrogating the Effects Agreement, on which the partnership's role in HealthConnect rests, management risks losing support built through promises of job security.

CHAPTER 10

Partnerships on the Front Lines

If strong and creative leadership was essential to the success of the partnership, so too was the involvement of front-line workers. That engagement was especially important in achieving the first two goals in the list of partnership objectives: to improve the quality of health care for Kaiser members and communities; and to help Kaiser achieve and maintain market-leading, competitive performance.

Such goals reflected the partnership's original vision, which was not only to realize peace on the labor relations front but also to serve as a vehicle for improving the quality and efficiency of health care and organizational performance. Realizing this vision proved more difficult than the original architects of the partnership anticipated.

Over the first decade of the partnership's existence, opportunities to engage front-line employees in partnership activities arose mainly when projects were launched to address specific problems or discrete tasks. The Office of Labor-Management Partnership counted more than 250 such projects, ranging from major initiatives, such as the opening of the Baldwin Park Medical Center (see chapter 3), to less visible efforts, such as joint staffing teams in Sunnyside Medical Center in Portland; service quality improvement teams in clinics in Fresno; and teams of physicians, social workers, nurses, and clerical employees that worked together to reduce waiting times for mental health patients in a psychiatric unit in Los Angeles. To use the

Los Angeles example, the team met for about three hours a week and conferred regularly with the full staff of the psychiatric unit. It took nearly a year, but the team developed an entirely new model of care delivery that changed the flow of patients through the unit, rebalanced the workloads of professionals, and provided for more rapid access and consistent care for patients. Based on its initial success in improving access, the team went on to develop and implement new productivity and scheduling standards for their unit.

Most successful team-based projects involved front-line employees working with supervisors, managers, and clinicians, including physicians, where appropriate, on the actual work processes involved in delivering health care. Such examples gave partnership leaders confidence that the team-based processes could be transformed from episodic projects into the standard practice for delivering and improving health care on an ongoing basis.

Notwithstanding these case-by-case occurrences, as of 2005 very few departments had an ongoing partnership process in place, and fewer than half of front-line employees had much direct involvement in partnership activities. According to a 2005 coalition survey of union members, 45 percent reported that they were "somewhat involved," only 16 percent said they were "very involved," and 39 percent reported they were "not very" or "not at all" involved. During roughly the same period, an internal employee survey by Kaiser found a similar level of involvement. Thirty-nine percent of respondents agreed or strongly agreed that they were "personally involved in structures or activities that are part of the partnership," 35 percent disagreed or strongly disagreed, and 27 percent were neutral. The challenge taken up in 2005 negotiations was to achieve an ongoing and widespread engagement of front-line workers and supervisors as a normal part of the way they carried out their work. The 2005 agreement called for unit-based teams (UBTs) to become the "basic unit responsible for work and results in a particular area."

The agreement laid out an aggressive schedule for implementing UBTs across the entire Kaiser system. The goal was to have teams in 15 percent of all units by December 2007, 40 percent by December 2008, 70 percent by December 2009, and 100 percent by the end of 2010. The agreement outlined the functions of UBTs: planning, setting goals, establishing metrics, reviewing performance, generating ideas to improve performance, participating in budgeting, identifying and solving problems, and participating in scheduling. To be effective, UBTs would need support, including open sharing of business information, timely performance data, access to department-specific training, enhanced meeting skills, facilitation, and backfill. To shore up this plan, many detailed recommendations were offered for how to implement, support, and evaluate UBTs.

On paper, this looked like a clear-cut strategy for achieving the key objective of transforming the partnership from a labor relations initiative to a plan for delivering efficient and high quality health care. The members of the bargaining task force that developed the UBT recommendations and their colleagues on the larger negotiating team were proud of the work they had done and excited about the new vision they had constructed for the partnership and for the overall Kaiser Permanente organization.

However, it was not a simple task to implement that vision. Unfortunately, the negotiators who generated the UBT vision and plans were not the ones who would be assigned the task of implementing them. Instead, the task of designing an implementation plan for those ideas was handed off to the partnership leaders. This handoff coincided with the transitions in leadership in both union and management. A number of false starts further slowed the process, including the hiring and firing of consultants who had been charged with developing an implementation plan (they had proposed an overly complex structure involving sixteen different oversight teams).

More than a year after the contract's ratification, partnership leaders developed an integrated approach that placed UBTs at the center of implementing the 2005 national agreement. By the time this decision was made, some of the regional leaders had already begun to take action on their own. To illustrate the process of introducing UBTs as a standard model for delivery, we focus on the first region to move forward, Southern California, and then summarize the efforts of the other regions. We found that the national goal of "wall-to-wall" unit-based teams by 2010 was daunting. It was one thing to roll out pilots that covered 15 percent of the workforce; it was another to implement this concept in all departments and areas. To the extent that joint committees were already in place, the transition to UBTs could be quite expeditious. However, in settings with no prior experience, or with experience that had been less than positive, the introduction of UBTs sometimes had to overcome skepticism that they were just the latest "program of the month."

"Targeted" Unit-Based Teams in Southern California

In Southern California, the UBT initiative was called "Targeted UBTs" (T-UBTs) to signify that these teams would differ from most of the prior teams in that they would be accountable for reaching region-defined performance goals for a battery of clinical, service, and quality indicators. This represented a significant shift from most prior partnership projects, which focused on *locally* defined, specific issues, such as budget crises and labor relations tensions. The new T-UBTs were to be the key operational means for achieving performance goals that were deemed critical to the *regional* strategic plan.

Launching UBTs

Coming out of the 2005 negotiations, the new Southern California regional president, Dr. Ben Chu, decided to aggressively implement UBTs. Chu viewed the partnership as a potential source of competitive advantage rather than an imposed constraint on management. And if 15 percent of the workforce was to be in UBTs by the end of 2007 and 100 percent by the end of 2010, there was no time to lose. Chu had prior successful experiences in working in partnership with unions as a physician and executive in New York hospitals organized by SEIU Local 1199 (also known as United Healthcare Workers-East) and had developed a personal friendship with then president of 1199 Dennis Rivera. He had also participated in some of the discussions of the performance improvement Bargaining Task Group that generated the UBT recommendations. Chu was anxious to move forward as quickly as possible.

The first key step was taken at the annual Southern California Leadership Conference, which brought together the region's top 200 to 300 management and medical leaders. The November 2006 meeting devoted considerable time to plans for launching UBTs. National labor coalition leader John August and Southern California coalition leader Walter Allen were invited, and sat next to Dr. Chu and Dr. Jeffrey Weisz, the regional medical director, explaining the new program and answering questions about it. This was the first time union people had participated in a Leadership Conference. The symbolism was lost on no one.

Regional management took the initiative in developing an implementation plan by assembling a group made up of some regional staff of the partnership, the organizational effectiveness unit, and several other staff groups. The coalition had one staff person participating in the design process. A sponsor team was created, led by Drs. Chu and Weisz and Walter Allen. Each medical center was asked to create a streamlined, top-level "strategy group," to be composed of the top three management and medical leaders, plus a high-level representative of each union present at the center to lead the T-UBT effort. For the first time in this region, union leaders were integrated into the management decision-making process at the most senior levels of each medical center.

It was decided to roll out the T-UBT in phases. The first phase called for a very aggressive schedule, tasking each medical center's Strategy Group to have seven to ten T-UBTs ready for launch by February 2007. The regional sponsors expected that the subsequent phases of the T-UBT roll-out would be planned in light of the results of this first phase.

Each medical center was asked to create one to three teams in inpatient care departments, one team in operating room departments, three to five teams in adult primary care, and one team in an area of their own choosing. Although it was recommended that these be composed of all the people who worked together in a given unit, the medical centers were given the option of creating "representative" teams if they thought a viable group would involve too large a number of front-line employees. In the end, 85 percent of the teams would be of the representative variety.

Senior union leaders at each medical center were asked to nominate labor co-leads for each team, meaning these would be appointed, rather than elected, positions. The partnership historically had relied on structures that allowed each union to have its own representative at every discussion table. The new T-UBTs represented a significant shift from this practice—the labor co-lead would be accountable for communicating with and representing whatever mix of union members were on the team or affected by the team's activities.

Some of the members of these T-UBTs had yet to receive the training normally required for partnership activities, such as consensus-based decision making. New, shorter versions of these courses were created and made available to team members on a "just-in-time" basis. Teams were to use the "rapid cycle improvement methods" (RIM) approach recommended by the Institute for Healthcare Improvement, a non-profit health care research and consulting group. This approach built on quality management guru Edward Deming's "plan-do-check-act" cycle. It encouraged work teams to identify local opportunities for improvement, try out ideas on a very small scale, test to see if these ideas were having the desired effect, then try the experiment on a larger scale, and eventually implement the change across the entire process. Training in this new approach was to be less extensive than the training on partnership processes provided to prior teams and similarly delivered on a just-in-time basis.

Initial Results

Between March and July 2007, about ninety-five teams were designated and began meeting. About half of the teams were converted from existing departmental teams. By the end of July, a majority of the teams had begun serious work. Many teams had enthusiastically taken up the challenge of generating, testing, and implementing performance-improvement changes. As one labor leader put it, "[Y]ou can only get so far with partnership only at the top level of the region and the medical centers. You have to get to the working level to make a real difference—that's why we need the T-UBTs."

Another local labor leader was similarly hopeful, but also saw challenges. "About half the labor co-leads and most of the labor representatives are new to partnership work," she said. "And the labor co-leads tend to be uncomfortable working with their management co-lead as an equal. They tend to become 'junior managers' [and] need a lot of support. So this is hard going, but we're in health care, and anything that helps our patients will get us involved. That, and support from management leadership, make me feel optimistic about the T-UBTs here."

Different teams focused on different kinds of outcomes. In an effort to reduce patient waits, some teams had dramatically reduced the waiting time for patients with the day's first appointments, in order to avoid a snowball effect of delays for all subsequent patients. They also rearranged schedules so that some medical assistants arrived and left earlier. Some teams had worked successfully on implementing "Care Boards" to show the status of patients as nurses rotated in. This was encouraged by nurses rounding and a program of (modest-sized) rewards for teams that systematically used the boards. Some teams dramatically reduced inpatient calls for pain medication by instituting procedures to ensure that nurses rotated regularly among the rooms and beds.

The region was pushing for faster "turn-around time" for operating rooms, which is arguably a classic case of work intensification. We observed one outpatient surgical T-UBT made up of RNs and clerical workers where team members expressed some frustration with the fact that the turn-around time goals had been "handed down from region." Yet the team tackled this challenge creatively. It first created teams by specialty. This had some downsides for those workers who liked more variation, but it smoothed and accelerated the workflow by eliminating unproductive changeovers. They then analyzed the work of the unit and decided that turn-around time would be reduced if they had a medical assistant to call in patients, take their vital signs, and help arrange transport. They were able to bring in a temporary worker and showed that this indeed improved performance. Next the management and labor co-leads developed a "business case" for a permanent addition to take to senior management. For one T-UBT meeting, workers from Environmental Services (janitors) were brought in to brainstorm their coordination with the OR team. In the team meeting, the management co-lead explained that the national association of operating room nurses had recently issued new guidelines on cleaning and that these guidelines allowed them to adjust the amount of cleaning. For instance, they would not need to do a complete cleaning, including wet-mop of floor, for minor surgeries—such as cataract surgery—that did not deposit anything on the floor. The cleaning team member and team leader discussed with the T-UBT several ways they might better coordinate along such lines. It was striking that all these ways of improving performance relied on eliminating unproductive activity, rather than adding tasks to the workers' already busy day.

Resource Issues

"Initiative overload" proved to be a major challenge for these teams, whose efforts came on top of a major push to implement HealthConnect, Kaiser's electronic medical records initiative. As we discussed in more depth in the previous chapter, the introduction of these new technologies, which was led by other executives and staff groups, was not seen as a core partnership activity. Although a few T-UBTs defined their tasks in terms of assuring effective HealthConnect implementation (by redesigning workflows), for the most part these two initiatives competed for very scarce time.

Indeed, time was already at a premium as most medical center managers felt they were understaffed, a view seemingly confirmed by high overtime costs. Resources were also very scarce for freeing up time for meetings. Unlike many of the pre-2005 partnership activities, T-UBTs were given no backfill budget. Moreover, newly formed Strategy Groups and T-UBTs often needed facilitation help, but the region allocated only a small budget for such support. Underlying these resource constraints was a policy issue that remained unresolved as of late 2007: Regional management saw the T-UBT program as a way to get away from the cumbersome and expensive pre-2005 form of partnership activity and governance; and their union counterparts worried that this "streamlining" risked undermining the program.

Moving Ahead in Southern California

By the end of 2007, the challenge of generalizing T-UBTs across all the region's departments within the next three years looked daunting. The regional leaders would need to put in place a mechanism that enabled regional labor and management leadership to hold the medical center strategy groups accountable for the implementation of T-UBTs across the entire staff and for sustaining their performance-improvement efforts over time. Similarly, the strategy groups themselves would need to develop mechanisms for holding all the T-UBTs accountable for their results and for ensuring that the representatives on the teams effectively engaged their entire work unit.

As T-UBTs generalized across the entire region, the resource constraints loomed large—the program would require a very considerable investment in training. Notwithstanding enthusiasm among management for the idea that short "huddles" might replace time-consuming formal team meetings, it seemed that T-UBTs would need time to meet. And as their number multiplied, this would create new tensions.

Despite such hurdles, enthusiasm ran high. Even recalcitrant safety and attendance problems seemed to be easier to address in the T-UBT structure. One labor co-lead of an outpatient clinic T-UBT noted:

> Before we had this T-UBT working on performance, it was hard to talk to your co-workers about these [safety and attendance] issues because many of them would just tell you it was none of your business. But now we are working on these performance goals, and if people are late or if they do something unsafe, it feels very natural to talk with them about it because their choices are making our work harder. On the safety stuff, [the management co-lead] and I have been doing some safety observations together, and that's worked out really well. We just watch someone working without getting in the way, and if we see something good, we praise them, and if we notice something dangerous, we point it out. On the attendance stuff, you used to hear people with attendance problems say sometimes, "But I just can't get up on time." And now you hear staff members challenge them, saying "That's no excuse. You should show more consideration for your co-workers." At Region, they see attendance and safety as some figures on paper; but here we see it in our work being harder, or our patients being delayed. So we can really make a difference when we talk about it with our co-workers.

UBTs in Northern California

While Southern California took the lead, other regions were not far behind. Northern California launched 100 teams in June 2007, focused on a subset of region-wide partnership goals, including improving attendance (reducing the use of sick days), decreasing missed meals and breaks (an indicator, at least in labor's view, of understaffing), decreasing the use of overtime, and improving the quality of both inpatient and outpatient service as measured by patient or member surveys and various team-selected metrics on the work environment.

As of late 2007, the Northern California region had implemented 123 UBTs and was carefully tracking their performance. Though it was still early in the process, there were some promising results. On most, though not all measures, the UBTs had been selected because they were lower than average performers in the areas of focus. The trajectory for the UBTs from July through December 2007 was generally positive, as was that for the region as a whole. For instance, the UBTs made steady progress toward the regional target for missed meals and breaks, going from 0.17 percent to 0.06 percent of total payroll, although still short of the target 0.05 percent. Similarly, departments with UBTs slightly decreased their use of overtime but still did not quite meet the regional target. The UBTs in the outpatient setting actually began above the target for service quality and above the regional average, but still experienced some small improvement in their service scores (78 percent to 79.1 percent of patients answering positively to a question about staff courtesy and helpfulness). Inpatient UBTs improved their service scores (rating of overall hospital stay from 73.7 percent to 76.4 percent), though their trend line was more or less the same as that of the region as a whole.

UBT performance on attendance was more mixed. Initial efforts to implement the attendance provisions in the 2005 agreement failed to produce the results intended. In particular, the new "cash-out" program seemed to have encouraged workers to use sick days early in the calendar year; this spike in sick leave in January was echoed by a smaller bump at the end of the year. Nor was there a real decline in the overall sick leave usage throughout the year. Labor took this setback as seriously as management and the parties actively began looking for other solutions, both in the governance and staffing of the attendance effort as well as its substance. One solution was to focus UBTs on attendance. Both the Northern and Southern California regions adopted this approach. As with the other initiatives, the UBTs in Northern California started out in units with higher than average sick leave usage. From July through October of 2007, the UBTs achieved a lower rate of sick leave usage than the regional target and the regional average. Unfortunately, that advantage did not last through the end of the year. As one regional manager said, "The teams were making progress by focusing on attendance, but then they took their eye off the ball and the numbers started creeping back up. Now [January 2008] our UBTs are again giving attendance priority attention, so we hope and expect to make progress on this issue again."

Overall, results from Northern California gave room for cautious optimism. A system had been put in place to carefully track UBT performance, an achievement in and of itself. There were also indications that UBTs could produce better than average performance improvements on at least some important regional metrics.

UBTs in Other Regions

In late 2007—more than two years after the 2005 agreement—most regions outside of California had also implemented UBTs. Colorado, for example, was systematically tracking results for fourteen teams, including five teams in pharmacies, one region-wide pharmacy team working on a particular project, and other teams distributed across diverse environments, including back-office/administrative areas, such as claims, and also chronic care, primary care, and behavioral health. The pharmacy teams all had the goals of increasing patient usage of the Kaiser patient Internet site, the use of mail order to fill prescriptions, and a decrease in "return to stock." Two teams were still getting started but the other three had made progress toward their goals, increasing the use of the Internet from 4 percent to more than 50 percent, though that was still short of the goal of 70 percent. The behavioral health UBTs were focused on increasing member access to providers and two of the three teams had met their access goals.

The Northwest region initially launched sixteen UBTs in the sole hospital in the region—Sunnyside—in early May 2007. These teams were converted from earlier teams that had been called Department Partnership Councils or Committees. The UBT effort was viewed, in part, as an opportunity to breathe new life into those Councils, only some of which were functioning well. A second wave of UBTs was launched in outpatient settings in July, bringing the total number of UBTs by the end of 2007 to forty.

In the Georgia region eight teams were launched toward an eventual goal of fifty to seventy-five teams. Ohio also started small but was increasing its number of teams. The emphasis in that region was on improved service in contrast to the earlier ambulatory redesign groups (discussed in chapter 4) that had focused on cost reduction. Also, many more people from the units were involved in the teams.

Summary: A Good Beginning but Challenges Ahead

Earlier efforts within Kaiser—such as bringing a new hospital on line (Baldwin Park), involving union stewards and members in service quality (Fresno), addressing staffing issues (Sunnyside), reducing costs in outpatient clinics (Ohio), and improving patient access (LA Metro Psychiatry)—confirmed the well-established principle that the organizational innovation represented by partnership can work well when labor and management see a compelling need to work together to solve a pressing problem. It has been far more challenging for labor and management to abandon their traditional roles and to work in partnership when there is no burning issue, when partnership is to be the standard everyday practice for assuring and improving operational quality and efficiency. Though Kaiser's success in this area has been limited, some useful lessons emerged.

Perhaps the greatest challenge facing UBTs is the need to sustain a sense of urgency. Where earlier project teams succeeded, it was because the environment gave them this sense of urgency. UBTs will need to have a rolling agenda of meaningful, energizing projects. This will require a new model of strategic management within the organization, in which strategy at the top level is "deployed" down to the operational units so that each unit understands its role in reaching critical strategic goals and understands why these goals are considered critical. The T-UBT process in Southern California took a promising approach to this challenge when it gave each team the task of reaching specified regional goals, but generalizing such top-to-bottom linkages for all the operating units will require a far more radical change in Kaiser's strategy process.

Another lesson is the fundamental difference between UBTs and many of the earlier examples of joint work. In the new UBTs, workers and union officials are present at the earliest stages, when problems are being defined. In the past, they were sometimes recruited to work on problems that management had already identified and to which it developed initial responses. This difference poses significant challenges to the standard leadership practices of many lower-level managers.

UBTs open the organization to a variety of process innovations that can improve efficiency, quality, and patient satisfaction through changes to operational policies. These critical dimensions in the production function for the delivery of medical service represent an agenda for joint work with big potential gains. However, even the limited experience to date reveals that capturing these potential gains requires a considerable investment in resources, such as time to engage in team activities, budgets for backfill and overtime, and time and budget for training and facilitation assistance. Partnership on the front lines requires considerable up-front investment before the payoff materializes.

Training is a crucial part of this up-front investment. Bringing union representatives up to speed on budget and performance information is a major challenge that must be faced. Worker representatives would often be teamed with people who had significant experience in finance or other specialized functions. As one medical director put it, "Two or three days of training is not enough."

Finally, UBTs will typically have to confront the challenges of representative participation. Although UBTs were initially to be composed of natural work groups—a type of committee of the whole—this proved impractical and a representative model emerged. But experience suggests that representatives face major role challenges in communicating with others in the department who are not members of the team.

Unless carefully managed, representative teams can create divisions between participants and non-participants in the larger group, leading to resentment and disconnects. One labor representative serving on a joint committee that pre-dated UBTs noted that management wanted information kept confidential. "We weren't allowed to talk about anything that was going on," he said. "And this blows up really big, because I was reporting back to the union. Then [word] came down to the manager whose reaction was, 'Don't you go saying anything to folks without talking to me first.'" Partnership on the front lines represents a deep challenge not just to management leadership practices, but to union democracy as well.

CHAPTER 11

Scorecard

From the start, partnership leaders have sought to build measurement and evaluation into the effort. Indeed, one of the first committees formed in 1997 was the metrics committee; in 2008, resources continued to be dedicated to substantive, quantitative evaluation of the partnership.[1] In this chapter we present the best data available within and across regions to assess progress to date in some of the major indicators related to goals established in the 1997 partnership agreement. None of these measures are available in a useful way for the time period prior to the creation of the partnership and, for the most part, the data for the latter years are very spotty.

We present results for the following partnership goals: improving the quality of health care; achieving and maintaining market-leading competitive performance; making Kaiser a better place to work; expanding Kaiser membership; providing Kaiser employees with employment and income security; and involving employees and their unions in decisions.[2]

Though it proved very difficult to collect process and outcome measures, particularly at the department and facility level, we are able to offer some conclusions, based on the data and surveys that have been conducted. Most significant, the partnership has had some positive impact on patients and a greater impact on how employees view their jobs and Kaiser as a place to get health care. Employee views of the partnership's positive effect on the quality of health care correlate with the assessments of Kaiser clients. Those regions where the partnership gained the most traction showed the most improvement; workers involved in partnership activities reported more positive views of their working conditions than those not involved. Other findings are clear, but not necessarily causal. For example, Kaiser is more financially successful than it was before the partnership, but we cannot definitively say that this improved performance is due to the partnership.

The root cause of the difficulty in clearly quantifying the partnership's effects lies in the decentralized tradition, culture, and structures of Kaiser. There was no single set of metrics to which everyone at Kaiser was held accountable. No one in either the Kaiser Federation or the Permanente Medical Groups had the power to compel everyone to provide common data to a single central body or functional group. Thus, it is not surprising that efforts to collect common performance data encountered great cultural and political barriers.

Consider the example of improving attendance. Though this was identified in 2002 as a high priority item for the partnership, regions tracked attendance differently, if at all. By early 2004, labor and management leaders on the National Attendance Committee had agreed to a common definition for measuring attendance (absenteeism), but a year later, only one region was able to collect data using this definition. And even that region remained unable to incorporate the results into their reports. Even when attendance became a central issue in the 2005 national negotiations, implementation of a new approach to the problem that was included in the contract was delayed in part because of the inability of the regional information systems to provide common data.

Similarly, the metrics committee identified workforce measures for the goal of "employment security," which included the number of represented employees redeployed, retrained, voluntarily and involuntarily laid off, and retired because of job elimination or reclassification. As of 2007, these critical variables were still not being reported by human resource departments in the different regions.

Efforts to relate the level of implementation of the partnership to various outcome measures were also difficult. A survey of facilities was undertaken by the Office of Labor-Management Partnership in late 2003 and early 2004 to determine the level of partnership involvement at Kaiser facilities, medical centers, and regional departments. Although useful results were obtained for some regions, others did not participate or participated in ways that made the information less useful. Facilities without basic partnership structures were far less likely to fill out the questionnaire. The Mid-Atlantic states and Georgia regions had minimal participation because their partnership leaders felt partnership was not "sufficiently advanced" to measure in their facilities. Southern California opted to complete the survey at the service area level, masking significant facility, medical center, and departmental variation.

Regions had a strong desire to customize survey questions, measurement tools, and other processes to meet their particular needs, and were often allowed to do so. Although this built support for measurement initiatives, it also undermined the ability to create standard, program-wide measures that were directly comparable to one another and needed for quantitative analyses. In 2007, all Kaiser regions agreed to use the same employee survey instrument and to have a unified approach to its administration. This action indicated a gradual shift toward more consistent and coordinated measurement within the organization.

While that new capacity may eventually produce more complete information, we had to rely on four main sources of data. First, we used Kaiser's internal employee survey, known as the People Pulse. Even though prior to 2007 People Pulse had not been administered evenly across the regions, many of the core questions had been standardized, thereby providing better consistency and trends than is the case for many other measures. Second, we used surveys the union coalition conducted of its members (see chapter 7 for more details). One of these surveys, conducted in 1998, was intended to be a baseline; another in early 2005 was conducted as the coalition headed into bargaining. Both of these surveys included questions regarding Kaiser performance and job satisfaction and provided useful additional information. Third, we drew on a survey we conducted of local union presidents in 2005: leaders of fifteen coalition locals covering about 85 percent of the coalition worker membership responded. Fourth, we report some aggregate quality, financial, grievance, and safety data drawn from either public sources or Kaiser's internal reports.

Improving the Quality of Health Care

Quality health care can be disaggregated into two dimensions. The first is clinical quality, which is the quality of the actual care provided and the health outcomes associated with that care. The second is service quality, or the satisfaction of patients and members with Kaiser health care experiences, such as access to care providers as well as politeness of the staff and doctors encountered. These dimensions, both of which were important to health plan members, were tracked within Kaiser and benchmarked externally.

Clinical Quality

One standard tool for measuring clinical quality is the Healthcare Effectiveness Data and Information Set (HEDIS), which is administered by the National Committee for Quality Assurance (NCQA) and is used by 90 percent of U.S. health plans. "HEDIS consists of 71 measures across 8 domains of care," including Effectiveness of Care (factors such as appropriate screenings and immunizations) and Access to Care, which are self-reported by the health care provider.[3] The specific measures included in HEDIS change regularly, which makes it difficult to determine significant trends. Table 11.1 presents a summary measure of HEDIS indicators from 2000 to 2006: the percentage of HEDIS Effectiveness of Care measures for commercial plan members (as opposed to Medicare) at the 75th percentile for all health plans. NCQA reports the percentile scores for its national database and Kaiser looks at both the 75th percentile and the 90th percentiles in its internal reporting. The current organizational targets for many specific HEDIS measures are at the 90th percentile but the Office of Labor-Management Partnership, reflecting earlier organizational practice, used the 75th percentile as its benchmark.

As is evident, there was variety in the performance of Kaiser's regions and no consistent trends across the regions. For instance, comparing the start and end points, Northern California improved substantially, whereas Ohio

Table 11.1. HEDIS Commercial Quality Measures at 75th Percentile, 2000–2004 (percent)

Region	2006[a]	2005[a]	2004	2003	2002	2001	2000
Colorado	67	69	78	72	70	83	86
Georgia	51	53	62	59	63	60	63
Mid-Atlantic	40	67	60	47	60	60	52
Northern California	65	72	68	63	57	53	41
Northwest	63	64	65	59	70	67	75
Ohio	28	36	30	38	40	37	54
Southern California	56	44	65	50	60	60	67

Source: Unless indicated otherwise, the data in each of the tables and figures in this chapter were provided by the Kaiser Permanente Office of Labor Management Partnership.

[a]2005 (based on 36 individual indicators) and 2006 (based on 43 individual indicators) were calculated by the authors and may not be trendable with earlier years.

went downhill. (It is worth noting that in 2007, NCQA rated all Kaiser regions as "Excellent" overall for commercial members.) Table 11.2 provides a longer trend for a single measure for illustrative purposes, using the "raw" rather than benchmarked data for screening for cervical cancer, one of many HEDIS measures, which the partnership could reasonably be expected to improve. This time we also included Hawaii, a non-partnership region, as a point of comparison. Despite some bouncing around in some regions, including Hawaii, an overall, gentle upward trend in this particular measure can be seen across the time periods reported.

These aggregate data would provide a more meaningful test of the effects of the partnership if the partnership had spread to the point where all or at least a significant majority of the workforce and work units were engaged in partnership activities and if we could have controled the myriad of other factors that influence variations in these outcomes. We know that the first is not the case—only about 40 percent of the workforce reported they were engaged in partnership activities in their work units, and at this aggregate level there was no way to control other factors affecting patient outcomes. Below, however, we report results from a more decentralized level of analysis where, for the first time, we were able to collect data that overcome these two problems.

We were able to test for the effects of the partnership on clinical outcomes with one set of data obtained as part of a study our PhD student, Adam Seth Litwin, carried out in the fifteen clinics in Kaiser's Northwest region for 2002 to 2006.[4] He compared units with varying levels of worker involvement in partnership activity and used a statistical procedure (called "fixed effects regression analysis") that controls for all other non-partnership factors, affecting outcomes across these units. Figure 11.1 reports the results

Table 11.2. One HEDIS Measure: Cervical Cancer Screening (percent of members receiving), every three years, 1997–2006

Region	2006	2003	2000	1997
Colorado	84.5	81.2	85.9	79.7
Georgia	94.2	91.8	84.5	79.0
Hawaii	74.6	80.5	82.2	76.5
Mid-Atlantic	82.2	84.4	85.1	81.7
Northern California	82.3	80.4	80.3	78.5
Northwest	80.5	85.6	83.0	80.4
Ohio	77.2	79.6	80.3	77.4
Southern California	82.1	80.5	80.0	76.4

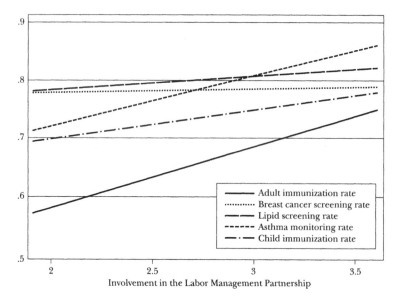

Figure 11.1. Effects of worker involvement in partnership activities on clinical outcomes
Source: Adam Seth Litwin, "Quantifying the Link from Partnership to Performance at Kaiser Permanente," MIT Institute for Work and Employment Research Working Paper, January 2008, available at http://mitsloan.mit.edu/iwer/workingpapers.

of Litwin's analysis of the relationship between worker involvement in the partnership, measured on a five-point scale, and five clinical outcomes. The measure of worker involvement comes from the People Pulse survey question, "I am personally involved in the structures or activities that are a part of the Labor-Management Partnership." The clinical outcomes are (1) adult immunization rates, (2) asthma monitoring rates, (3) breast cancer screening rates, (4) child immunization rates, and (5) lipid screening rates. The trend lines in figure 11.1 track the effects of increases in worker involvement in the partnership on each of these patient outcomes. All five clinical outcomes improved with more partnership activity and the upward trends in three of the five outcomes are statistically significant. Translating the statistical results into practical terms, the results indicate that a one-point increase in the average People Pulse involvement score in a unit (for example, moving from an average response of two to an average response of three on the five-point scale) increased the adult immunization rates by 10 percent, the asthma monitoring rate by 9 percent, and the lipid screening rate by 2 percent.

Although limited to one region, these results indicate that higher levels of employee engagement in partnership activities were associated with improvements in several key clinical outcomes. We view these as only preliminary results that should be interpreted with caution. Although the statistical technique used here does control for other factors that may be associated with cross-clinic performance differences, we are hesitant to make the argument that all of these improvements were *caused* by increased partnership engagement. The bottom line is that these are the first data establishing a clear quantitative association between partnership activities and clinical outcomes. It would be useful to have such data available in more units.

Service Quality

One of the dimensions of HEDIS is "satisfaction with the experience of care," measured in large part by the CAHPS (Consumer Assessment of Healthcare of Providers and Systems) survey of health plan members.[5] CAHPS includes questions about access to care, doctor communications, compassionate and courteous staff, and customer service. It is the most inclusive of all Kaiser service quality surveys because the sample frame is all current members. Below, we present two different tables with CAHPS data. Because of changes in the question mix and in question wording over time, it is not possible to provide a trend for a summary measure of CAHPS. It is, however, possible to establish trends in a couple of specific questions. Table 11.3 shows the trend in percentage of plan members answering 8, 9, or 10 to the question: "Using any number from 0 to 10, where 0 is the worst health care possible and 10 is the best health care possible, what number would you use to rate all your health care in the last 12 months?" The bottom two rows show the scores at each of two percentiles derived from NCQA's national database—these are Kaiser's benchmarks. While Kaiser improved fairly steadily in most regions, the organization's scores remained below the 50th percentile (which is not shown) in almost all regions in all years. Kaiser was well aware of its poor performance on this crucial metric, which was why most of the initial unit-based teams focused on improving service quality, along with their other goals. Table 11.4 presents organization-wide results for one dimension of service, "Courteous and Helpful Staff," that can be tracked for a slightly longer period given the consistency in questions and answer categories. The measure is a composite of two questions; the results presented are for the top two answers ("usually" and "always"). There is no clear trend upward across the regions on this particular measure.

Table 11.3. CAHPS Scores, Overall Rating of Health Plan, 2000–2006 (percent)

Region	2006	2005	2004	2003	2002	2001	2000
Colorado	76	71	75	68	67	66	62
Georgia	73	70	75	73	70	69	73
Mid-Atlantic	67	69	69	65	65	63	65
Northern California	76	75	70	67	65	64	66
Northwest	72	73	70	73	64	69	63
Ohio	77	74	76	76	72	69	70
Southern California	74	73	68	68	67	65	64
90th percentile	84	83	82	82	80	79	78
75th percentile	81	81	80	79	78	76	75

Table 11.4. CAHPS Scores, Courteous and Helpful Office Staff Composite, 2000–2006 (percent)

Region	2006	2005	2004	2003	2002	2001	2000
Colorado	92	93	93	92	91	91	90
Georgia	92	91	92	92	92	92	94
Mid-Atlantic	86	89	90	90	89	89	90
Northern California	92	92	91	90	88	89	90
Northwest	93	93	94	94	92	92	93
Ohio	94	93	93	93	95	93	93
Southern California	90	92	90	88	90	97	89

It is also instructive to look at how Kaiser workers and union leaders view Kaiser's quality performance, especially because most Kaiser workers get their own medical care through Kaiser. Figure 11.2 presents evidence of a link between 2003 HEDIS measures and the "Care Experience Index" as measured in the 2003 People Pulse survey. The actual questions in the index are listed in table 11.5. This index includes questions that are, for the most part, direct or indirect indicators of worker perceptions of the quality of the service and the health care offered by Kaiser. Note the correlation at the regional level between the HEDIS percentages from table 11.1 and the employee service results from table 11.4. Although the sample size is of necessity small, the connection between employee perceptions of care and the HEDIS indicators is strong. Scores on the Care Experience Index are also highly correlated with other aspects of worker satisfaction, such as the degree of involvement in decision making in their units. This is another indicator that worker engagement and partnership activities can affect service

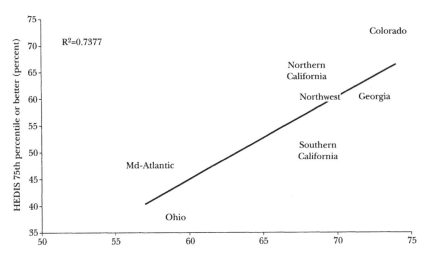

Figure 11.2. Correlation between HEDIS and employee perceptions of the care experience, 2003

Table 11.5. Employee Survey Results: Care Experience Index, 1998–2006 (percent)[a]

Region	2006	2005	2004	2003	2002	2001	2000	1999	1998
Union-represented employee scores[b]									
Colorado			74	68	67	61	54	47	49
Mid-Atlantic			62	56	58	58	52	N/A	54
Northern California	68	67	69	67	63	56	47	N/A	47
Northwest			66	67	62	61	58	52	N/A
Ohio			62	56	57	59	55	44	52
Southern California	66	65	67	66	60	56	55	N/A	55
Managerial employee scores									
Colorado			92	92	92	89	82	76	80
Mid-Atlantic			74	68	69	71	55	N/A	53
Northern California	85	86	87	85	82	77	59	N/A	64
Northwest			82	86	84	87	81	76	N/A
Ohio			78	72	70	72	71	62	67
Southern California	85	85	84	85	83	79	77	N/A	74

[a]Care Experience Index = percent responding favorably to the following ten questions:
I would recommend KP to a close friend as a good place to get health care.
I understand how my work fits into the goals of the organization.
Our leaders are committed to making customer satisfaction a high priority in the organization.
The physicians in my work unit support me in providing quality service to our customers.
In general, I am supported to do what is necessary to satisfy customers.
Day-to-day decisions and activities in the organization demonstrate that quality is a top priority.
How much do you know about the goals of your department?
I receive training that helps me give good service to customers.
The organization does a good job of letting me know what's going on.
In general, how much say or influence do you have over decisions affecting your work?
[b]Northern and Southern California, partnership unions represented only.

quality: partnership and teams enable workers to influence the care delivery process; worker influence leads to higher satisfaction with the quality of care delivered; higher worker satisfaction with the quality of care delivered correlates with higher patient satisfaction.

Trend data for the People Pulse survey "Care Experience Index" also contain interesting findings. Table 11.5 presents the results from 1998 to 2004 for most regions and 2006 for the California regions. Because union members and managers tend to have substantially different viewpoints, these two groups are presented in two separate tables. The managers' survey results are dominated by first- and second-level managers; the union members included in the first table are represented by partnership unions. Three things are worth noting. First, managers consistently held more positive perceptions of Kaiser than union members. Second, variation occurred across the regions, with Colorado workers being the most positive in the later years. Third, a steady upward trajectory in worker views of the "care experience" can be noted for the first several years of the partnership, although that trend appears to have leveled in the regions for which we have recent data.

These results are reinforced by the coalition survey of members done at the beginning of the partnership in 1998 and again shortly before national bargaining in 2005 (table 11.6). The percentage of union members feeling positive about the quality of care at Kaiser reached 89 percent by 2005. Furthermore, the perception that the partnership has been good for quality of care grew from 68 percent to 78 percent over the seven-year period.

Table 11.6. Union Coalition Survey Results Regarding Quality of Care, 1998 and 2005 (percent)

	2005	1998
Quality of care was good or excellent	89	73
Would recommend KP as a good place to get care (agree/strongly agree)	90	74
LMP is good for quality of care (agree/strongly agree)[a]	78	68

Source: Coalition of Kaiser Permanente Unions.
[a]1998 question was prospective ("LMP will have a positive impact") rather than retrospective.

Finally, table 11.7 presents results from the survey of local union presidents. Looking at the measures listed under "Health Care Operations," union leaders were moderately positive about the impact of the partnership on quality and clearly more positive than they were about its impact on other outcomes discussed below.

Taken together, these data suggest that the partnership was having a positive effect on key clinical (patient) outcomes in units where there was significant partnership activity. The challenge ahead is to continue to expand the reach of partnership activities on the front line to more units. That task is being addressed by the unit-based teams discussed in chapter 10.

Table 11.7. Union Leaders Survey, 2005: Evaluation of Partnership Effectiveness on Organizational Performance

Has the LMP been effective in making significant improvements in the following areas:	Mean
Health Care Operations	
Cost Structure Improvement	3.50
Quality of Care	3.43
Attendance	2.77
Working Conditions and Environment	
Workplace Safety	3.67
Less Authoritarian Work Environment	3.20
Less Stressful Work Environment	3.07
Job and Employment Security	
Job Security	4.33
Enhanced Skill Development	3.64
Workforce Planning	3.07
Union and Employee Involvement	
Increased Decision Making for the Union	3.87
Better Understanding of the Business	3.53
Access to Information	3.33
Increased Worker Responsibility	3.27
Increased Worker Decision Making	3.13
Influence over the Introduction of New Technology	3.07

Source: Coalition of Kaiser Permanente Unions.
Note: 5=very effective; 1=not effective.

Achieve and Maintain Market Leading Competitive Performance

Operating Margins

We know Kaiser's overall financial performance improved consistently since the beginning of the partnership. However, due to data limitations, we cannot determine what causal role, if any, was played by the partnership. As the data in table 11.8 indicate, financial performance improved across all of Kaiser's regions, most impressively in California. These results clearly reflect a number of factors and demonstrate that it is possible to improve financial performance while working in partnership. But as with other indicators, it is necessary to look at the results of specific partnership efforts to improve financial performance. A number of examples from Southern California, Ohio, and Northern California have been summarized in prior chapters. Here we draw on People Pulse data to get a view from employees engaged in partnership efforts.

Cost Reduction Efforts

Since 2001, the People Pulse survey included a question asking employees about efforts by their department or work unit to reduce costs. About two-thirds of union members reported such efforts in the baseline year and most regions showed a modest but steady increase in this number through 2004. Managers again reported higher levels of effort. Table 11.9 tells us that union leaders saw the partnership as modestly effective in dealing with cost issues.

Table 11.8. Operating Margin (percent)

Region	2005 (October)	2004	2003	2002	2001	2000	1999	1998
Colorado	0.6	2.7	6.6	4.5	3.1	4.8	2.4	−1.7
Georgia	0.4	1.2	1.7	1.4	4.0	1.9	0.9	1.9
Mid-Atlantic	2.7	1.7	0.0	−1.4	−1.4	−2.8	−1.2	0.7
Northern California	4.0	5.4	3.6	2.8	3.9	3.4	2.4	−3.2
Northwest	3.9	5.3	4.2	5.7	2.4	3.0	0.7	0.6
Ohio	5.0	−0.3	2.1	0.0	1.0	2.3	2.4	4.2
Southern California	5.1	6.6	5.1	3.3	4.7	4.4	2.5	−3.5

Table 11.9. Employee Survey Results: "My department or work unit seeks improvements in an effort to reduce costs," 2001–2006 (percent)

Region	2006	2005	2004	2003	2002	2001
Union-represented employee scores[a]						
Colorado			74	69	67	65
Mid-Atlantic			62	59	59	64
Northern California	69	66	70	70	65	61
Northwest			72	73	71	69
Ohio			74	65	66	67
Southern California	67	65	70	68	61	59
Managerial employee scores, 2001–2006						
Colorado			92	92	89	86
Mid-Atlantic			79	73	79	82
Northern California	89	87	88	91	85	83
Northwest			86	93	90	90
Ohio			82	83	84	87
Southern California	88	88	89	87	84	85

[a]Northern and Southern California, partnership unions represented only.

Make Kaiser a Better Place to Work

Wages and Benefits

Given that the union coalition initially came together to resist wage and benefit concessions forced by Kaiser one local at a time, an important coalition goal was to return to and maintain industry-leading compensation levels. The coalition was quite successful in that regard. In preparation for the 2005 bargaining, Kaiser hired Watson Wyatt, a consulting firm, to evaluate coalition member salary and benefit levels against those of specific competitor health care institutions in each Kaiser region. Wyatt found that Kaiser was paying above market for almost all occupations in all regions, except for Northern California, where Kaiser's base (though not total) compensation across several health care occupations was a bit below market. The margin above the market was even greater for non–health care occupations. Although the coalition rejected some of Watson Wyatt's findings, arguing that it had used the wrong comparators, most labor leaders agreed with the basic message of these data: over the first decade of the partnership's existence, Kaiser regained and maintained its position as a market leader in compensation and benefits.

Survey Results

The People Pulse survey did not ask any direct job satisfaction questions until 2007. The closest question to gauging worker sentiment about working conditions and the work environment was, "I would recommend Kaiser as a good place to work." Although the distribution of answers differed among the regions, there was significant improvement in every region since the start of the partnership (see table 11.10). As with almost every People Pulse question, managers reported higher scores than did union members in most regions. This is consistent with job satisfaction surveys in other organizations, where managers nearly always score higher than professionals and hourly employees. The regions where this was not always true were those that struggled financially and whose survival had sometimes been doubtful.

The union coalition survey shows similar results (see table 11.11). Overall job satisfaction—were respondents satisfied or very satisfied with their jobs— rose from 74 percent in 1998 to 91 percent in 2005. Despite continuing difficulties in joint staffing initiatives and anecdotal evidence to the contrary, satisfaction with workload showed a similar improvement. Other specific measures of satisfaction showed significant gains (e.g., training for job) whereas others were flat (respect and relationships with co-workers).[6] Overall, Kaiser workers appeared increasingly satisfied. Interestingly, in 1998, about 60 per-

Table 11.10. Employee Survey Results: "I would recommend KP as a good place to work," 1998–2006 (percent)

Region	2006	2005	2004	2003	2002	2001	2000	1999	1998
Union-represented employee scores[a]									
Colorado			85	81	82	72	57	48	N/A
Mid-Atlantic			70	60	70	65	55	N/A	60
Northern California	85	85	85	81	77	68	56	N/A	52
Northwest			79	79	72	72	66	56	N/A
Ohio			67	74	68	74	66	48	53
Southern California	83	83	83	81	76	71	65	N/A	58
Managerial employee scores, 1999–2006									
Colorado			97	97	96	95	89	87	
Mid-Atlantic			74	61	69	68	38	N/A	
Northern California	90	92	92	89	90	83	69	N/A	
Northwest			82	89	90	92	81	79	
Ohio			85	74	60	72	72	39	
Southern California	91	92	92	90	89	85	86	N/A	

[a]Northern and Southern California, partnership unions represented only.

Table 11.11. CKPU Survey Results, Job Satisfaction Indicators, 1998 and 2005 (percent)

	2005	1998
Job satisfaction (satisfied or very satisfied)		
Overall	**91**	**74**
Relationships with co-workers	93	94
Policies that allow work-family balance	87	79
Respect from supervisor	80	76
Training for job	83	74
Workload	75 ˙	59
Would stay in current job if you could get the same pay and benefits elsewhere	73	56
Would advise a child/friend/relative to work at Kaiser (definitely or probably yes)	93	82
LMP has had positive impact on (agree or strongly agree)		
Working conditions[a]	59	61
Workplace safety	64	N/A

Source: Coalition of Kaiser Permanente Unions.
[a]1998 question was prospective ("LMP will have a positive impact") rather than retrospective.

cent felt that the partnership *would* improve working conditions, and, in 2005, 59 percent indicated that they had, in fact, seen a positive impact. Two-thirds of employees thought the partnership had a positive impact on safety, thus corresponding with the actual improvement in injury rates and worker compensation costs reported in chapter 4.

Grievance Rates

Grievance rates are a complex, though potentially important, indicator of the overall state of labor relations. Grievance rates may reflect individual or collective worker discontent in the workplace, borne of poor management or organizational issues; concerted effort by the union to put pressure on management, often in the context of collective bargaining; or some combination of these factors. Grievance rates are important, because they reflect underlying organizational problems and also because they can be costly. For example, studies of General Motors plants and paper mills have found strong and negative relationships between grievance rates and plant-level quality and productivity.[7] In both of those studies, grievance rates were correlated with and possibly served as indicators of the overall quality of labor-management relations; that is, they were correlated with employee attitudes/relationships with supervisors, discipline rates, and length of time needed to negotiate new labor contracts.

Labor-management partnerships frequently experience lower grievance rates through a variety of mechanisms. These may include revisions to collective bargaining agreements that increase managerial flexibility and reduce the numbers of rules violations and related grievances, improved supervision, improved communication between union representatives and managers, formal and informal problem solving by union and management, and reduced union effort in pursuing grievances.[8] The Kaiser partnership included two core processes that could be expected to reduce grievances: issue resolution and corrective action. Both processes were originally negotiated in 2000 and continued to be part of the national collective bargaining agreement. The processes were intended to be used in tandem, with the latter focused on a non-punitive, corrective approach to individual employee performance problems that, in a traditional relationship, often would lead to discipline. The former was defined by the parties as "a system for raising and quickly resolving workplace issues using interest-based problem solving by those directly involved in the issue."[9]

Table 11.12 presents Step 3 (the highest level, short of arbitration) grievance rates from 1998 to 2005 for both partnership and non-partnership unions. There was a steady and substantial system-wide decrease (23 percent) in Step 3 grievance rates for partnership unions over this period. This overall trend masked continued variation across regions, including regions that did not experience a consistent or sustained decline (Colorado had a low rate and the mid-Atlantic region had a high rate). The large California regions, which dominate the program-wide averages, experienced fairly steady declines in grievance rates for *both* partner and non-partner unions, suggesting that either a spillover of the partnership effect or something else was responsible for the reductions. Either some factor outside the partnership was driving down grievances or the improvement in the labor relations climate driven by the partnership carried over to manager interactions with non-partnership unions. Finally, it is interesting to note that, contrary to what is typically the case, there was no spike in most regions in grievances in the negotiations years of 2000 or 2005. The spike in 2000 in Northern California may reflect the fact that CNA (not a member of the partnership) was also in negotiations with Kaiser that year.

Table 11.12. Step 3 Grievance Rates, 1998–2005 (percent)

	2005	2004	2003	2002	2001	2000	1999	1998
Partner Unions								
Colorado	4.5	4.2	1.7	1.5	0.7	4.1	2.3	1.8
Georgia	8.9	11.4	14.1	0.0	N/A	N/A	N/A	N/A
Mid-Atlantic	13.3	22.3	16.0	16.1	15.5	7.6	7.5	20.2
Northern California	4.2	5.3	6.7	3.5	2.3	8.0	8.2	7.2
Northwest	4.6	4.5	4.0	8.6	7.7	7.7	16.7	22.4
Ohio	5.6	2.0	3.1	5.0	5.0	8.5	7.5	N/A
Southern California	5.3	7.0	7.3	9.0	12.1	16.6	15.0	20.7
Program	**5.3**	**6.9**	**7.1**	**6.9**	**7.9**	**11.9**	**11.7**	**14.9**
Change from previous year	−23.0	−3.0	3.0	−12.0	−33.0	1.0	−21.0	
Non-Partner Unions								
NCAL	0.3	0.8	0.7	1.1	3.8	8.7	4.5	6.2
NW	0.0	0.0	0.0	14.7	2.6	5.6	10.8	3.6
OH	0.0	0.0	12.5	16.7	0.0	0.0	24.4	N/A
SCAL	4.2	1.5	4.5	2.6	4.7	7.5	10.4	18.5
Program	**0.6**	**0.9**	**2.0**	**2.3**	**3.9**	**7.9**	**4.8**	**6.6**

Finally, we present union leaders' perceptions of the effectiveness of the partnership in improving working conditions. Returning to table 11.7, we see that union leaders rated the effectiveness of the partnership in improving workplace safety high compared to most other outcomes, including the more day-to-day issues related to work environment.

Expand Kaiser Membership in Current and New Markets

Increasing Kaiser's market share was a key goal of the partnership. But though of vital concern to both management and labor, joint marketing efforts were slow to develop. As with many aspects of the partnership, there were many small-scale, local success stories that did not translate into a larger trend. Table 11.13 presents overall changes in Kaiser's "Commercial Membership" (the non-Medicare portion of Kaiser plan members) by region, from 1998 to 2005. In 2007, Kaiser's customers, management, and union leaders generally agreed that the prices of Kaiser's health plans were not competitive and were becoming even less competitive over time. Both labor and management leaders of the partnership were fully engaged in figuring out how best to respond. Some regions engaged in joint cost-cutting efforts,

Table 11.13. Commercial Membership Growth, 1998–2005 (percent)

Region	2005 (October)	2004	2003	2002	2001	2000	1999	1998
Colorado	8.4	3.0	2.0	−1.2	9.4	1.1	−1.5	6.6
Georgia	6.5	−3.1	−2.2	0.8	1.9	1.9	1.2	3.4
Mid-Atlantic	0.6	−2.0	−2.9	−1.7	−3.3	1.5	−1.6	−0.6
Northern California	1.7	−0.4	−1.6	2.1	2.5	1.9	2.5	4.7
Northwest	5.2	4.6	−3.1	−0.6	−1.6	2.7	0.1	3.4
Ohio	1.9	−1.3	−7.4	−5.1	−4.6	−7.5	−8.7	−4.2
Southern California	1.9	−0.5	−2.6	1.6	2.8	0.8	2.8	7.9

while all regions pinned their hopes on the implementation of unit-based teams to improve the quality of care, cut costs, and increase revenue. However, expanding overall membership and capturing more of the new market opportunities remain challenges for Kaiser and the partnership.

Provide Employees with Employment and Income Security

Economic security is of central importance to all workers, and given Kaiser's performance problems, this was especially true for Kaiser workers when the partnership was formed. A decade earlier, unions had struggled with the distinction between job security (protection of the worker's current job at the current employer) versus employment security (broader employability within the employer organization or the industry). As described in chapter 3, the Kaiser union coalition struck middle ground early on by seeking guarantees of redeployments within Kaiser, rather than guarantees of existing jobs. The coalition also saw that such security would be facilitated by a comprehensive workforce development program that included workforce planning and individual skill building. Various survey results presented below address these aspects of employment security.

Kaiser held to its employment security guarantees, laying off no partnership union members for several years, though occasionally redeploying individuals or small groups, especially due to the implementation of Health-Connect. This is reflected in the results of the Kaiser employee survey (table 11.14) and the coalition's member survey (table 11.15). Note that both of these surveys reference "job" rather than "employment" security.

The People Pulse question about job security produced some of the survey's most positive results. The results improved significantly after the question was first asked in 1999, reflecting Kaiser's adherence to the employment security agreement, even in the face of budget crises that occurred in some

Table 11.14. Employee Survey Results: "KP offers a level of job security as good or better than job security in most other health care organizations" (percent)

Region	2006	2005	2004	2003	2002	2001	2000	1999
Union-represented employee responses, 1999–2006[a]								
Colorado			88	84	84	77	63	44
Mid-Atlantic			71	60	68	63	54	N/A
Northern California	87	88	89	87	85	77	67	N/A
Northwest			79	79	73	71	68	53
Ohio			60	44	57	68	61	36
Southern California	85	86	86	86	83	79	72	N/A
Managerial employee responses, 1999–2006								
Colorado			94	96	93	94	84	69
Mid-Atlantic			64	44	56	61	39	N/A
Northern California	90	92	91	90	90	86	69	N/A
Northwest			68	85	81	87	80	70
Ohio			76	54	48	66	67	21
Southern California	92	93	93	90	92	90	82	N/A

Source: Coalition of Kaiser Permanente Unions.

[a]Northern and Southern California, partnership unions represented only.

Table 11.15. CKPU Survey Results, Income and Employment Security Indicators (percent)

Job satisfaction (satisfied or very satisfied)	2005	1998
Income Security		
Wages	78	56
Benefits	92	75
Employment Security		
Job security	93	74
Ability to advance	73	55

Source: Coalition of Kaiser Permanente Unions.

regions. This is one metric where there was little difference in recent years between union member and manager responses. The coalition member survey showed similar advances in the levels of satisfaction with job security and a related concept, "ability to advance."

Union leaders also gave the partnership the highest grade for any item on the list for its impact on job security (see table 11.7). Union leaders also gave the partnership relatively high marks for improving skill development for the workforce, but a much lower rating for workforce planning, both of which received more attention in the two years after the 2005 negotiations (and after this survey) were completed. That contract included workforce development language and a training trust fund.

Involve Employees and Unions in Decisions

Another original partnership goal was increased involvement by employees and union. Table 11.16 presents the results of a People Pulse question about individual employee involvement in the partnership, beginning when the question was first posed in 1999 in some regions. Although there was some variation across regions, we see steady growth in the proportion of positive answers. Roughly twice as many managerial employees reported participation. Table 11.17 sets a higher bar, looking at the degree to which employees felt they had a say or influence in decisions affecting their work. The results for union members—in fact, for all employees—remained among the lowest on the entire People Pulse survey. Nevertheless, we see a substantial increase in most regions.

The union coalition survey results were very similar (table 11.18). Substantially higher percentages of workers reported having a say over how work was

Table 11.16. Employee Survey Results: "I am personally involved in the structures or activities of the LMP," 1999–2006 (percent)

Region	2006	2005	2004	2003	2002	2001	2000	1999
Union-represented employee responses (favorable)[a]								
Colorado	N/A	N/A	41	41	31	24	16	13
Mid-Atlantic	N/A	N/A	35	34	31	18	14	N/A
Northern California	44	42	40	38	33	25	20	N/A
Northwest	N/A	34	31	31	22	24	22	17
Ohio	N/A	26	21	21	16	22	16	13
Southern California	41	36	40	38	34	29	22	N/A
Managerial employee responses (favorable)								
Colorado	N/A	N/A	84	77	76	64	63	48
Mid-Atlantic	N/A	N/A	63	61	54	40	35	N/A
Northern California	82	79	80	80	69	62	45	N/A
Northwest	N/A	N/A	76	70	64	59	48	49
Ohio	N/A	65	63	63	50	35	38	41
Southern California	79	79	78	74	74	65	45	N/A

Source: KP People Pulse Survey.
[a]Northern and Southern California, partnership unions represented only.

Table 11.17. Employee Survey Results: "In general, how much say or influence do you have over decisions affecting your work?" 1998–2006 (percent)

Region	2006	2005	2004	2003	2002	2001–02	2000	1999	1998
Union-represented employee responses ("a great deal" or "quite a bit")[a]									
Colorado			38	33	33	30	23	17	17
Mid-Atlantic			24	21	24	22	21	N/A	28
Northern California	33	32	32	31	27	23	18	N/A	32
Northwest			32	33	28	27	24	24	N/A
Ohio			22	17	17	16	16	12	27
Southern California	29	28	31	26	22	22	21	N/A	30
Managerial employee responses ("a great deal" or "quite a bit")									
Colorado			89	89	88	86	78	78	
Mid-Atlantic			68	60	65	62	55	N/A	
Northern California	75	75	75	76	71	66	59	N/A	
Northwest			83	84	85	88	80	82	
Ohio			76	63	57	65	71	56	
Southern California	76	77	73	75	76	73	64	N/A	

Source: KP People Pulse Survey.
[a]Northern and Southern California, partnership unions represented only.

Table 11.18. Union Coalition Survey Results, Employee Involvement, 1998 and 2005 (percent)

	1998	2005
Satisfaction with (satisfied or very satisfied)		
Say over how work is done	70	82
Being kept informed about policies and decisions	54	69
LMP has helped give me a large role in decision making (agree or strongly agree)[a]	42	50

Source: Coalition of Kaiser Permanente Unions.
[a]1998 question was prospective ("LMP will help give me a larger role") rather than retrospective.

done and being kept informed of policies and decisions in 2005 than in 1998. There was similar growth in the numbers crediting the partnership with improving their role in decision making, although the percentage answering that question positively remained at only 50 percent in 2005. This reflected the difficulties in bringing the partnership to the front lines discussed in other chapters.

Linking Partnership and Other Outcomes

These reported results do not definitively establish the success of the partnership in achieving its stated goals. And the wide array of measurement problems noted earlier makes it impossible to present a quantitatively compelling story for the effects of the partnership across Kaiser or for all workers covered by the partnership agreement. At the same time, a more disaggregated look at survey data, comparing employees who were involved with the partnership with those who were not, lends credibility to the case for partnership.

Table 11.19 presents results for one year of the Kaiser employee People Pulse survey for partnership union members only, with the results divided by involvement in the partnership. The questions are ordered by the degree of gap between the involved and not involved, shown in the third column. There were differences that are both statistically and substantively significant between these two groups on every question, especially those involving partnership goals that have been the focus of this chapter.

In all cases, workers who were involved in the partnership reported more positive attitudes than those who were not involved. Not surprisingly, the greatest differences were in questions about influence ("management uses employee ideas," "say and influence over decisions") and communication ("Kaiser lets me know what's going on," "trust information from leaders"). However, there were also large gaps in employee views of important organi-

Table 11.19. Employee Attitudes, Comparisons by Involvement in the LMP, 2003–2004 (percent)

Pulse question[a]	Not involved in LMP	Involved in LMP	Gap
Management uses good ideas employees have	28.4	67.4	39.0
Organization lets me know what's going on	32.7	69.8	37.1
Valued in organization for diversity	47.2	81.9	34.7
Can influence decisions affecting work	15.0	48.7	33.7
Decisions/activities demonstrate quality is priority	43.9	77.5	33.6
Trust information from leaders	43.3	75.1	31.8
Opportunities for career growth/development	46.5	76.9	30.4
Work together to ensure safe place to work	52.9	80.8	27.9
Supported to satisfy customers	57.5	83.7	26.2
Department seeks improvement to reduce costs	56.1	81.6	25.5
Recommend KP as place to work	66.5	90.5	24.0
Leaders committed to making customer satisfaction a priority	63.4	85.0	21.6
Recommend KP for health care	70.2	91.2	21.0
KP job security equal to other health care organizations	74.6	93.2	18.6

Note: Results are for employees in partnership unions only.
[a]Percent answering agree or strongly agree.

zational goals, such as "decisions and activities demonstrate quality is an important goal" and "leaders are committed to customer satisfaction."

Although these People Pulse results show a strong relationship between partnership involvement and positive employee attitudes, they do not provide evidence of causation. It could well be that workers with positive attitudes were simply more likely to participate in the partnership. The union coalition survey results allow for a test of this explanation. Table 11.20 presents results from the union survey, dividing workers into three categories: those who reported involvement, those who reported they were not involved but would like to be ("wannabes"), and those who were not involved and did not want to be ("don't wannabes"). If workers with positive attitudes chose to participate in the partnership (a "selection effect"), we would expect the "wannabes" to be very similar to "the involved." Conversely, if the partnership was really improving worker attitudes (a "program effect"), we would

Table 11.20. LMP Involvement and Attitudes toward the Job and KP (percent)

	Very/somewhat involved in LMP($N=920$)	Not involved/ would like to be ($N=214$)	Not involved/ don't want to be ($N=350$)
Job Satisfaction (satisfied or very satisfied)			
Overall	92	87	90
Relationships with co-workers	95	89	91
Job security	94	88	94
Say over how work is done	84	74	82
Respect from supervisor	83	69	79
Workload	77	65	73
Being kept informed about policies and decisions	73	55	68
Would stay in current job if you could get the same pay and benefits elsewhere?	75	65	73
Would advise a child/friend/relative to work at Kaiser?			
Definitely or probably yes	94	88	91
Definitely yes	61	47	49
Quality of Care			
Quality of care was			
Good or excellent	93	87	86
Excellent	48	35	39
Would recommend KP as a good place to get care (agree or strongly agree)	94	87	85

Source: Coalition of Kaiser Permanente Unions.

expect the two categories of not involved employees to be similar to one another *and* to be lower than the involved.

The results provide strong support for a partnership effect with respect to at least some questions. Workers who were involved in the partnership reported greater satisfaction with all the specific dimensions of work listed than the "wannabes." They were also more likely to stay in their jobs, more likely to advise someone close to them to work for Kaiser or to get care from Kaiser, and more likely to report that that care was excellent. Especially important to Kaiser's competitiveness in both the labor and product markets are the findings that workers who had participated in the partnership were more likely to recommend Kaiser as a place to work or receive care.

Summary: The Bottom Line

With other factors undoubtedly also at play, these data demonstrate that employee involvement made a positive difference. Although we cannot conclude that the partnership was responsible for all of the general improvement in Kaiser performance and worker satisfaction that occurred over the first ten years of the partnership, we can see that employees attributed their improved attitudes to the partnership and that Kaiser was successful in managing the partnership and improving important aspects of its performance.

The conclusion from the data we have been able to obtain is that where the partnership was active, it had significant effects on reducing costs, improving workers' views of their jobs and of Kaiser as a place to get health care, and, at least in one region where the data were available, improving clinical performance. Combined with the examples presented throughout this book, these quantitative data illustrate how partnership initiatives contributed to important performance outcomes.

CHAPTER 12

Partnerships:
The Future

As we write this the United States once again appears to be on the brink of trying to address the crises in both labor relations and health care that we used to motivate this study in chapter 2. Thus, it is fitting to use this final chapter to first summarize what we have learned from our study of the largest and most complex labor-management partnership in U.S. history and then to draw out implications for the coming debates over labor policy and health care reform.

Accomplishments

The hardest question to answer is what would have happened at Kaiser if the partnership had not been formed. Absent the partnership, it seems clear that the financial pressures confronting Kaiser in the mid-1990s and at various times since then would likely have led management to continue to impose layoffs, seek wage and/or benefit concessions, and take other unilateral actions, which would have provoked a major confrontation with its unions. Even if labor peace had been somehow maintained, it would have been at the cost of financial and job security losses for the workforce. With reduced morale, employees would have been less committed and willing to accept changes in the future, such as those associated with the introduction of medical records technologies. The partnership's most significant achievement may be that it stopped and reversed the downward spiral in which the parties were caught in the mid-1990s. The partnership produced a decade of labor peace and positioned labor and management to work together to meet the organizational and health care delivery challenges of the day.

Another important accomplishment is the fact that the partnership has survived for over a decade. As noted in chapter 2, although most labor-management partnerships in the United States tend to have short half-lives, this one demonstrated an ability to work through the various pivotal events that come along in the course of partnerships. These pivotal events included negotiation of a comprehensive employment security agreement in response to conflicts over how to restructure operations that were no longer competitive; negotiation of a restructuring plan that both saved and improved the performance of the Northern California Optical Laboratory, which consultants had advised management to close; successful negotiation of three national bargaining agreements after significant concern that national agreements meant threats of national strikes; continuity of the partnership through a controversial CEO transition; response to budget crises in Southern California and several other regions; resolution—or at least a truce—of a bitter inter-union dispute over organizing and raiding of bargaining units involving coalition unions and the California Nurses Association; and a leadership succession from the coalition's initial executive. Any one of these events held the potential for derailing the partnership. But in each case the parties were able to draw on the relationships developed from working together and used their collective skills in negotiations, problem solving, and conflict resolution to work through the various crises.

Labor relations in the day-to-day functioning of the organization improved markedly, as evidenced by the decline in grievance rates and many examples of the effective use of issue resolution tools developed by the parties. Another benefit—harder to measure yet equally if not more important—lies in problems that never grew into actual conflicts because of better communication that had developed between front-line managers and union leaders.

We believe the extensive and creative use of interest-based bargaining in the negotiations of the national-level agreements will be recorded as historic achievements in U.S. labor relations. To date, these are the largest (in terms of number of workers, geographic scope of operations, and number of unions covered) and the most extensive (in terms of range of issues addressed and numbers of participants involved) applications of interest-based bargaining in U.S. labor relations. And though the national bargaining processes required huge financial, human, and organizational resources and support, they concentrated all of the negotiations into a single time frame, rather than requiring Kaiser and its unions to engage in multiple negotiation processes that would have entailed a much higher likelihood of work stoppages.

The partnership was favorably received by a majority of the front-line workforce. A 70 percent majority preferred partnership over a more arm's-length labor-management relationship. Moreover, although only about 40 percent of front-line workers and union members participated directly in partnership activities, those who did so reported higher levels of job satisfaction and influence in decision making than those who did not participate in partnership initiatives. Although diffusion was slow and remained partial as of 2008, that is arguably the nature of change efforts in most large-scale organizations.

The partnership created a capacity for labor and management to jointly resolve new, unexpected challenges, whether it was the opening of a new facility such as Baldwin Park or the restructuring of a troubled facility such as the Optical Lab, or the joint response to financial crises that arose in a particular region. In these and other instances, the parties were able to work together to meet the immediate need. Moreover, with each new challenge, they came out of the experience with more people more deeply committed to working in partnership in the future. In an era as turbulent as our own, such a capability is especially valuable.

Although we lack the data needed to track the effects of the partnership on patient outcomes on a broad scale, the one such study we were able to carry out in the Northwest region's clinics showed that employee participation in partnership activities was associated with significant improvements in patient outcomes, such as adult and child immunization rates and breast cancer screenings. Though these results are encouraging, a definitive test of the effects of the partnership on patient outcomes must await more such data.

More generally, Kaiser benefited because the partnership taught both employees and managers important new skills in problem solving, meeting management, conflict resolution, and business understanding—all valuable resources in meeting challenges Kaiser would face in the future.

These skills represented a considerable achievement from the employees' point of view as well. The expanded training and development and opportunities for direct participation on a wide array of issues upgraded employees' skills and abilities. Some employees took advantage of these opportunities to develop the knowledge and skills needed to become facilitators or issue specialists, such as coordinators for workplace safety and HealthConnect; some took on new leadership and representative roles within their unions or the coalition; some benefited from new job opportunities outside of Kaiser. The capacity of employees to influence decisions increased, both at an individual level and collectively, through their unions. Unions too were given the opportunity to develop new capabilities. Many individual leaders, at all levels, learned new skills and the new organizational arrangements within and across the unions helped them develop new capacities for collective action, such as working in coalition and participating in decision making on topics and processes, including the design and planning of new facilities, that heretofore had been out of their reach.

Employees benefited in additional ways. Wages rose at least in tandem with, and perhaps somewhat more than, wages of other health care workers across the country. Wages for those at the bottom of the occupation and wage distribution ladder increased even faster than wages of their peers in health care and other industries. Kaiser workers avoided the travails of other workers who have experienced declining coverage and increasing costs of health care and the elimination of defined benefit pensions. The overall partnership agreement's employment and income security language and the more specific protections and adjustment provisions subsequently negotiated to facilitate the introduction of new technologies were among the strongest in the country. These gains were all good news for Kaiser employees—and for a society that is suffering from increases in income inequality and stagnant wages.

The introduction of electronic medical records technologies, which many health care leaders, including those at Kaiser, believe have a high potential to improve the quality of health care in the United States, was actively supported by the partnership. The collectively bargained agreement outlining how workforce issues would be handled in the transition and in the implementation of the new technology is a national benchmark for others to emulate. It paved the way for acceptance of this initiative and provided the guidelines for involving workers and union leaders at the local level in fitting the new technologies to their specific circumstances.

To be clear—the evolving partnership at Kaiser did not mean the elimination of conflict. It did not create some idyllic world of pure cooperation. Differences in interests are a natural and ongoing part of all employment relationships, union or non-union, adversarial or partnership. To expect that workers will always go along with management directives or initiatives or that all managers will always go along with what workers or their unions want is neither realistic nor good for the long-term interests of any of the stakeholders to an organization or an employment relationship. The question is whether partnership provides a better way of addressing problems and conflicts than the alternatives. On this dimension Kaiser's labor-management partnership proved its value in the first decade of its existence.

Finally, and of particular importance to a labor movement facing continued union decline and continuous conflicts in union organizing drives, Kaiser's unions expanded and organized approximately 20,000 new members. Some of this growth came from expansion of employment in existing bargaining units, and some came by activating the negotiated rules governing organizing of new employee groups. In doing so, Kaiser and the coalition unions were able to avoid the diversion of scarce health care dollars from patient care to battles that enrich lawyers and consultants.

Limitations

In other dimensions, the record of the partnership has been more mixed. Despite many examples of specific project successes in reducing costs, improving service, and solving problems, it is difficult to see clear performance improvements in patient care outcomes at the aggregate level. Kaiser's financial performance improved considerably over the years of the partnership and remained strong through the first part of 2008, but real and ominous storm clouds—discussed later in this chapter—were on the horizon.

A key goal of the partnership was to expand patient membership. As with other aspects of organizational performance, there were many small-scale successes—examples where the unions working through their networks were able to convince employers to offer the Kaiser option for health care to their workers—but these successes were not sufficient to impact the overall trajectory of Kaiser's membership base. Union efforts could not overcome the price considerations that drive employer decisions regarding whether to offer Kaiser as a service provider. Nevertheless, union involvement in marketing opened up another new vista for joint efforts.

Building and maintaining the partnership was a costly endeavor. Though less than 1 percent of Kaiser's total operating budget, the approximately $16 million annual budget of the Office of Labor-Management Partnership was considerable by any measure. And this amount does not reflect the full costs of time and energy of executives, physician leaders, union leaders and staff, and front-line managers and union representatives devoted to making the partnership work. At the same time, these partnership costs need to be compared to the full or potential costs of alternative possible relationships, especially the costs and risks associated with adversarial union-management relations, the costs of union avoidance efforts in non-union settings, and the opportunity costs of not having the collective capabilities the partnership has developed. Although the direct costs and investment of time and energy needed to manage the partnership are measurable and/or visible to those involved, the avoided costs are much harder to quantify.

The partnership's many-layered and sometimes slow-moving governance structure and process was a matter of significant and seemingly constant debate. However, in designing that structure, the parties had little choice but to match the organizational complexity of Kaiser and its multiple unions. A key effect of this weakness in governance in both the partnership and management was the limited ability of senior leaders to communicate their own commitment to partnership down to lower, local levels. As one went farther down management and union organizations and farther from California headquarters, the partnership's support and capacity declined. A decade after Kaiser and the coalition announced their commitment to partnership as a "new way of operating throughout the organization," most operating units still had no partnership structures or processes in place. The unit-based team initiative promised to turn that situation around, but this would take at least several more years.

The units most resistant to partnership were outside of California and in regions with lower union density. In environments less accepting of labor, it was harder for top management and labor leaders to diffuse partnership principles. Moreover, most of the unions representing Kaiser workers outside of California were mixed locals where leaders had responsibilities beyond Kaiser and often beyond health care. Such mixed responsibilities reduced identification with the partnership and required union leaders to balance multiple constituencies, some of which had no concept or experience with partnership and therefore reinforced a more adversarial style among their leaders. This often created a schizophrenic-like challenge for union leaders and staff that few could handle without occasional lapses to a more adversarial approach.

Partnership leaders made only limited progress in realizing their vision of evolving from a labor relations program to a full-fledged new model for delivering health care. Though the 2005 contract codified this as a major objective, as of 2008 leaders were still in the process of implementing it, focusing on the creation and diffusion of unit-based teams. This is a good first step. But if Kaiser's experience with these teams is consistent with that of other industries, it will require complementary changes in workflows and full integration of new medical information technologies to realize the full potential of teams for improving productivity and service quality.

In summary, we judge first decade of the Kaiser Permanente labor-management partnership's existence a success—but still a work in progress. It turned around dangerously deteriorating labor-management relations; deepened the organizational capacity of Kaiser to meet challenges and crises as they arose; demonstrated that workers, unions, managers, and physicians could work together in delivering high quality health care; and yielded significant benefits for management, employees, and unions. This positions the partnership in stark and favorable contrast to the restructuring underway in other industries, such as airlines, where restructuring has exacted a terrible toll on wages, working conditions, and employment security of the workforce. Although still not as far along as leaders hoped, the partnership offers a collaborative model for addressing the health care crisis facing the country. At the same time, it has yet to reach a majority of the workforce. And, though we have documented numerous examples of improved patient care and cost reduction brought about through partnership efforts, to date no broad-scale data are available to link the partnership to a system-wide, general improvement in patient care.

Looking Forward

Is this partnership sustainable? Here we are cautiously optimistic, yet, given the long history of labor-management partnerships in the United States, we are also realistic. The partnership has made it possible to negotiate two national contracts. It took major leadership transitions in stride and showed an ability to learn and adapt to new challenges. However, Kaiser faces major competitive challenges in costs and products and growing its membership base will be increasingly difficult. Not all regional or local management or labor leaders are strongly tied to the partnership mode and, facing serious pressure, they could easily revert to adversarial tactics if management, not wanting to wait for the slow deliberations of the partnership, opts to implement changes unilaterally and union leaders react aggressively and defensively. Holding the union coalition together will also be challenging in the face of different union priorities, leadership changes, conflicts—like the one that erupted between Sal Rosselli and Andy Stern that eventually put Rosselli's union under trusteeship—and the types of work reorganizational issues that are likely to continue to arise as technology and industry restructuring move forward. At some point, it is possible that the partnership could go into eclipse or be scaled back in some way. It will require continued vigilance by all who share a commitment to the partnership to work through these issues as they arise.

Lessons for Labor-Management Relations Practice

The Kaiser Permanente partnership demonstrates that labor and management, working together, can step up and meet the higher expectations in employment relationships long sought by workers, employers, and the public. While battles over the process by which workers gain a voice at work raged in the halls of U.S. Congress and on the front lines of practice, Kaiser and its unions agreed on and implemented codes of conduct and procedures ensuring that workers would make their own choices about whether or not to be represented and then offered the opportunity to directly participate in improving workplace conditions and performance.

Viewed in this light, partnership must be seen as a valuable tool for the nation's labor-management system. A partnership clearly will not work in all circumstances; but it deserves to be an option available to labor and management practitioners ready to give it a try. We identify three main lessons from this case about what it takes to lead and sustain a partnership.

First, partnership as a new mode of labor-management relations cannot develop without strong top-down leadership. In a field as contentious as labor relations, a partnership model cannot develop if it relies exclusively on horizontal diffusion across units that imitate each other in adopting the new approach. Nor will partnership take root if it is driven only by the upward influence efforts of local champions. Strong, top-down leadership and influence are needed to drive changes in behavior of lower-level leaders in both the management and union structures. This is even more important for management than unions, because leaders are selected in the former and elected in the latter, and mid-level managers are averse to taking labor relations risks to which their superiors are not committed.

Second, Kaiser's partnership experience teaches us that the path from adversarial or arm's-length labor relations is arduous. Rather than allowing crises or pivotal events to be viewed as signs that the parties are falling back into prior adversarial patterns, the challenge is to ensure that people learn from their mistakes and setbacks in ways that strengthen their capabilities as well as the partnership as it moves forward.

Third, it is hard work for managers to learn to partner without abdicating responsibility. "It takes very savvy leaders to deal with what I call the partnership trap," said a top executive in one Kaiser region. "We need to keep in mind that partnership is about a business strategy and trying to change a culture. But it does not excuse us from our management responsibility. I have to help labor understand that I still have a whole group of people that I have to work with to achieve results."

Similarly, union leaders have to learn to partner without abdicating their responsibilities to represent their members. They need deeper understanding of financial matters and more meeting management skills. Above all, they need to develop deeper forms of union democracy so that any enrichment of their dialogue with management is paired with enriched dialogue within their union.

Lessons for Non-Union Employment Relationships

When presenting some of our results to other health care management groups, we have often gotten a predictable—and sometimes not so polite—response. "These are interesting and particularly relevant to us if we are unionized," goes this response. "In that situation, clearly partnership is preferable to traditional adversarial relationships. But what relevance does this case have for the vast majority of us who are not unionized?"

This is a good and reasonable question that poses a significant strategic dilemma for non-union managers, union organizers, and public policy makers. Managers walk a fine line. If there was no interest from their workers in organizing, it would be impossible and indeed inappropriate for them to propose or to introduce a formal labor-management partnership. The decision of whether to be represented properly rests with the workforce. Labor law appropriately prohibits management from sponsoring or supporting employee representation. If union organizing is underway in their organizations, management faces a razor-edge choice. If it aggressively opposes unionization (as opposed to staying neutral or agreeing on rules of conduct to allow workers to make their independent choices), it risks laying a foundation of low trust that will likely result in an adversarial relationship if the union gains recognition.

Our answer to the generic question posed by non-union health care managers is that they need to learn about the costs and benefits of partnership and consider partnership as one option in their professional toolkit, to be drawn upon when the circumstances are appropriate. Their challenge is to avoid waiting until the conflicts associated with traditional organizing efforts escalate to the point that it becomes difficult, if not impossible, to use this option.

The same point applies to union leaders, who also face a dilemma. They cannot simply offer management the option of forming a partnership without workers expressing a strong desire to be represented. This would neither generate a positive response from employers nor be consistent with national labor policy. Instead, they have to demonstrate significant if not majority worker interest in representation to gain the attention of management. The problem is that the traditional way by which unions engage management is negative campaigning and/or by applying political and increasingly public pressure on employers to abort opposition to unionization. The more union leaders engage in such tactics, the more likely they are to end up in an adversarial relationship.

This double game of "chicken" seems almost inevitable, given the current labor law, management and labor culture, and labor relations environment. Absent a change in these baseline features of employment relations, the best suggestion is to do what some are now doing. Increasingly, labor union leaders are expressing a desire and willingness to engage in partnerships with willing employers and interested workers. They are making this part of their public statements and campaigns. At the same time, they are taking steps to build support from rank-and-file workers and to demonstrate their credibility and power to employers. Some are offering to negotiate rules of the game that limit the negative campaigning and the time and costs associated with organizing drives. This offers the possibility of a more independent and non-coercive environment for workers to decide whether or not to be represented while laying a better foundation for building a partnership right from the start of the union-management relationship. For example, the SEIU has made its commitment to building partnerships and alliances with employers a visible part of its organizing strategies, often combined with a willingness to use its political influence to address issues of mutual concern to employers and the workforce, all in exchange for employer neutrality and sometimes card-check recognition. More than any other union, SEIU has used the lessons learned at Kaiser to make union representation more attractive to employees and employers alike. However, this approach has its critics within the labor movement as witnessed by CNA's challenge to SEIU organizing efforts in Ohio and elsewhere. The challenge is to know how to extend the hand of cooperation to management and simultaneously mobilize workers to assert their interests.

Lessons for U.S. Labor Policy

What are the implications of our study for the future of employment relations for the nation as a whole? Speculating about this is timely: there is likely to be an active debate in Congress in 2009 over whether and if so how to reform labor law. So what can we say based on the experience and evidence amassed during the first decade of the Kaiser partnership's existence? Given the choice between adversarial union-management relations and partnership, the choice is obvious: workers prefer partnerships; managers and physicians who have experienced both approaches prefer and recognize the clear benefits of partnership; and society gains from the externalities.

Yet because this model of union-management relations remains fragile, the question facing policy makers is whether they can do anything to strengthen the resiliency and/or increase the likelihood of adoption of a partnership approach. We believe they can and should take a number of steps.

The first would be to fix labor law so that workers have the ability to form a union if they wish, without having to risk their jobs or undergo a prolonged, costly, and conflict-riddled ordeal. But this is only a necessary starting point. Equal attention needs to be given to improving the quality of labor-management relations and to putting them to work to address the pressing problems facing the industry and the economy. Partnerships such as between Kaiser and its unions should be encouraged and, at a minimum, obstacles in current labor law that limit them should be eliminated. This would start with the reversal of recent National Labor Relations Board (NLRB) and Supreme Court decisions that take away the rights of union membership for charge nurses, for example, or other professionals who now assume some of the duties and responsibilities heretofore handled by "managers." Doing so would not only support the diffusion of partnerships in health care, it would get on with the task of updating labor law doctrines to match accepted principles for organizing and carrying out work in today's organizations.

Broader changes in labor policy are also needed to encourage labor and management to break out of the "NLRB Box" illustrated in figure 2.1. Artificial boundaries around what labor and management can or should talk about constrain innovation and no longer make sense in a knowledge-based economy, where employees have so much to offer by way of improvement ideas, both radical and incremental. Partnership is a way to bring lagging U.S. organizations into the twenty-first century.

In short, labor policy makers should no longer be agnostic about the shape and character of labor relations practice. In recent years, policy makers have largely taken a hands-off or even hostile approach to labor or issued regulatory decisions that set practice back. On their watch, collective bargaining has continued to decline in coverage and in performance. This was not always the case. As far back as World War II, government leaders recognized the value of helping labor and management implement and institutionalize innovations such as grievance procedures, wage and salary standards that achieved equity without inflating prices, private pensions and health insurance, and joint safety and productivity committees. Those innovations were deemed to be essential for meeting the challenges of their day. In the decades following the war, similar leadership ensured that peaceful labor relations developed and were maintained in critical industries and installations dealing with atomic energy and space exploration, the postal service, and in specific negotiations where national health or safety were at risk.

In 1978, Congress took the affirmative step of enacting the Labor Management Cooperation Act to provide funds for promoting joint efforts to improve labor-management relations. The vision and leadership behind such initiatives are now absent in the highest levels of labor relations policy making and administration. Today, the key challenges facing labor and management are to restore worker voice and to engage workers' knowledge and skills in improving their work environment and the performance of their organizations and enterprises. A return to the type of policy leadership once present in U.S. government would encourage labor-management partnerships to be put to use in pursuit of these goals and would create an environment in which partnership would no longer be such a precarious experience. With this type of leadership, partnership might just evolve to become standard labor relations practice.

Lessons for Health Care Organizations

The United States once again appears to be poised to undertake another effort at comprehensive health care reform. What implications can we draw from the Kaiser case for this effort? By now, it should be clear that the type of partnership implemented at Kaiser is more complex, larger, and perhaps more ambitious than what most other health care employers and unions are ready to undertake. But if we have been successful in pointing out the strengths and weaknesses of this partnership, others need not try to replicate the Kaiser partnership in its full dimension. Few, if any, other health care organization structures are as complex or have as many unions representing their employees as Kaiser. Clearly, less complex partnership structures are possible in other, less complex health care organizations. Instead, we believe the key lesson for health care reformers is that any strategy for reform should attend to workforce, technology, and labor-management relations issues as a priority, rather than as an afterthought.

One way to view the Kaiser partnership is as a lead experiment in how to link these issues and engage the workforce and its representatives in the re-structuring and reform of health care processes that lie ahead. More experiments like this are needed. But to jumpstart more of them will require that an outmoded labor law and the adversarial ideologies that it reinforces be cast aside. Rather than wait for the national debates over labor law reform to be resolved, health care could serve as the experimental setting for a new set of labor policy principles that promote the types of teamwork, coordination of care, cooperation, and engagement of the workers and their representatives needed to create a high performing health care system. In this way, partnerships and/or other innovative forms of labor-management relations can be part of the solution to the nation's health care crisis. If, however, these issues are not addressed in a sensible way, or worse, if health care reform and restructuring exact a high price on the health care workforce, we can expect labor-management relations to be part of the problem.

Notes

Chapter 1. To Fight or Talk?

1. See for example, Thomas Kochan and Joel Cutcher-Gershenfeld, *Institutionalizing and Diffusing Innovations in Industrial Relations* (Washington, DC: U.S. Department of Labor, Bureau of Labor Management Relations and Cooperative Programs, 1988).

2. Thomas A. Kochan, Harry C. Katz, and Robert B. McKersie, *The Transformation of American Industrial Relations* (New York: Basic Books, 1986).

3. Saul Rubinstein and Thomas Kochan, *Learning from Saturn* (Ithaca, NY: Cornell University Press, ILR Press, 2001).

4. Examples of this work include Adrienne E. Eaton and Saul A. Rubinstein, "Tracking Local Unions Involved in Managerial Decision-Making," *Labor Studies Journal* 31, no. 2 (Summer 2006): 1–30; Adrienne E. Eaton and Paula B. Voos, "Productivity-Enhancing Innovations in Work Organization, Compensation, and Employee Participation in the Union Versus Nonunion Sector," *Advances in Industrial and Labor Relations* (JAI Press) 6 (1994): 63–109; and Adrienne E. Eaton, "Factors Contributing to the Survival of Participative Programs in Unionized Settings," *Industrial and Labor Relations Review* 47, no. 3 (April 1994): 371–389.

5. See, for example, Paul Adler, "The New 'Learning Bureaucracy': New United Motors Manufacturing, Inc.," in *Research in Organizational Behavior*, ed. Barry Staw and Larry Cummings (Greenwich, CT: JAI Press, 1993): 111–94.

6. See, for example, the compendium of papers on the partnership published in *Industrial Relations*, January 2008.

Chapter 2. Partnerships: Great Challenges, Greater Opportunities

1. This was the central conclusion of a national commission on labor-management relations in the mid 1990s. See *The Commission on the Future of Worker Management*

Relations: Fact Finding Report (Washington, DC: U.S. Departments of Commerce and Labor, 1994).

2. See Joel Cutcher Gershenfeld, Thomas Kochan, John Paul Ferguson, and Betty Barrett, "Collective Bargaining in the Twenty-First Century: A Negotiations Institution at Risk," *Negotiations Journal* (Fall 2007): 249–66; Richard B. Freeman and Joel Rogers, *What Do Workers Want?* (Ithaca, NY: Cornell University Press, ILR Press, 1999).

3. For the most up-to-date summary of the polls on worker interest in unions see Richard B. Freeman, "Do Workers Still Want Unions? *More Than Ever*," *Economic Policy Institute Briefing Paper*, no. 182 (22 February 2007), available at http://www.shared prosperity.org/bp182. See also Seymour Martin Lipset and Noah Meltz, *The Paradox of American Unionism* (Ithaca, NY: Cornell University Press, ILR Press, 2004).

4. For a broad sample of the editorials, press reports, and media coverage of debates over labor law reform see http://www.americanrightsatwork.org/press/news.cfn (accessed 13 September 2007).

5. See, for example, Janice Fine, *Work Centers: Organizing Communities at the Edge of the Dream* (Ithaca, NY: Cornell University, ILR Press, 2006).

6. *Crossing the Quality Chasm: A New Health System for the 21st Century* 2001. (Washington, DC: Institute on Medicine, National Academy Press), 125.

7. http://www.unionstats.com (accessed 29 January 2007).

8. Eileen Appelbaum, Peter Berg, Ann Frost, and Gil Preuss, "The Effects of Work Restructuring on Low-Wage, Low-Skill Workers in U.S. Hospitals," in *Low-Wage America: How Employers Are Reshaping Economic Opportunity in the Workplace*, ed. Eileen Appelbaum, Annette Bernhardt, and Richard J. Murnane (New York: Russell Sage, 2003), 77–120.

9. Surprisingly little has been written about the 1199/League partnership. The description here is drawn from one author's involvement in training related to the partnership and years of conversations with staff and consultants who support the partnership. Readers can also visit 1199's website for additional information: http://www.1199etjsp .org/training/labor_management.aspx (accessed 16 May 2008).

10. See Gil Preuss and Ann Frost, "The Rise and Decline of Labor-Management Cooperation: Lessons from Health Care in the Twin Cities," *California Management Review* 45, no. 2 (Winter 2003): 85–106.

11. For more on the first phase of this partnership, see Preuss and Frost, "The Rise and Decline of Labor-Management Cooperation."

12. Mary E. O'Leary, "Y-NH Broke Labor Laws, Union Pact, Arbiter Says," *New Haven Register*, 14 December, 2006, available at http://www.nhregister.com/articles/2006/ 12/14/import/17589251.txt.

13. Lawrence Darmiento, "Unions Step up Drive to Organize Cedars' Nurses," *Los Angeles Business Journal* 27 (January 2003).

14. Paul Clark, "Health Care: A Growing Role for Collective Bargaining," in *Collective Bargaining in the Private Sector, ed.* Paul Clark, John Delaney, and Ann Frost (Champaign, IL: Industrial Relations Research Association, 2002), 91–135.

15. The changes at Beth Israel Hospital and their effects on nursing and patient care are documented in Suzanne Gordon, *Life Support: Three Nurses on the Front Lines* (Boston: Little Brown Press, 1997) and Dana Beth Weinberg, *Code Green: Money Driven Hospitals and the Dismantling of Nursing* (Ithaca, NY: Cornell University, ILR Press, 2003).

16. For a detailed discussion, see Adrienne E. Eaton and Saul A. Rubinstein, "Tracking Local Unions Involved in Managerial Decision-Making," *Labor Studies Journal* 31, no. 2 (Summer 2006): 1–30.

17. John Paul Ferguson, "The Eyes of the Needles: A Sequential Model of Union Organizing Drives, 1999–2004," *Industrial and Labor Relations Review*, forthcoming.

18. For a classic summary of the poll data on the public's views of labor management relations see Derek Bok and John Dunlop, *Labor and the American Community* (New York: Simon and Schuster, 1970). For data on workers' views, see Richard Freeman and Joel Rogers, *What Workers Want* (Ithaca, NY: Cornell University, ILR Press, 1999).

19. Paul Adler, "The New 'Learning Bureaucracy': New United Motors Manufacturing, Inc.," in *Research in Organizational Behavior*, ed. Barry Staw and Larry Cummings (Greenwich, CT: JAI Press, 1993), 111–94.

20. Saul Rubinstein and Thomas Kochan, *Learning from Saturn* (Ithaca, NY: Cornell University, ILR Press, 2001).

21. For a general description and study of the steel industry partnerships, see Saul A. Rubinstein, "Partnerships of Steel? Forging High Involvement Work Systems in the U.S. Steel Industry: A View from the Local Unions," *Advances in Industrial and Labor Relations* 12 (2003): 115–144.

22. For a description of the Workplace of the Future partnership when it was still thriving see Adrienne E. Eaton, "Educating for AT&T, CWA and IBEW's Workplace of the Future," *Proceedings of the Forty-Seventh Annual Meeting of the Industrial Relations Research Association*, Washington, DC, 1995, 383–90.

23. See for example, Jody Hoffer Gittell, "Coordinating Mechanisms in Care Provider Groups," *Management Science* 48, no. 11 (2002): 1408–25.; Ingrid M. Nembhard, Anita L. Tucker, Jeffrey D. Horbar, and Joseph H. Carpenter, "Improving Patient Outcomes: The Effects of Staff Participation and Collaboration in Healthcare Delivery," Harvard Business School Working Paper, 2007. For a summary of a range of health care commission and study group reports calling for greater teamwork in health care see, "Teamwork in Health Care and Professional Training," Tufts Managed Care Institute, 2001, available at www.tmci.org/downloads/topic5_01.pdf.

Chapter 3. To Fight or Partner: Forming the Partnership

1. Rickey Hendricks, *A National Model for Health Care: The History of Kaiser Permanente* (New Brunswick, NJ: Rutgers University Press, 1993), 35–37.

2. Hendricks, *A National Model for Health Care*, 35.

3. Hendricks, *A National Model for Health Care*, 13–14.

4. John J. Sweeney, "America Needs a Raise," *Perspectives on Work* 1, no. 3 (1997): 21.

5. *The New American Workplace: A Labor Perspective* (Washington, DC: AFL-CIO, 1994).

6. See the "Understanding Kaiser Permanente: Hawaii's Success" (28 December 1999), report issued by KP's internal Consulting Services unit, which documents some of the positive aspects of the partnership among management, physicians, and employees in Hawaii. The report is available on request from the Kaiser Permanente office of Labor Management Partnerships.

Chapter 4. Early Challenges, Early Wins—But More to Do

1. See for example, John P. Kotter, "Leading Change: Why Transformation Efforts Fail," *Harvard Business Review* (March–April, 1995): 59–67.

2. Joel Cutcher-Gershenfeld, "The Impact on Economic Performance of a Transformation in Industrial Relations," *Industrial and Labor Relations Review* 44, no. 2 (January 1991): 241–60.

3. For issues of *Hank* and other articles on the partnership see www.lmpartnership.org.

Chapter 5. Slow Diffusion

1. Joel Cutcher-Gershenfeld, "The Impact on Economic Performance of a Transformation in Workplace Relations," *Industrial and Labor Relations Review* 44 (January 1991): 241–60.

2. Joel Cutcher-Gershenfeld, *Tracing a Transformation in Industrial Relations: The Case of Xerox and the Amalgamated Clothing and Textile Workers Union* (Washington DC, U.S. Department of Labor, Bureau of Labor Management Relations and Cooperative Programs, 1988).

3. See for example, Kurt Lewin, "Frontiers in Group Dynamics," *Human Relations* 1, no. 1 (1947): 5–41; Thomas A. Kochan and Lee Dyer, "A Model of Organizational Change in the Context of Union-Management Relations," *Journal of Applied Behavioral Science* 12, no. 1 (1976): 59–78; John Kotter, "Leading Change: Why Transformation Efforts Fail," *Harvard Business Review* 73, no. 2 (March-April, 1995): 59–67; Richard E. Walton, Joel Cutcher-Gershenfeld, and Robert B. McKersie, *Strategic Negotiations: A Theory of Change in Labor-Management Relations* (Boston: Harvard Business School Press, 1994).

4. Kaiser Permanente's partnership model, from the Kaiser Permanente Office of Labor Management Partnership.

5. See Paul S. Adler, "The New 'Learning Bureaucracy': New United Motors Manufacturing, Inc.," in *Research in Organizational Behavior*, ed. Barry Staw and Larry Cummings (Greenwich, CT: JAI Press, 1993), 111–94.

6. See Jody Hoffer Gittell, *The Southwest Airlines Way* (New York: McGraw-Hill, 2003).

Chapter 6. Negotiating in Partnership: The 2000 and 2005 National Negotiations

1. See Roger Fisher and William Ury, *Getting to Yes* (New York: Houghton Mifflin, 1982).

2. Richard E. Walton and Robert B. McKersie, *A Behavioral Theory of Labor Negotiations* (New York: McGraw-Hill, 1965).

Chapter 7. The Union Coalition

1. In 1997, the unions estimated a population of about 7,300 unorganized but union-eligible workers in the newer, less organized regions of KP (Georgia, Kansas, MO, North Carolina, Northeast, and Texas). These numbers did not include many small pockets of unorganized employees on the West coast and in Colorado and Ohio.

2. Joint News Release, 15 December 2003, SEIU/CAN (available from the authors).

3. In fact, those three unions developed their own written agreement along with the IUD for organizing Kaiser/CHP. The unions divided the employer into five system-wide bargaining units, including one for doctors. Each of the occupationally based units was assigned to one of the unions. This agreement included a separate dispute resolution procedure.

4. Adrienne E. Eaton and Jill Kriesky. "Union Organizing Under Neutrality and Card Check Agreements," *Industrial and Labor Relations Review* 55, no. 1 (October 2001): 42–59.

5. It is important to note that these are not the contractual wage levels. Because these data are from wage surveys they reflect the seniority, assignments, and other variations at the individual level.

6. See Kochan et al., "The Kaiser Permanente Labor Management Partnership: 2002–2004," research report, Institute for Work and Employment Research, MIT, May 2005.

7. Adrienne E. Eaton. "Factors Contributing to the Survival of Participative Programs in Unionized Settings," *Industrial and Labor Relations Review* 47, no. 3 (April 1994): 371–89.

8. Howard Raiffa, *The Art and Science of Negotiations* (Boston: Harvard Business School Press, 1982).

9. "RNs Speak Out: The SEIU Track Record," available at http://www.calnurses.org/seiu-watch/pdf/ohio_seiu_talkinghead.pdf.

10. Deborah Burger, Geri Jenkins, Malinda Markowitz, and Zenei Triunfo-Cortez, "Letter From the Council Presidents," *Registered Nurse: The CNA/NNOC Journal of Patient Advocacy* 2 (April 2008), published by the California Nurses Association.

Chapter 8. Leading in Partnership

1. See, for example, James P. Spillane, *Distributed Leadership* (San Francisco: Jossey Bass, 2006).

2. See Deborah Ancona, Thomas W. Malone, Wanda J. Orlikowski, and Peter M. Senge, "In Praise of the Incomplete Leader," *Harvard Business Review* (February 2007): 92–100.

3. Saul Rubinstein, "The Impact of Co-Management on Quality Performance: The Case of the Saturn Corporation," *Industrial and Labor Relations Review* 53, no. 2 (January 2000): 197–218.

4. The story of Leslie Margolin's time at Kaiser was like Pauline's in *The Perils of Pauline* (1914), a silent film episodic serial considered the most famous suspense serial in cinema history. Pearl White was the most famous star of the silent serials, known for their archetypal cliff-hangers that left audiences wondering what would happen next. This well-known, multi-chaptered, much-celebrated, archetypal play was originally 20 episodes in length (but many have since been lost), and now only exists as nine chapters (rearranged). The daring, athletic and active female star performed some of the riskiest, hair-raising stunts in these films (stranded on the side of a cliff, in a runaway balloon, in a burning house, etc). Week after week, Pauline (Pearl White) evaded attempts on her life. She fought pirates, Indians, gypsies, rats, sharks, and her dastardly guardian. (http://www.filmsite.org/peri.html.)

5. Janice Klein, "Why Supervisors Resist Employee Involvement," *Harvard Business Review* (September/October 1984): 87–95.

Chapter 9. Partnership and HealthConnect

1. This case study was carried out by Adam Seth Litwin as part of his PhD dissertation at the Massachusetts Institute of Technology. See Adam Seth Litwin, "Essays on Information Technology and the Employment Relationship: Work, Workers, and IT in American Healthcare," 2008.

2. Alison L. Booth, *The Economics of the Trade Union* (New York: Cambridge University Press, 1995).

3. Thomas A. Kochan, Harry C. Katz, and Robert B. McKersie, *The Transformation of American Industrial Relations* (New York: Basic Books, 1986).

4. Sumner H. Slichter, James Joseph Healy, and E. Robert Livernash, *The Impact of Collective Bargaining on Management* (Washington, DC: Brookings Institution Press, 1960).

5. See, for example, Sandra E. Black and Lisa M. Lynch, "How to Compete: The Impact of Workplace Practices and Information Technology on Productivity," *Review of Economics and Statistics* 83, no. 3 (2001): 434–45; Sandra E. Black and Lisa M. Lynch, "What's Driving the New Economy? The Benefits of Workplace Innovation," *Economic Journal* 114 (2004): 97–116; Erik Brynjolfsson and Lorin M. Hitt, "Computing Productivity: Firm-Level Evidence," *Review of Economics and Statistics* 85, no. 4 (2003): 793–808; Erik Brynjolfsson, Lorin M. Hitt, and Shinkyu Yang, "Intangible Assets: Computers and Organizational Capital," *Brookings Papers on Economic Activity*, no. 1 (2002): 137–81; Casey Ichniowski, Kathryn Shaw, and Giovanna Prennushi, "The Effects of Human Resource Management Practices on Productivity: A Study of Steel Finishing Lines," *American Economic Review* 87, no. 3 (1997): 291–313; John Paul MacDuffie, "Human-Resource Bundles and Manufacturing Performance: Organizational Logic and Flexible Production Systems in the World Auto Industry," *Industrial and Labor Relations Review* 48, no. 2 (1995): 197–221; John Paul MacDuffie and John F. Krafcik, "Integrating Technology and Human Resources for High-Performance Manufacturing: Evidence from the International Auto Industry," in *Transforming Organizations* (New York: Oxford University Press, 1992), 209–26.

6. Paul S. Adler, "The Learning Bureaucracy: New United Motor Manufacturing, Inc.," in *Research in Organizational Behavior*, vol. 15 (Greenwich, CT: JAI Press, 1993), 111–94; MacDuffie and Krafcik. "Integrating Technology and Human Resources for High-Performance Manufacturing: Evidence from the International Auto Industry."

7. Robert J. Thomas, *What Machines Can't Do: Politics and Technology in the Industrial Enterprise* (Berkeley: University of California Press, 1994).

8. Thomas A. Kochan, John Paul MacDuffie, and Paul Osterman, "Employment Security at DEC: Sustaining Values Amid Environmental Change," *Human Resource Management* 27, no. 2 (1988): 121–43; George P. Shultz and Arnold R. Weber, *Strategies for the Displaced Worker: Confronting Economic Change* (New York: Harper & Row, 1966).

9. Center for Studying Health System Change, *Community Tracking Study Physician Study, 2000–2001* (Ann Arbor: Inter-University Consortium for Political and Social Research, 2003); Center for Studying Health System Change, *Community Tracking Study Physician Study, 2004–2005* (Ann Arbor: Inter-University Consortium for Political and Social Research, 2006).

10. Richard Singerman (Office of the National Coordinator for Health Information Technology, U.S. Department of Health and Human Services), interview with Adam Seth Litwin, 17 November 2005.

11. Ashish K. Jha, Timothy G. Ferris, Karen Donelan, Catherine DesRoches, Alexandra Shields, Sara Rosenbaum, and David Blumenthal, "How Common Are Electronic Health Records in the United States? A Summary of the Evidence," *Health Affairs* 25, no. 6 (Web exclusive) (2006): 496–507.

12. David Woodwell and Donald K. Cherry, "National Ambulatory Medical Care Survey: 2002 Summary," *Advance Data from Vital and Health Statistics*, no. 346 (2004).

13. For a detailed account and econometric evidence, see Litwin, "Essays on Information Technology and the Employment Relationship."

14. Elizabeth A. McGlynn, Steven M. Asch, John Adams, Joan Keesey, Jennifer Hicks, Alison DeCristofaro, and Eve A. Kerr, "The Quality of Health Care Delivered to Adults in the United States," *New England Journal of Medicine* 348, no. 26 (2003): 2635–45.

15. Anthony G. Bower, *The Diffusion and Value of Healthcare Information Technology* (Santa Monica: RAND Corporation, 2005); George C. Halvorson and George J. Isham, *Epidemic of Care* (San Francisco: Jossey-Bass, 2003); Richard Hillestad, James Bigelow, Anthony Bower, Federico Girosi, Robin Meili, Richard Scoville, and Roger Taylor, "Can Electronic Medical Record Systems Transform Health Care? Potential Health Benefits, Savings, and Costs," *Health Affairs* 24, no. 5 (2005): 1103–17; McGlynn et al., "The Quality of Health Care Delivered to Adults in the United States."

16. Institute of Medicine, *To Err Is Human: Building a Safer Health System* (Washington, DC: National Academies Press, 2000); Institute of Medicine, *Key Capabilities of an Electronic Health Record* (Washington, DC: National Academies Press, 2003); Institute of Medicine, *Preventing Medical Errors* (Washington, DC: National Academies Press, 2006).

17. Terhilda Garrido, Brian Raymond, Laura Jamieson, Louise Liang, and Andrew Wiesenthal, "Making the Business Case for Hospital Information Systems: A Kaiser Permanente Investment Decision," *Journal of Health Care Finance* 21, no. 2 (2004): 16–25.

Chapter 11. Scorecard

1. One of the authors of this report, Adrienne Eaton, has also served since 1998 as an external consultant to the Metrics Workgroup and its measurement efforts.

2. As discussed in earlier chapters, the parties added a seventh goal in 2002, consultation and joint advocacy on public policy issues when possible and appropriate. This goal, though a very interesting one, does not lend itself to any sort of quantitative analysis.

3. "What is HEDIS? HEDIS and Quality Compass," http://www.ncqa.org/tabid/187/Default.aspx.

4. Adam Seth Litwin, "Quantifying the Line from Partnership to Performance at Kaiser Permanente," MIT Institute for Work and Employment Research Working Paper, available at http://mitsloan.mit.edu/iwer/workingpapers.

5. Unfortunately, the quality of service for hospital patients—a different though overlapping population from Kaiser plan members—has not been measured by a survey that provides any reliable trending. Suffice to say, Kaiser hospitals in California, despite some variation among them, tend to perform somewhat below average.

6. The flat result on relationships with co-workers is worth noting. Many labor critiques of labor-management partnership suggest they increase peer pressure around work performance. In fact, we certainly saw evidence of that dynamic at work at Kaiser, but it was not reflected in any *increased* tension among workers, at least according to these surveys' results.

7. Casey Ichniowski, "The Effects of Grievance Activity on Productivity," *Industrial and Labor Relations Review* 40, no. 1 (October 1986): 75–89; Harry C. Katz, Thomas A. Kochan, and Kenneth R. Gobeille, "Industrial Relations Performance, Economic Performance and QWL Programs: An Interplant Analysis," *Industrial and Labor Relations Review* 37, no. 1 (October, 1983): 3–17.

8. Michelle Kaminski, "New Forms of Work Organization and Their Impact on the Grievance Procedure," in *Employment Dispute Resolution and Worker Rights in the Changing Workplace,* ed. A. Eaton and J. Keefe (Champaign, IL: Industrial Relations Research Association, 1999); Adrienne E. Eaton and Saul A. Rubinstein, "Tracking Local Unions Involved in Managerial Decision-Making," *Labor Studies Journal* 31, no. 2 (Summer 2006): 1–30.

9. 2005 National Agreement, 29. Available at http://www.lmpartnership.org/contracts/agreements/docs/2005_national_agreement_agreement.pdf.

Index

Milton Keynes UK
Ingram Content Group UK Ltd.
UKHW010136280324
440206UK00006B/511